GENESIS

Readings: A New Biblical Commentary

General Editor
John Jarick

GENESIS

Second Edition

Laurence A. Turner

SHEFFIELD PHOENIX PRESS

2009

For Anne, Jonathan and Lisa
'Bone of my bones and flesh of my flesh' (Gen. 2.23)

Copyright © Sheffield Phoenix Press, 2009
First published by Sheffield Academic Press, 2000

Published by Sheffield Phoenix Press
Department of Biblical Studies, University of Sheffield
Sheffield S10 2TN England

www.sheffieldphoenix.com

A CIP catalogue record for this book
is available from the British Library

Typeset by Vikatan Publishing Solutions, Chennai, India

Printed by
Lightning Source in the UK and USA

ISBN 978-1-906055-65-3 (hardback)
ISBN 978-1-906055-66-0 (paperback)

Contents

Preface

My first memories of Genesis go back to the Primary Sabbath School class at Croscombe Seventh-day Adventist church, Somerset. There, in the rear room, Sister Benwell brought to life the stories of Abraham, Isaac, Jacob and Esau, with nothing more sophisticated than a sand tray and cardboard cut-out characters. I have learned much about Genesis over the years from erudite tomes written in closely argued English, French and German. But the *magic* was initiated in that childhood experience. The first scholarly impetus I received to work on Genesis was provided by Professor Bernhard Anderson at Princeton Theological Seminary, whose lectures on Genesis 1–11 opened up totally new perspectives for me. My later research at the University of Sheffield showed me just how profound this book can be, when I studied it under the unrelenting perfectionist eye of Professor David Clines.

The writing of this slim volume has taken much longer than it should have. More than full teaching loads, an international move from Australia back to my homeland of England, and an increasing administrative load have all played their part. Nevertheless, the burden was lightened by a grant from the Avondale College Foundation in Australia which allowed me to spend six weeks at Tyndale House, Cambridge, and by Newbold College which granted me a sabbatical term towards the end of the project. For both acts of generosity I am most grateful.

Any commentator is greatly indebted to those who have gone before. I have learned much from others, including those whose methodological stance is radically different from my own. However, the nature and length of the commentary mean that I do not usually have space to dialogue with them. My bibliography lists works that I have found to be particularly stimulating.

The task of a commentator, among other matters, is to provide the results of his or her working with the text. That procedure, however, does not work only in one direction. For myself, I can say that in the writing of this commentary I have discovered numerous things I did not know previously. Indeed, I have had to revise some of the things that I thought I did know about the text. If only, I tell myself, I had seen then what I see now, I would not have written what I did in some of my previously published material. But working with a text like Genesis not only provides occasion to change one's mind about words on the page, but also about oneself. Genesis has touched my life, challenged me to reconsider who I am, and shaped many of my perspectives on the world. One might say that all great literature should do that. For myself, as a member of a community of faith, I see it as part of the role of Genesis as Scripture.

I would like to thank those who have helped me during the writing of the commentary. Paul Kissling read the entire manuscript and contributed many insightful comments (and some protests!). Robert McIver read the first half of the commentary with characteristic attention to detail. Karl Wilcox brought his perspective as an English literary critic to bear, particularly on the Jacob story. My former student Hayden Bland was encouraging in his assessment of the general thrust of the work.

My transliterations often indicate the root of the Hebrew word rather than its actual form in the text. This is done to make clearer stylistic matters such as repetition and plays on words, which might not be apparent to a reader unfamiliar with the way in which Hebrew words mutate in various verbal and nominal forms. Citations of the English text are taken from the New Revised Standard Version, Anglicized Edition (NRSV), except where I have indicated that the translation is my own. The verse references follow those found in English versions. Portions of the commentary on chs. 18–19 have been taken from 'Lot as Jekyll and Hyde: A Reading of Genesis 18–19' (Turner 1990b).

This volume is dedicated to my wife Anne, and children Jonathan and Lisa. Our life together over the past few years has shown me that there are some things more important than writing books.

Abbreviations

AB	Anchor Bible
AnBib	Analecta biblica
ASV	American Standard Version
Bib	*Biblica*
BSac	*Bibliotheca Sacra*
CBQ	*Catholic Biblical Quarterly*
ETR	*Etudes théologiques et religieuses*
EvQ	*Evangelical Quarterly*
FOTL	The Forms of the Old Testament Literature
ICC	International Critical Commentary
JBL	*Journal of Biblical Literature*
JSOT	*Journal for the Study of the Old Testament*
JSOTSup	*Journal for the Study of the Old Testament, Supplement Series*
JPSV	*Jewish Publication Society Version*
KJV	King James Version
NEB	*New English Bible*
NICOT	New International Commentary on the Old Testament
NIV	New International Version
NRSV	New Revised Standard Version
OTL	Old Testament Library
RSV	Revised Standard Version
TD	*Theology Digest*
TEV	Today's English Version
TOTC	Tyndale Old Testament Commentaries
VT	*Vetus Testamentum*
WBC	Word Biblical Commentary
ZAW	*Zeitschrift für die alttestamentliche Wissenschaft*

Introduction

The present volume, in keeping with the aim of the series, reads the book of Genesis as a literary whole. This approach no longer elicits the surprise that it once did. However, it is still not greeted with equanimity by many who see the exegete's primary task as that of disassembling a biblical book in order to trace the historical development of, and posit historical contexts for, its constituent parts. From such historical-critical preoccupations we can arguably learn a great deal about the evolution and contexts of biblical books, the ideologies of their putative sources, and by extension of the societies that produced them. The book of Genesis is a parade example of such scholarly endeavour. The Documentary Hypothesis of Graf and Wellhausen, modified in many ways over the last century or so, has had an enormous impact not only on the interpretation of Genesis itself, but also upon scholarly understanding of the history of Israel. Briefly, the hypothesis holds that the Pentateuch as a whole is the end-result of editorial activity that brought together material from four main sources. Arranged chronologically, they are J (Yahwist), E (Elohist), D (Deuteronomist) and P (Priestly), with several centuries separating the earliest J material from the latest P traditions. The details, including the number and nature of the sources, and their historical sequence and contexts, have been debated. Nevertheless, some form of the hypothesis has provided the bedrock upon which research on the Pentateuch has been built. Such study has, by definition, not set out to read the text as a unified literary work. Rather, its *raison d'être* is to foreground elements which it sees as being, for example, inconsistent, redundantly repetitious or contradictory. From such evidence, the underlying sources can be reconstructed, their individual ideological concerns explicated and the evolution of the text clarified. Generally speaking, sections of the text deemed to derive from different sources (e.g., Gen. 1.1-2.4a [P], and 2.4b-25 [J]), are read in isolation from one another, except when the contrasts between the two are being set out. Such scholarly approaches have at times produced work of breathtaking erudition. Its approach, however, to use a helpful analogy, is that of eating a cake in order to reconstruct the recipe from which it has been baked, and assessing the origins and qualities of its individual ingredients, rather than savouring the cake as a finished product. There are still those who hold to some version of the Documentary Hypothesis, but it no longer commands the respect of all. A number who accept that its historical analysis of the text's conception and growth is correct, concede that its predominantly historical and atomistic approach to the text should not veto all other readings. The present commentary is not written as a polemic against the Documentary Hypothesis, or other source-critical theories, though I must admit to more than a mild scepticism.

In most respects the methodology I have adopted is similar to that employed in my previous volume, *Announcements of Plot in Genesis* (Turner 1990a). Since Genesis is a narrative book, I have chosen to foreground *plot*, which gives a narrative its essential quality and the absence of which would relegate it to being a mere chronicle. Many episodes in Genesis that appear on the surface to be simple and independent, are actually complex and interconnected. Thus, to use the example of the two creation stories cited above, which source critics assign to different traditions and historical periods, the commentary will ignore such hypothetical source divisions. However, the tensions between the two narratives that elicit the source critical analysis will not be ignored but interpreted from a holistic final form perspective.

Plots are traditionally surveyed as they move from exposition to complication and on to resolution. Numerous individual stories in Genesis could be cited to illustrate that movement. For example, in the story of Cain and Abel, the initial announcement of the birth of the pair, their vocations and sacrifices (4.1-4a), is complicated by God's reaction to Cain's sacrifice and his reaction to God's disapproval (4.4b-8). The rest of the narrative moves towards a resolution (4.9-16), though a rather uneasy one it is to be sure. Such plotted movements are not confined to individual stories, but span whole blocks. Thus the initial announcement to Abraham concerning land, nationhood and blessing (12.1-3), initiates the plot that runs throughout the subsequent chapters in which complications threaten each of those elements. To cite just one of the most obvious examples, the potential sacrifice of

Isaac (22.1-19), complicates the promise of nationhood in a most dramatic way. In these larger blocks, as in individual stories, the resolutions are rarely neat and absolute. They usually leave behind some unresolved issues for the reader to carry over into the next episode. For example, the statement concerning Joseph's resting in a coffin in Egypt, which brings the Genesis narrative to a conclusion (50.26), is a reminder that some complications have been resolved—the ancestral family have escaped famine and thus preserved their potential for nationhood, but they are not in the land promised to them. That is a complication that will require resolution beyond the confines of Genesis.

In giving attention to plot development, in places I emphasize *intertextuality*. Given the limitations of space placed upon contributors to this series I have chosen, on the whole, to read episodes in Genesis in light of other episodes in Genesis, rather than in light of the whole Hebrew Bible. Thus the term *intratextuality* might be more appropriate. Frequently, two or more passages with numerous explicit similarities cry out to be interpreted in the light of each other (e.g., the 'wife-sister' stories of chs. 12, 20 and 26). In others, connections are more allusive, but the resulting intratextual readings no less rewarding. For example, reading the Flood account (chs. 6–9) in light of Creation (chs. 1–3); Lot's offer of his daughters in Sodom (19.8) against Abraham's abandonment of his wife in Egypt (12.10-20); Jacob's wrestling at the Jabbok (32.22-32) as a reprise of his deception of Isaac (27.18-29), and so on. These and a host of other examples make of Genesis a sophisticated and complex literary work.

The intertextual reading I provide is predominantly a 'first-time' reading. That is to say, I provide intertextual readings retrospectively, looking back to previous episodes, rather than prospectively looking forward to passages not yet encountered at that point in the book. Thus, for example, in the wife-sister episodes, I provide only a cross-reference to the later episodes in commenting on 12.10-20. In ch. 20 I look back to ch. 12. I reserve comments that compare and contrast all three episodes until I come to ch. 26. As a consequence of this, intertextual readings occupy an increasingly prominent part as one works through the commentary from beginning to end.

To comment on the book as a first-time reader is not to claim, as one uncomprehending reviewer of my earlier volume seemed to think, that I have read Genesis only once. Of course not. But reading the book *as if* for the first time, is a helpful way to foreground its surprises, ironies, innovations and so on, and to enter into the plot with the characters, experiencing narrative developments through their eyes. Everyone of us has at some stage been a first-time reader of these narratives. So a first-time reading is an attempt to recapture the impact of that initial encounter.

For example, to read Gen. 22.1-19, the dramatic 'sacrifice' of Isaac, entirely as a second-time reader who knows the outcome from the beginning, divests the narrative of much of its tension. If we read already knowing that Isaac is rescued, then Abraham's 'test' generates no suspense, and as readers we do not enter into his angst. It is only by suspending our knowledge, entering into the story *as if* for the first time, and with the characters wondering what the outcome will be, that we can appreciate fully the literary genius of the story.

First-time reading, however, incorporates elements of second-time reading. First-time readers who read passage A and then proceed to passage B might well find in the latter all manner of elements that draw them back to the former as second-time, intertextual readers. To use the words of Rashkow,

> The reader confers meaning retrospectively, earlier narrative elements retain a provisional status until the reader reaches another meaning based upon subsequent episodes ... The plot develops and events become sequential rather than redundant, providing a grid through which antecedent scenes are re-examined, not to enhance an initial impression, but to qualify and complicate it. (Rashkow 1992: 61-62)

Sometimes, when encountering a passage for the first time, I pause to consider how a first- and second-time reading might differ. On occasions, I also consider how a reading that incorporates perspectives from further afield in the Hebrew Bible might differ from, or add to, one confined to information divulged within Genesis (e.g., the connotations of the rivers mentioned in 2.10-14, or the role of Moabites and Ammonites in 19.30-38).

Plots require characters. More than anything else it is the depth of *characterization* that adds interest and verisimilitude to the narratives. In a book crammed full with a vast array of characters, not every individual can be developed fully. To use the terminology of Berlin (1983: 23), there are *flat characters* who contribute something to plot development, but do not emerge as individuals. They 'are built around a single quality or trait' (e.g., Onan, 38.8-10). There are *agents*, who act as functionaries to move the plot along to a new stage, but whose characterization is not developed (e.g., the cupbearer, 41.9-13). Much of the appeal of Genesis is produced, however, by numerous *fully fledged* characters who emerge from the text as believable and complex. The Genesis text constantly challenges us to readjust our assessment of a character. For example, when readers encounter Abraham who obeys God's command to leave his country (12.4), yet lies about his 'sister' (12.13; 20.2); believes God's amazing promise (15.6), but objects to God's plans (17.18); attempts to persuade the Lord to change his mind (18.22-33), though unquestioningly obeys the divine imperative to sacrifice his own son (22.1-10), they realize that here is a complex character indeed. And he is no exception, as I hope to demonstrate in the commentary.

The poetics of Hebrew narrative art has been extensively analysed in recent years. The reader who wishes to have a detailed treatment of this is referred to volumes such as Alter 1981; Berlin 1983; Bar-Efrat 1989 and Gunn and Fewell 1993. I provide a few selected examples here of how Hebrew narrative style is employed in Genesis.

Wordplay abounds, as part of the narrative's strategy to underline the truly significant, or to encourage a reader to read one passage in the light of another. Sometimes this forms the basis for a motif such as *'ādām / 'ªdāmâ* ('man/ground'), which occurs in the primaeval history (e.g., 2.7; 3.17; 6.1). More often it is the narrative's way of emphasizing details in individual episodes, as with *'ªrûmmîm / 'ârûm* ('naked/crafty') in 2.25–3.1, or with *yaªqōb* (Jacob), *yē'ābēq* ('wrestled') and *yabbōq* (Jabbok) in 32.22-32.

Multivalence is exploited at many points, alerting the reader to the possibility of more than one interpretation of a passage. So, for example, the fact that the root *gnb* can mean 'steal' or 'deceive' adds to a reading of Jacob's and Rachel's encounter with Laban (30.33; 31.19-20). When Potiphar's wife brandishes Joseph's 'garment' (*beged*) as evidence of his attack on her, the fact that the root *bgd* also conveys the concept of treachery or adultery, adds silent comment on her accusation (39.16-19).

Ambiguity is exploited in many a passage, emphasizing the subtlety and profundity of ostensibly simple narratives. Some passages exploit ambiguity by providing different interpretations of the same scene by narrator and characters, as in for example, Jacob's wrestling at the Jabbok (32.22-32). Ambiguity also appears on the larger conceptual scale, as when, for example,

Abraham's dialogue with God and Lot's subsequent rescue from Sodom raise more than one possible view about the nature of human-divine relationships (18.16–19.38).

Irony is embedded throughout Genesis. For example, Hamor and Shechem's speech to the city elders, in which they assess Jacob's family as being 'friendly' (34.21), is seriously at odds with the information divulged by the narrator (34.13). Similarly, the news that Esau has prospered greatly (33.9; 36.6-7), can not be anything but ironic to a reader who has traced the complications caused by the dispensing of blessings throughout the narrative.

Repetition serves, among other things, to reinforce the important, remind the hearer of antecedent steps in the plot, or sometimes merely to delight in the aesthetics of hearing the cadences of familiar phrases. The first chapter of Genesis is an obvious example of repetition, with its hypnotic presentation of creation in six days. Days 1–6 have an almost identical structure. The seventh day contains none of those elements, and reveals another function of repetition. Climaxes are often underlined by departing from the repetitive patterns that precede them. Repetition can also heighten the reader's emotional involvement, as in 'your son, your only son' (22.2, 12, 16) and 'so the two of them walked on together' (22.6, 8), in the heart-stopping 'sacrifice' of Isaac.

The recurrence of concepts and/or vocabulary so as to form *motifs* aids integrative reading. The fact that the chaos motif occurs at the beginning and end of the primaeval history (1.2, cf. 11.7-9), as well as in its heart (e.g., in the reversal of creation in the Flood), provides a perspective for enhancing a reading of chs. 1–11 as a whole. Similarly, the clothing motif in the story of Jacob's family alerts a reader to significant transitions likely to transpire (37.23; 38.14; 39.12; 41.14). While some motifs are confined to particular blocks, others span the entire book. One of the most pervasive is that of the reversal of primogeniture, that is the younger being preferred to the older (e.g., 4.1-16; 17.18-19; 25.23; 37.3-10).

Investigating the plot, intertextuality, character and aspects of Hebrew narrative style, however, is not an end in itself, nor can it be done without imagination. This simply provides a way into the text, a sounding of various possibilities for elucidating the narrative. Thus, I do not subject every passage to the same analysis. In some the emphasis will be on plot, in others on character, in others intertextuality will predominate, in others any one or more of these will be muted or nonexistent.

I have deliberately left unanswered some questions raised by the text. The literary power of these narratives is sometimes best preserved by signalling the questions that they raise, rather than positing a neat solution. I hope that this will draw the reader into the Genesis text, rather than viewing it just through the prism of the commentary.

The significance of Genesis is based on more than the fact that it is the first book of the biblical canon. While every biblical book in one way or another touches on human life, Genesis addresses matters of human existence more fundamentally and vividly than most others. Issues such as the creation of the universe; the origins of life; what it means to be human; the nature of the human-divine relationship; God's destiny for people in general and for Israel in particular, and so on, are painted in graphic detail in the Genesis narratives, some of which rank with the greatest ever written.

A cursory reading of Genesis is enough to discover that the book is divided into two distinct blocks. The primaeval history comprising 1.1–11.26, takes the reader from the creation of the heavens and earth to the erection of the tower of Babel. The ancestral history, 11.27–50.26, transports us from the call of Abraham in Haran to the death of Joseph in Egypt. The ancestral history itself is divided into sections dealing primarily with Abraham (11.27–25.18), Jacob (25.19–36.43) and Jacob's family, especially Joseph (37.1–50.26).

The literary style of the book is not static, and a general development can be plotted as one moves through the book from beginning to end. The primaeval history is more than a miscellaneous collection of diverse stories, but its parts are less interconnected than those of the rest of the book. There is certainly a sense of plot and forward momentum, and motifs function to hold the material together, but in a less sophisticated way than in the ancestral history. Characterization is also more sparse. Individuals are not allowed enough space in their narrative worlds to become as well-rounded as any of the major and many of the minor characters in the ancestral history. Even Noah, the major protagonist of chs. 6–9, remains a relatively flat character. What the narratives in this section do more vividly than any other, however, is set out the basic polarities of human existence—dependence/autonomy; blessing/curse; chaos/order, and so on.

The Abraham story is much more cohesive, with the initial call to Abraham (12.1-3) setting the stage for the rest of the narrative.

Reading subsequent episodes in this section invariably causes the reader to ponder the issues raised in these initial verses. The characterization is also more complex, and not only of the major characters such as Abraham, Sarah and Lot; we are also provided with detailed cameos of minor characters such as Pharaoh, Hagar and Abimelech. An overarching plot is more discernible than in chs. 1–11, but the expectations of the characters, and with them those of the readers, are regularly raised and then disappointed.

The plot of the Jacob story is every bit as complex as that of Abraham, but its central character is more enigmatic. By the end of the Abraham story a reader will have recognized the complexity of Abraham, but will probably have been able to paint a cohesive portrait of the character. The character of Jacob, however, is not only more complex but also elusive, and certainly less sympathetically drawn. The complexity of Jacob's character is a reflection of the intricate interrelationships set up within the Jacob story by numerous allusions to episodes in both chs. 1–25 and within the Jacob story itself. They provide particularly rich opportunities for intertextual reading.

With the Joseph story, or more correctly the story of Jacob's family, we reach the most sustained, almost seamlessly constructed narrative block in Genesis. It is human activity, rather than the divine, that is at the centre of attention. God is present, though more often than not he is invoked by characters rather than being explicitly active. Yet, as if to underline the nature of the book, Joseph might be the most finely portrayed character in Genesis, but he is the most enigmatic of all, more so even than Jacob.

The brief outline above indicates something of the complexity, subtlety and interconnectedness of the book. Too often in the past Genesis has been treated as an amalgam of disparate sources cobbled together by dull redactors. Thankfully, that assessment is being increasingly challenged in contemporary scholarship. Viewed as a whole, and allowed to display its integrity as a cohesive composition, the book emerges as a coherent and well constructed literary work that rewards repeated investigation.

Genesis 1.1–11.26:
The Primaeval History

Genesis 1

Genesis begins with breathtaking comprehensiveness. It commences with the limits of time ('in the beginning'), and proceeds immediately to the limits of space ('the heavens and the earth'). The style of the book's first major section (1.1-2.4a) is characterized by symmetry, simplicity and repetition, all of which have an impact on a reading of the account.

The symmetry of the account of creation can be set out diagrammatically. As often noted, days 1–3 see the formation of the various 'environments', and days 4–6 witness the filling of these environments, in the same sequence as their creation, with appropriate 'creatures'. The luminaries (day 4) assume responsibility for light (day 1); flying creatures and water creatures (day 5) inhabit the dome/firmament and waters respectively (day 2); land animals and humans (day 6) inhabit the land and are sustained by vegetation (day 3, cf. 1.29-30). These matching horizontal pairs between the two triads form a balanced framework for Genesis 1. What is not noted so often, however, is that the introductory and concluding statements of 'chaos' and 'rest', form a complementary pair (see below).

Chaos (1.2)

Day 1. Light (1.3-5)	Day 4. Luminaries (1.14-19)
Day 2. Dome/Firmament Waters (1.6-8)	Day 5. Flying creatures Water creatures (1.20-23)
Day 3. Dry land Vegetation (1.9-13)	Day 6. Land animals Humans (1.24-31)

7. Rest (2.1-4a)

The description of creation on each day contains repetitive common elements which may be set out as follows:

1. Announcement: 'And God said ...' (1.3, 6, 9, 11, 14, 20, 24, 26, [29]).
2. Imperative: 'Let there be ...' and so on (1.3, 6, 9, 11, 14, 20, 24, [25]).
3. Report: 'And there was ...'; 'It was so' (1.3, 7, 9, 11, 15, [21], 24, 30).
4. Evaluation: 'And God saw that it was good' (1.4, 10, 12, 18, 21, 25, 31)
5. Temporal framework: 'and there was evening and there was morning, a first day ... second day ...' and so on (1.5, 8, 13, 19, 23, 31)

Each of these common elements (with one exception, see below), occurs once on each day, but on the third and sixth days (i.e., the climax of each triad), elements 1 to 4 are repeated, before the temporal framework concludes in the usual way. Thus the second repetitive pattern of common elements complements and emphasizes the first symmetrical pattern of unique elements.

At one level therefore, the creation account appears to be concerned with the physical universe, and with the symmetry and regularity of its creation. It is, however, more complex than this. While the chapter does indeed recount the creation of 'the heavens and the earth', its structure actually places primary emphasis not on matter, nor on space, but on *time*.

Time (1.1)

'In the beginning'

1. Time (Creation of light producing temporal cycle of day/night)	4. Time (Luminaries for signs/seasons/days/years)
2.	5.
3.	6.

7. Time

(Sanctified time)

Thus the first words in the account concern time, as do the first acts of creation in each triad. Days 1–6 are punctuated by '... first day ... second day ...' and so on. And the final statement of the account concerns time—God's sanctification of the seventh day. Thus the account's concern with simple time culminates with holy time. The chapter's agendum is not limited to a catalogue of God's physical creation.

The balance between the first and second triad is *almost* exact. The lower waters separated on the second day are not gathered together or named 'seas' until the third day. Thus there is some ambiguity as to whether their creation belongs to the second or third day (and 'waters' of course were present before God's first creative command, 1.2). The symmetry elsewhere in the account tempts one to favour day 2, thus balancing the creation of aquatic creatures on day 5, but a case could be made for opting for day 3, thus producing an 'asymmetrical' reading. Similarly, the repetition of common elements on each day is *almost* precise. The fourth element, that of evaluation, is missing from the second day (producing *seven* evaluations in the whole week). And the non-conformity of the seventh day is absolute. Such disturbances to exact symmetry in the creation account give advance notice of a tendency to be found throughout Genesis. The book confounds the reader's expectations. Chapter 1 reveals at the outset that not everything can be predicted, and that the narrative will contain surprise, complication and interest.

1.1-2

There is a great deal of debate about the translation of the opening paragraph of Genesis and its precise syntactical relationship to 1.3 (e.g., NIV, RSV cf. NRSV, NEB). The most likely reading of the text, in my opinion, is that 1.1 is a separate sentence and acts as a summary of the rest of the chapter—that is, that in the beginning God created the 'heavens and the earth', an idiomatic use of polar opposites to express 'universe' (see 3.1-7). Genesis 1.2 details the condition of the 'earth' before God spoke his first command, and 1.3 marks the beginning of his creative act. How the 'heavens' came into existence is taken up by the account of day 2.

New sections of Genesis are regularly introduced with the formula 'These are the descendants of (*tôleḏōt*) ...' (5.1; 6.9; 10.1; 11.10; 11.27; 25.12, 13, 19; 36.1; 37.2), and all human characters in Genesis 1–11 have genealogical relationships with one another. Yet here, God, the major character in Genesis 1–11, is given neither *tôleḏōt* formula nor genealogy. The concluding formula (2.4a) refers to the *tôleḏōt* of the 'heavens and earth', not God. With no family tree, God is the unique character in the story.

He transcends the creative and procreative processes, as the creator of the 'universe'.

Before God's first creative word the earth is 'a formless void' (*tōhû wābōhû*), an expression conveying the sense of 'chaos' (cf. Jer. 4.23-28). That is, the earth lacked order and structure. An integral part of God's creating, as we shall see, is the *organizing* of the cosmos. For example, the separating of day from night, waters above from waters below, dry land from seas. Before this separation the earth was an undifferentiated mass. This is the starting point for the account of Genesis 1, and as order increases with each successive day, chaos is left further and further behind.

Yet in these introductory verses, where chaos rules, with darkness covering the deep, we are given notice that God is present. The spirit (or 'wind') of God is moving, presaging God's first command in the next verse.

1.3-5
Throughout the account imperative monologue and lack of dialogue underlines the ease with which God creates. The first step away from chaos is the creation of light and its subsequent separation from darkness—the first of the two elements of chaos mentioned in the introduction. The separation of light from darkness initiates the temporal rhythm of 'evening and morning', forming the first day. Once 'darkness' is set in its place, given a function, and named 'Night', it ceases to be an element of chaos. Creation, therefore, involves not only the advent of a new element ('light'), but also the 'domestication' of previously existing chaos.

1.6-8
God's action on the first day dealt with the first of the two elements of chaos—darkness; on the next day, the creation of the dome (often translated 'firmament'), makes possible the separating of the other element of chaos—the waters. The dome is set above the earth (Job 37.18) and acts as a barrier against the waters above. The waters above the dome form a 'heavenly ocean', and are apparently complete in themselves, while the waters below will need further separation (1.9-13), before they fulfil God's purpose. The introductory statement to the chapter announced that God created 'the heavens (*šāmayim*) and the earth (*'ereṣ*)'. Here on the second day the 'sky' (*šāmayim*) is created. The earth will soon follow (see 9.8-19).

1.9-13

The climax of the days of preparation is brought about by the organization of the earth into its environments of dry land and sea.

This day includes all of the main elements found in the introductory statement (1.1-2): 'heavens'; 'earth'; 'waters'; and the transformed 'darkness' ('evening' of 1.3). However, because they have now been organized and given their respective functions they are no longer *tōhû wābōhû*. The first triad has moved from chaos to order. Because the earth is ordered it may now participate in the ongoing act of creation by itself 'bringing forth' vegetation (1.11). Not only does the earth bring forth, but what it does 'bring forth' is capable of 'bringing forth' itself—plants 'yielding *seed*', trees 'bearing *fruit*' (1.12).

1.14-19

The fourth day brings us to the mid-point of the seven day week. It is concerned primarily with the government of time (i.e., with 'signs and ... seasons ... days and years', 1.14.). Thus the first, middle and last days of the week share a common theme and illustrate the narrative's primary concern, that is God created everything, but his primary creation was *time*. At first sight it seems strange that luminaries are needed when light and the cycle of day and night have been present since the first day. However, the creation of light-bearers shows that God desires to operate through intermediaries. Since day 1 he has governed day and night by himself, but now hands over that function to the heavenly bodies. The repetitious account of the fourth day emphasizes the precise nature of God's abdication of authority to the heavenly bodies; they will govern only time. In doing so they are not autonomous, nor do they usurp God's authority in any other area. There will be a similar surrender of power on the sixth day.

1.20-23

Just as the earth 'brought forth' vegetation on day 3, so the waters are here commanded to 'bring forth' aquatic (and possibly also flying) creatures. As with all previous commands there is an immediate and positive response (1.21). However, a new element occurs on the fifth day: God *blesses* the creatures of sea and air. This element occurs just twice during days 1–6, the other blessing being on humans in 1.28. These blessings anticipate events beyond 'creation week'. All other commands of God receive a positive response on the same day they are uttered. But the fulfilment of the blessing/command to multiply (1.22), lies beyond the scope of the fifth day (note the omission of 'and it was so'). Given creation's previously consistent response to God's command the reader might assume that these blessings will also translate easily into fulfilment. But, as already noted, the symmetry of the account, despite its general balance, indicates that consistency cannot be guaranteed. The fate of the blessings here and on day 6 is one element of interest carried over into the ensuing narrative.

1.24-31
The first act of the sixth day sees the earth 'bringing forth' land animals as it had previously produced vegetation on the corresponding third day (1.11-12). Its primary interest, however, indicated by the bulk of its content, is with the creation of humanity (1.26-31).

Within Genesis 1 the divine self-imperative is unique to the creation of humans: 'Let *us* make ...' (1.26), though widely debated, with no suggestion being without problems, is best seen as a 'plural of deliberation', (see Westermann 1984: 145). This switch to the plural seems to be a Hebrew idiom underlining the significance of the statement being made (cf. Gen. 11.7-8; Isa. 6.8; 2 Sam. 24.14). Humans are thus distinguished from the rest of creation, and their significance is further highlighted by God's command to make them 'in our image, according to our likeness' (1.26).

While the text of Genesis 1 does not state explicitly what the image is, it does provide hints. If humans are in God's image then there must be some analogy between God and humans. One such analogy is provided in 1.26b, with its granting of dominion over creation. God has just demonstrated his dominion by creating these creatures; the granting of human dominion over these same creatures is one way, perhaps the major way, in which human activity reflects the divine and thus indicates something of the 'image of God' in humans. The blessing on humans in 1.28 adds two more elements. The first, 'be fruitful and multiply, and fill the earth' is shared with the creatures of sea and air (cf. 1.22), but the second, 'subdue [the earth]', is a separate and uniquely human destiny. The creation account has given ample evidence of God's subjugation of the earth as he has ordered it according to his will and transformed it from its chaotic origin. Thus human subjugation of the earth and dominion over animals bears analogy with divine activity and represents at least part of the human condition of being in the image of God. Just as God previously created light (day 1) and then transferred this responsibility to the heavenly luminaries (day 4), so here he transfers dominion over creation to human beings. This suggests that the 'image of God' in humans refers not only to what humans *are* but primarily to what they *do* (see 9.1-7).

The threefold blessing on humans in 1.28, like the blessing of fertility on the creatures of water and air in 1.22, projects beyond the time-scale of ch. 1. Reasonable questions for readers to ask are, 'If this is what is expected of humans at their creation, do they in fact fulfil this divine requirement? If they do not, what will be the consequences?' As we shall see in the subsequent chapters, the struggle of this blessing/command to translate itself into reality provides part of the connective tissue in the unfolding of the narrative's plot.

2.1-4a

The description of the seventh day begins with a peculiar statement: 'Thus the heavens and the earth were finished, and all their multitude. And on the seventh day God finished his work ...' (2.1-2a). So, God had already finished his work by the sixth day, and on the seventh he finished it! This apparent contradiction has inspired some to emend the text from 'seventh' to 'sixth' (as in LXX), which also conveniently lets God escape the accusation of Sabbath-breaking. Others suggest rendering 2.2a as a pluperfect, '*By* the seventh day God *had* finished his work ...' (cf. NIV). However, the conventional translation makes coherent sense: by the sixth day the 'heavens and the earth' (i.e., the physical universe) had indeed been created. But the seventh day is concerned with a different order of 'work', an item that transcends the physical universe and is concerned with the non-physical intangibilities of sacred time. Thus the seventh day is concerned with a different matter than days 1–6, a point reflected in the form of the passage.

The monotonous regularity of description that has built up in days 1–6 is broken by day 7. Here is a thoroughly different day, containing no Announcement, Imperative, Report, Evaluation, or Temporal Framework (see above). Days 1–3 saw God's naming of his creation; days 5 and 6 his blessing; but day 7 itself uniquely receives his blessing and sanctification. The two previous blessings of sea and air creatures (1.22) and humans (1.28), were immediately understandable. But what does the blessing of a *day* imply? And is it not strange that the day that is blessed is, at first sight, the least significant of all—the day on which God rests? No physical object in the whole of God's creation is 'sanctified', not even human beings created in his image, but the seventh *day* is (2.3).

This final day, unique in its content and narrative form, forms the apex and goal of God's creativity. It is God's final act of 'separation'. Previously he has separated light from darkness, waters above from waters below, dry land from seas. Here the seventh day, containing no recurring elements from other days, standing outside the two triads of preceding days, is blessed and sanctified like no other. It is separated from the preceding six; unique; blessed; holy. The final day thus reminds readers that in a text seemingly preoccupied with balance and repetition, non-conformity to set patterns and expectations is not a disruption, but an indication of what is truly important. Rest, in comparison to the activity of days 1–6, may seem to be an anticlimax; but in comparison to the chaos that preceded the creative activity, rest is an appropriate, climactic and paradoxically counterbalancing conclusion (see 4.17-26; 5; 10; 11.10-26; 46.1-27).

Genesis 2

While *tôlᵉdōt* ('generations') formulas elsewhere in Genesis introduce a section, 2.4a forms a very poor introduction 2.4b-25 which is not a description of the creation of the heavens and earth, nor of what heaven and earth generated, but a description of the creation of humans, trees, the garden, land animals and birds. Chapter 2.4a functions better as a conclusion, bringing the description of creation week to a natural resting place and forming an inclusion with 1.1:

> 1.1: 'In the beginning God created the heavens and the earth'.
> 2.4a: 'These are the generations of the heavens and the earth when they were created'.

Genesis 2.4b thus forms the introduction to the following narrative. By reversing the standard 'heavens-earth' sequence (cf. Ps. 148.13), it also forms a chiasm with 2.4a, the conclusion of the previous narrative:

	A	B	C
2.4a	Heavens (*šāmayim*)	earth (*'ereṣ*)	created (*bārā'*)
	C'	B'	A'
2.4b	made (*'āśâ*)	earth (*'ereṣ*)	heavens (*šāmayim*)

The chiasm binds the consecutive creation narratives together. It suggests that the two episodes, despite their differences, should be read in an integrated manner, and not simply as two independent units.

Chapter 1 set out a simple chronology of creation. Chapter 2 produces some dissonance when read in this context, as the following comparison of common elements, and the sequence of their creation shows:

	Ch. 1	Ch. 2
1.	Vegetation (1.11-12) (Day 3)	Man (2.7)
2.	Land animals (1.24-25) (Day 6)	Vegetation (2.9 cf. 2.5)
3.	Humans (1.26-27) (Day 6)	Land animals (2.19)
4.		Woman (2.21-22)

When the two episodes are read together, the chronological dissonance indicates that the interest in time displayed in ch. 1, with the climactic seventh day focusing on the quality of time, is not translated into an overriding concern with absolute chronology. NIV's use of the pluperfect is an unconvincing attempt to harmonize the chronologies of the two chapters (see 3.20-24; introductory comments to ch. 6).

Another noticeable difference from ch. 1 is the term used for God. In ch. 1 the term *Elohim* is used. This is continued in 2.4b–3.24, together with the compound term *Yahweh Elohim* ('Lord God'). However, the two terms are not mixed haphazardly. The Woman and the Serpent consistently use *Elohim*. Strangely, the Man gives names to all the animals, but never utters the name of God. The narrator uses *Yahweh Elohim* exclusively. The different terms used by the narrator and characters indicate that they have differing perspectives of God. Indeed, the narrator's shift in vocabulary from that of ch. 1 indicates that there is more than one possible perspective on God. (Cf. how Amnon's term for Tamar shifts as his perspective changes, 2 Sam. 13.6, 11 cf. 17. Also, see Berlin 1983: 60-61.) The distinctions apparent in Genesis 2–3 are a reminder to us to distinguish between the perspectives of narrator, characters and reader in this and any other plotted narrative.

2.4b-9

The action begins 'when no plant of the field (*śîaḥ haśśādeh*) was yet in the earth' (2.5a). We are never told, however, when the plants of the field do appear, though they are on the scene by 3.18 (i.e., *'ēśeb haśśādeh*). We are told that the Lord God planted a garden (2.8) and created trees (2.9), but presumably the term 'plants of the field' refers to more than these, as the distinction between plants (*'ēśeb*) and trees (*'ēṣ*) in 1.11 would indicate. The reason why there are no such plants initially is because first, there is no rain, and secondly, there is no one to till the earth (2.5b). Yet if there is a 'stream' which waters the 'whole face of the ground' (2.6), why is there need for rain? The rest of the chapter introduces us to the Man whose vocation is 'to till and keep' the garden (2.15), but nowhere is rain introduced. Additionally, in the description of the trees formed by the Lord God (2.9) we learn of the 'tree of the knowledge of good and evil', but nowhere do we receive an explanation for this enigmatic expression. Thus ch. 2 forms a contrast to ch. 1. The form of ch. 1 was characterized by almost precise symmetry and balance. The content of ch. 2, however, leaves many loose ends to intrigue the reader. The contrast between the orderliness of the 'generations of the heavens and the earth' (2.4a) and the account of 2.4b-25 is continued in subsequent chapters, where the regularity of human genealogies contrasts with the unpredictability of the narratives (see ch. 5).

God's creation of trees (2.9) includes the tree of life, and the tree of the knowledge of good and evil. All trees are 'pleasant to the sight and good for food' (2.9a), but these two trees have additional properties which will play a crucial part in the development of the narrative (see ch. 3).

2.10-14

The description of the division of the rivers recalls the separation of the waters in ch. 1. The different emphases of the two narratives on this point underline their general perspectives.

Chapter 1 was concerned with the 'heavens and the earth', and in its description of the 'waters above' and 'waters below' (1.7) appropriately considered the vertical dimension. Chapter 2 limits its concerns to the earth, ignoring the heavenly bodies, and thus its description of the separation of the waters takes in only the horizontal dimension, with an outline of the geographical distribution of the rivers over the surface of the earth.

The names of the rivers form two pairs, one known, the other unknown. The Pishon is unique to this passage, while the Gihon, unknown as a river, has a name identical with the spring in the Kidron valley outside Jerusalem (e.g., 2 Chron. 32.30). The mention of the eastward flowing Tigris and Euphrates (2.14) is the first of a number of references in Genesis to movements eastward. Elsewhere, such movements are generally associated with banishment (cf. 3.24; 4.16; 25.6). To a reader familiar with Israel's history of exile in Mesopotamia, this detail linked with the specific mention of Assyria, and the connotations of 'Gihon' mentioned above, could have ominous overtones concerning the fate of humans in Eden.

2.15-25

The recapitulation of Man's placement in the garden (cf. 2.8), is not essential for the reader's information, but juxtaposes this information with mention of the rivers of exile in the preceding verse (2.14). The source of the rivers of exile is in Man's home itself (see 3.20-24).

Part of the commission given to humans in 1.28 was to 'subdue' the earth. No definition of this task was given previously, but here the first hint is provided. Being placed in the garden 'to till it and keep it' (2.15) is at least part of what is entailed in 'subduing the earth'. By tilling the earth, Man makes it conform to his will, and serve his desires, thus 'subduing' it.

The permission given to the Man to eat from any tree in the garden (cf. 1.29b) excludes the 'tree of the knowledge of good and evil', but presumably includes the tree of life (confirmed implicitly in 3.3). The effect of eating from the former tree would be death (2.17). The term $b^e y \hat{o} m$, translated 'in the day' in 2.17 and previously in 2.4b, does not necessarily connote 'on that very day'. NRSV translates the same term with the general 'when' in 5.1-2 (cf. 1 Kgs 2.37 and context). It does, however, indicate a short period between eating and dying. Effectively, therefore, the garden contains a tree of life and a tree of death.

This stark contrast underlines the ominous note introduced by the rivers of exile that emanate from Eden. In a passage that has previously informed us that God gave life, is an announcement that God can also take it away.

In ch. 1 the evaluation formulas stated six times that God's creation was 'good' (1.4, 10, 12, 18, 21, 25) with a concluding seventh pronouncement that everything God had made was 'very good' (1.31). In 2.18 we encounter something that is 'not good'. The Male, in his solitary state, is incomplete. He needs 'a helper (*'ēzer*) as his partner (*keneḡdô*)'. Why does the Man need a helper? The human task has already been outlined in 1.28 and consists of three aspects: to multiply, subdue the earth and exercise dominion over animals. In his single state the Man cannot fulfil any of these. He can hardly be fruitful and multiply by himself. And the fulfilment of this first requirement is necessary for the next two to be realized.

Why does God create animals at this point? Is it, as some suggest, a divine experiment to see whether any can be Man's helper (2.20)? Surely not. No helper could be found *among* the animals because Man needs a helper to have dominion *over* the animals. Chapter 1 had underlined the distinction between animals and humans by stating that only humans were created in the image of God (1.26-27). This, in part, means to have dominion over the animals. Likewise, ch. 2 underlines that difference by showing that animals are not partners for humans—only another human can fill that role. The purpose for God's action in creating animals here is thus not to satisfy God's curiosity, but to impress on the Man the inadequacy of the animals for the task God has given him. Retarding the creation of the Woman, from the Man's perspective, underlines how crucial she is. Before her arrival, he is impotent to fulfil his God-given vocation. Hence the cry of released frustration on meeting her, 'This at last ... !' (2.23). Woman was derived from the Man, as Man was derived from the dust of the ground. The Man's task, in part, is to till the ground (2.15) and the Woman's is to help the Man (2.18). Their vocations are related to their origins. Reminders of their origins will become significant again in the next chapter (see 3.8-19). The Man names 'non-helpers' and 'helper' alike. This underlines his authority within creation, as God's naming in ch. 1 illustrated his authority over creation (see Clines 1990: 37-40).

The chapter concludes with two images that convey the nature of the relationship between the two. First, in their procreation they will replicate their own creation, becoming once again 'one flesh' (2.24). Secondly, the intimacy implied by that image is heightened by their mutual nakedness which lacks all embarrassment (2.25). In contrast to God's announcement before the Woman's arrival that the situation was 'not good' (2.18), it is fair to assume that circumstances at the end of ch. 2 are once again those at the end of ch. 1, namely 'very good' (1.31).

Genesis 3

As the first two main episodes (1.1-2.4a; 2.4b-25) were linked by chiasm (2.4a cf. 2.4b), so ch. 3 is linked to ch. 2 through parono-masia. Verse 2.25 states that the human couple were naked (*ᵃrûmmîm* from *ārôm*); 3.1 that the Serpent was 'crafty' (*ārûm*). The nakedness of 2.25 is positive—a state in which the Man and Woman are in harmony with one another. However, the term *ārûm* is ambiguous. Whether the Serpent will be merely clever/prudent (e.g., Prov. 14.8, 15, 18), or more ominously, crafty (Job 5.12; 15.5), becomes apparent almost immediately.

3.1-7

This is a most enigmatic episode, raising many questions and providing few answers. The Serpent and his actions remain shrouded in mystery. How does the Serpent know about the divine directive against eating (3.1)? The prohibition in 2.17 was given to the Man alone, before the creation of the Serpent (2.19) or the Woman (2.22). This raises another question—how does the Woman know of the prohibition? If one assumes that the Man told her, did the Serpent gain his knowledge from the same source? Has the Serpent himself already eaten the fruit, and thus gained forbidden knowledge—which gives him supernat-ural insight of some kind which he demonstrates in his ques-tioning? None of these questions is answered and this silence allows the possibility that neither the Serpent nor the Woman knows fully what they are talking about. The Serpent's initial question is misleading; God had not prohibited all trees (3.1 cf. 2.16). But the Woman's reply is also at odds with the reader's knowledge; God had made no mention of not touching the tree (3.3 cf. 2.17). The Serpent's 'mistake' may well reveal the nature of his cleverness (*ārûm*)—a deliberate lie or stab in the dark to test the Woman's resolve to obey God. But the Woman's mistake may well reveal a misunderstanding of the original command, or even her perception that it is a petty restriction.

Another obvious question arises. Why does the Serpent engage the Woman in such a conversation? The Serpent nowhere tells the Woman to eat, but he incites her to do so by impugning God's motives for prohibiting the fruit. Is the Serpent privy to the command of 1.28 (as he seems to be to the command of 2.17), that humans are to have dominion over the animal creation? If so, is this an attempt to reverse that God-given human destiny? Even if it is, we still do not know *why*. The reader is as beguiled by the unknown as the Woman is by the Serpent.

Having been made in the image of God, the Man and Woman are already like God in certain respects (1.26-27). The Serpent states that they can become like God in another area—knowing good and evil. Ironically, they arc already like God in having dominion over the animals and here an animal subtly seduces the Woman to do *its* will. But what does the Serpent mean when he says, 'you will be like God, knowing good and evil' (3.5)? The inherent mystery of the passage should warn us against the possibility of a definitive understanding. Nevertheless, the Serpent's prediction contains three points: on eating the fruit they will (a) 'know', (b) 'good and evil' and (c) 'be like God'. The verb 'to know' (*yd'*) has a wide range of connotations of which 'intellectual knowledge' is but one. For example, Gen. 4.1 informs us that 'the man knew (*yd'*) his wife'—a banality indeed if 'intellectual knowledge' is in mind. However, the result of such knowledge was the birth of Cain, indicating that Adam's knowledge amounted to an 'experiencing' of his wife in a sexual encounter (cf. Gen. 19.5, 8; 1 Kgs 1.4). There is the possibility therefore, that *yd'* carries similar experiential connotations in 3.5. In addition, the use of the term 'good and evil' (*ṭôb wārā'*) could well be an example of merismus, that is a linking of polar opposites to convey the idea of totality (cf. 'heavens and earth', 1.1). Thus 'good and evil' expresses the totality of experience (cf. 2 Sam. 13.22; Zeph. 1.12). It is likely, therefore, that the Serpent's statement is an idiomatic way of saying 'you will experience everything'. He is telling the Woman that she and the Man will be able to experience life with no restrictions. God's one restriction—prohibition of the tree—will be swept away, and they will be 'like God' in experiencing whatever they wish.

The Woman now looks at the tree from the Serpent's perspective. She makes three observations. The first two, that the tree was 'good for food' and 'a delight to the eyes' (3.6) do not distinguish it from any other tree in the garden (see 2.9). Her third confirms her seduction by the Serpent: it is no longer a tree distinguished from all others by its ability to deliver death, but is now 'desired to make one wise', that is the experiential wisdom of 'good and evil'. The Man unquestioningly eats the fruit offered to him by his wife, indicating that he shares her new perspective.

The Serpent had predicted that eating the fruit would open their eyes (3.5). This does in fact occur (3.7)—but what they see is not their expected autonomy, but the knowledge that they were naked—a disappointment in the extreme (see Good 1981: 84). Their reaction to this outcome, making clothes to hide their nakedness, indicates that while there it nothing new to see, they now perceive their true status. It also marks the transformation of their nakedness from an expression of mutuality (2.25) to reason for shame (3.7).

3.8-16
Having just hidden their nakedness from each other with leaves of the fig tree (3.7), the human pair now hide from God among the 'trees of the garden' (3.8). Eating from one of the trees made them aware of their nakedness, and now ironically they use the trees to hide that self-same nakedness. God's question, 'Where are you?', is not asking for information of the pair's geographical whereabouts (cf. 4.9-10). The Man's reply understands God's question to mean, 'Why are you hiding?' (Hamilton 1990: 193), 'I heard the sound of you in the garden, and I was afraid, because I was naked; and I hid myself' (3.10). The Man states that he was afraid because he was naked. But his true fear must surely be that God had pronounced the death penalty if he ate from the tree. The Man responds to God's second question, 'Who told you that you were naked?' (3.11), with a statement of beguiling honesty: 'The woman, whom you gave to be with me, she gave me fruit from the tree, and I ate' (3.12). This is perfectly true, but one can hear his tone of voice, in which he first betrays his wife and then blames God. Verse 2.24 had spoken of a man's 'clinging' to his wife. We see now how the former 'one flesh' (2.24) has disintegrated into two naked people. God had previously stated, 'It is not good that the man should be alone' (2.18). Now, the Man's response to God's interrogation shows that the Man and Woman are both alone.

The Woman, questioned next, answers similarly, 'the Serpent tricked me, and I ate' (3.13). Unlike her husband she does not remind God who created the Serpent, but all characters and readers know that he is one of the wild animals 'that the Lord God had made' (3.1). Thus, like her husband she blames another of God's creatures and ultimately, therefore, God himself.

Significantly, the Serpent is never questioned. We are never given his perspective on the turn of events. If given the chance, whom would *he* have blamed? His motivation remains a mystery, but for having done his deed he is cursed. When introduced to the Serpent we were told he was 'ārûm (wise, crafty, 3.1); on his exit from the narrative he is deemed to be 'arûr ('cursed', 3.14). He may have beguiled the Woman (3.13), but he cannot outwit God. The first part of the curse reads most naturally as indicating, among other things, a change in the Serpent's mode of locomotion. From now on he will crawl on his belly and 'eat dust'—a posture of humiliation ensuring the human dominion over the animal that his seduction of the Woman had threatened to overturn (cf. 1.28). This relationship between humans and animals is expanded on in 3.15. While enmity between the Serpent and humans will continue through the generations (3.15a), humans will have the advantage (3.15b). They will each 'strike' at the other, but the human target of the Serpent's head suggests a more serious blow than the Serpent's striking a human's heel. This is all the more likely in a divine speech which is a curse on the Serpent (3.14a). The curse announces a decisive shift in human-animal relations: the intended dominion (1.28) will be heightened into enmity.

The reason for the Woman's creation was to be the Man's helper to fulfil the mandate of 1.28. She has failed lamentably in one aspect—exercising dominion over the Serpent, a representative of the animals. The curse on the Woman (3.16) relates to another aspect of the original mandate—being fruitful and multiplying. The process of reproduction will become a painful affair, but the Woman's continued sexual craving for her husband will negate this seeming disincentive to human reproduction. And in any case, the fact that her husband shall 'rule' over her, suggests she will not be left with any choice in the matter (see 4.1-7).

The curse addressed to the Man is actually a curse on the ground (3.17). The narrative did not indicate previously that the Man's 'tilling' and 'keeping' would be effortless, but now 'thorns and thistles' will cause him to 'sweat' and 'toil' over his task. The earth will become a less hospitable environment, thus the Man must struggle more in order to subdue the earth. In fact, one is left wondering whether the Man will ever be able to fulfil this God-given vocation. The statement that he would struggle to sustain himself, and eventually return to the dust of the ground (3.19), suggests that ultimately it is the earth that subdues the Man.

The curses complicate humanity's destiny outlined in 1.28. Dominion over the animals is challenged by the struggle with the Serpent; multiplication will now be accompanied by pain in childbirth; subduing the earth will now need to contend with the curse on the ground.

The curses also recall the origins of the Man and the Woman. The Man was formed from 'the dust of the ground' (2.7), and so he will return to the dust (3.19). The Woman was formed from the Man, and she will be dominated by the Man. Each becomes subordinate to its origins. However, what of the Serpent? The Serpent was formed from the ground (2.19) and he will eat the dust of the ground (3.14), to which the Man returns after death. Will the Serpent, whose seduction resulted in eating forbidden fruit, continue his dominance, even through the very curse of eating the dust to which the Man returns?

3.20-24

Despite the sombre tone of the curses, the Man gives his wife a name that expresses optimism. Eve (*ḥawwâ*) is so named because 'she was the mother of all who live' (*ḥay*, 3.20). She has not yet, however, given birth to anyone. Her name shows that the Man is confident that she has indeed been provided as a 'helper' towards the human goal of reproduction (1.28; 2.18), and will give birth despite the increase of pain predicted in the curse (3.16). In ch. 1 God's acts of naming showed his sovereignty over creation; in ch. 2 the Man named the animals (2.20), thus displaying his dominion over them. His naming of Eve in ch. 3 demonstrates that he is the senior partner (cf. 2.23b). The naming of his wife shows that he is more willing to conform to the divine words of curse— '[your husband] shall rule over you' (3.16)—than he was to the original command not to eat from the tree (2.17).

The Man gives his wife a name, while God gives them both clothing. The substitution of the flimsy covering of fig leaves with the more durable one of animal's skin might demonstrate God's care, but at the same time confirms the permanence of the human dilemma (Hauser 1982: 32). Ironically, an animal was instrumental in humans becoming aware of their nakedness, and animals are used to hide that nakedness, just as eating from a tree produced knowledge of nakedness, and leaves from a tree were used to hide that nakedness.

The Lord God's words show that the Serpent was a seducer rather than a blatant liar. He had merely been economical with the truth. His prediction that on eating the fruit the couple would become like God, knowing good and evil (i.e., achieving autonomy), is confirmed by God (3.22), though apparently not realized by the couple (see 3.1-7). The Serpent's reassurance that they would not die (3.4), however, while true in the short term, is not confirmed for the long term. The Lord God has already announced that humanity will return to the dust (3.19), and here he denies access to the tree of life, which would have bestowed immortality (3.22b). That is to say, the Man and Woman achieved the autonomy they desired, but it would not last. Denied access to the tree of life they are exiled eastward. This is the first enforced move to the east that is experienced by the dispossessed in Genesis, and confirms the negative connotations introduced in the earlier description of the rivers (see 2.10-14; 4.8-16; 11.1-9; 13.8-13; 29.1-14).

A backward glance at chs. 1–3 shows once again the complementary nature of the narratives. The narrative of creation week (1.1-2.4a) had emphasized time and culminated with holy time (see introductory comments to ch. 1; 2.1-4a). The story of the human couple in the garden of Eden emphasizes the concept of holy space through its use of sanctuary imagery. Just like the sanctuary/temple the garden is entered from the east (3.24 cf., e.g., Ezek. 47.1); is associated with river imagery (2.10-14 cf. Ezek. 47.1-12; Ps. 46.4), one of which is named Gihon. (3.13 cf. 2 Chron. 32.30). The vocation of the man within Eden is to 'till' (*'bd*) and 'keep' (*šmr*) it (2.15), verbs used elsewhere to describe priestly duties in the sanctuary/temple (Num. 3.7-8; 8.26; 18.5-6). Most obviously, the garden is protected by cherubim (3.24, cf. Exod. 25.18-22; 26.1; 1 Kgs 6.23-29) (for more detail see Wenham 1986: 20-24.) The first three chapters of Genesis therefore, are concerned with time and space, but more particularly with holy time and holy space. In such a context, the chronological discrepancies between the two narratives are hardly surprising (see introductory comments to ch. 2.) The account of creation week moved from chaos to order and as it did so also moved from time to holy time. The Eden account moves from protection to expulsion and as it does so moves from holy space to common space outside the garden. Chapters 1–3 are cocooned in holiness; the action of chs. 4–11 will inhabit a very different world.

Genesis 4

Events inside the Garden have forewarned us that life away from Eden will be qualitatively different from life within it. But what exactly will be the nature of human existence in this new environment? How might God's ideal for humanity originally stated in 1.28 and subsequently modified by the curses of 3.14-19, concerning fertility, subjugation of the earth and dominion of the animal creation, actually work out?

Verses 4.1-16 contain a large number of verbal echoes of the previous narrative. For example, 'know' (3.5, 7, 22; cf. 4.1, 9); 'till' (3.23; cf. 4.2, 12); 'drive out' (3.24; cf. 4.14); 'ground' (3.17, 19, 23; cf. 4.2-3, 10-12, 14). Also, the similarity between 4.7b and 3.16b is striking. In addition, events in chs. 3 and 4 follow a similar sequence. Each contains a succinct description of an offence (3.6; cf. 4.8); pointed questions from God (3.9; cf. 4.9; 3.13 cf. 4.10); curses which focus on the ground (3.17; 4.11); God's giving an item to the offenders—clothes to the Man and Woman and a mark to Cain (3.21; 4.15); banishment of the transgressors east of Eden (3.24; 4.16) (see Wenham 1987: 99). The sum of these connections shows that despite the fact that the Man and Woman appear only in 4.1-2a, the story of 4.1-16 has a vital connection with what has preceded.

4.1-7

No sooner does the Man 'know' good and evil (3.22), than he 'knows' his wife (4.1). No sooner have they been barred from the Tree of Life (3.24), than they procreate new life in the form of their two sons (4.1-2a). These ironies show that events in the Garden, once again, cast their shadow over the story, as indeed does the original divine command (1.28) and its subsequent adaptation in the curses (3.14-19). Not only do the Man and Woman reproduce (multiplication), but their progeny keep sheep (dominion over the animals) and till the ground (subjugation of the earth) (see 1.24-31; 2.15-17; 3.8-19).

Verses 4.1-7 introduce us to two new characters. The way they are described emphasizes that this is above all a story of brothers.

After giving birth to Cain, Eve 'bore his brother Abel' (4.2). These two are self-evidently brothers, yet the narrative persists in reminding us of the fact: 'his brother Abel' (twice in 4.8); 'Where is your brother Abel?' (4.9a); 'am I my brother's keeper?' (4.9b); 'your brother's blood is crying out to me' (4.10); '... your brother's blood from your hand' (4.11). This is a story of two *brothers*.

The main action of this passage, however, is precipitated by a crucial distinction made between the two in 4.4b-5a, emphasized by its chiastic formulation:

> A And the Lord had regard
> B for Abel and his offering,
> B' but for Cain and his offering
> A' he had no regard.

God's favouritism, in which the younger brother is preferred to the older is a recurring motif in Genesis (see 9.20-29; 11.10-26). Possible reasons for such divine favouritism will be discussed below.

The cry of Eve in 4.1b is very difficult to understand. The Hebrew text places the particle *'et* before Yahweh. Elsewhere this is used to indicate the definite object or is occasionally translated 'with'. But Eve can hardly be claiming to have produced Yahweh, while the usual translation 'with the help of' has no other Old Testament attestations to support it. It is just possible that it could be translated, 'I have created a man *as well as* the Lord'. Understood this way, it would be an arrogant cry directed against God, in which she proclaims that she has become like God (Gibson 1981: 143; cf. Cassuto 1964: I, 198-202). If so, we see how the influence of the Serpent lingers.

In Eve's exclamation the name of the firstborn, Cain (*qayin*), is related through assonance to *qānîtî*, 'I have produced/created/acquired'. His brother is called Abel (*hebel*), meaning 'breath/shadow' (e.g., Eccl. 1.2; Ps. 144.4), a name provided by the narrator, not Eve, as an ominous foreshadowing of his role in the story.

The reason for God's rejection of Cain's offering is enigmatic. It is unlikely that lack of blood rendered it unacceptable because *minḥâ* ('offering', 4.3-5) elsewhere describes both animal (e.g., 1 Sam. 2.17; 26.19) and cereal offerings (e.g., Lev. 2.1-15). Yet Yahweh's reaction might not be entirely inscrutable. The narrative does seem to underline the generosity and quality of Abel's sacrifice. His contribution was 'the firstlings of his flock, their fat portions' (4.4). By contrast, Cain brought a minimal contribution, some of 'the fruit of the ground' (4.3). There are no 'first-fruits' (e.g., Exod. 23.19; 34.26; Lev. 2.14) to correspond to Abel's 'firstlings' (e.g., Lev. 27.26; Deut. 12.6). This distinction between the offerings must reflect differing attitudes to Yahweh (cf. Heb. 11.4). Once again 'fruit' seals the fate of a human character. Eating the forbidden fruit led to expulsion from the garden (3.23-24); offering fruit results in separation from Yahweh (4.16).

Yahweh's confrontation with Cain reads more like fatherly advice to a wayward child than a condemnation. Yahweh gives Cain hope, 'If you do well, will you not be accepted?'; a warning, 'And if you do not do well, sin is lurking at the door; its desire is for you'; and a task, 'you must master it' (4.7). The fact that Yahweh can give Cain advice on how he can be 'accepted', shows that whatever the reason for the rejection of his sacrifice, the rupture in their relationship was not final—but its continuation was in the hands of Cain. The warning and task given by Yahweh recall the curse given to the Woman. In 3.16 the Woman's 'desire' (*tᵉšûqâ*) would be for her husband, and he would rule (*mšl*) over her. In 4.7, 'Sin' has a 'desire' (*tᵉšûqâ*) for Cain, but he must 'master' (*mšl*) it. In the first case the one desired *will* rule, and in the second *is exhorted* to rule over the party desiring him. Yet 3.16 is a curse, and 4.7 brings hope. We see in the next paragraph that Cain is unable to 'master'/'rule' the 'sin' that desires him. This raises the question of whether the Man will be able to rule over the Woman who desires him.

4.8-16
Cain proceeds to murder Abel. We are not told why he does so. This continues the trend of the narrative so far in which characters' motives are largely ignored. Thus, we were not told why the Serpent seduced the Woman, nor in this story why Yahweh rejects Cain's sacrifice (though there are implicit hints). Like much Hebrew literature, this narrative engages the reader's interest and participation through withholding such information. This feature is underlined in this passage by a gap in the text. The Hebrew text does not include what 'Cain said to his brother' (4.8a) prior to despatching him. Many modern versions insert words found in some ancient traditions, but such attempts remove the mystery designed to heighten the senselessness of his act.

The passage contains a number of comparisons and contrasts with preceding narratives. In 2.18 the Lord God had said, 'It is not good that the man should be alone'. Now, Cain also stands alone, without his brother. In ch. 3 Eve had to be seduced by the Serpent to disobey God. But Cain cannot even be persuaded by God not to succumb to sin. When the Man and Woman were questioned concerning their crime they admitted it, though claiming mitigating circumstances (3.12-13). Cain is even more evasive, showing an arrogant attitude to divine authority with his impertinent reply to God's question, 'I do not know; am I my brother's keeper?' This witticism, which could be paraphrased, 'am I to shepherd the shepherd?' (cf. von Rad 1972: 105), shows no remorse or willingness to confess. His words contain two motifs from the previous narrative, those of 'knowing' (*yd'*) and 'guarding'/'keeping' (*šmr*), which were bound up with the original offence (3.5, 7, 22) and its consequences (3.24) (cf. Cassuto 1964: I, 217). Their repetition here, in the tone of voice delivered by Cain, underlines the callous nature of his act. There is a concomitant increase in the severity of Yahweh's punishment. The Man was told, 'cursed is the ground because of you', (3.17), while Cain's curse shifts the focus from the ground to the offender, 'you are cursed from the ground' (4.11). Cain's *livelihood* has been derived from the ground; Cain's *crime* arose out of his involvement with the ground; his *punishment* is to be driven from the ground as 'a fugitive and a wanderer on the earth'. His ability to subdue the earth is thus severely curtailed (cf. Miller 1978: 32).

Cain's reaction to his new destiny is instructive. Though the meaning of 4.13 has been debated by some, it would appear that Cain bewails his punishment rather than his criminal act, 'My *punishment* is greater than I can bear!' His curt reply to God's initial question (4.9) has already revealed his true attitude to his brother's death. There is more of the whimpering self-pity of an apprehended criminal than contrition in his words. It is ironic to hear the murderer confess his fear of being murdered (4.14). Given the facts of the narrative so far, he must mean that his mother and father are likely to take vengeance. The Lord prevents this from happening by placing a mark on Cain to indicate the sevenfold penalty that will come upon any perpetrator of vengeance. The mark thus announces both his guilt and his safety (Brueggemann 1962: 160), in much the same way as Yahweh's gift of clothes to the human couple are reminders of their offence yet also of Yahweh's 'grace' (3.21).

Cain journeys on to 'the land of Nod' (*nôd*, 4.16), a destination which provides a linguistic echo of the curse which condemned him to a life as 'a wanderer' (*nād* 4.12). Thus 'land of Nod' conveys not only the continual physical movement of Cain, but also the state of his relationship with God, humans and the turmoil of his own guilt. Yet his situation could be worse. Despite his banishment, Cain is a man who stands simultaneously under the condemnation and protection of God (see 27.41–28.9).

4.17-26
The heavens and earth were generated in one week, culminating in the unique seventh day (see 1.1-2.4a). The list of generations in 4.17-24 similarly takes us down to Lamech, the seventh generation from Adam. The earlier generations are passed over hurriedly, but the seventh generation is obviously of greatest importance, with the activities of Lamech (4.19-24), occupying more space than all of the previous generations combined. As if to emphasize the number seven, Lamech's song concludes, 'If Cain is avenged sevenfold, truly Lamech seventy-sevenfold'. This seventh element in the genealogy, however, contrasts with that of the creation account. There, the seventh element contained blessing and sanctification (2.1-3); here, arrogance and vengeance (4.23-24). The reason for the contrast is provided by the events described in 2.4b-4.16 (see 2.1-4a; ch. 5; ch. 10; 11.10-26; 46.1-27.)

The continuation of the human line, beginning in 4.17, presents a precise verbal echo of 4.1. Just like Adam, Cain 'knew his wife, and she conceived and bore ...' The repetition of this information makes the reader wonder whether this narrative will go the same way as the former, with conflict and murder. These fears are fulfilled by 4.17-24 which commence with one murderer, Cain, and conclude with another, Lamech. The wife through whom Cain fathers his line arrives on the scene with no introduction, but presumably is one of the daughters born to Adam (5.4). Thus, Cain threatens the family line by murdering one sibling and ensures its continuation by marrying another.

In the previous narrative Cain was condemned to a life of wandering (4.12b, 14b), yet after the birth of Enoch, he builds a city. This would appear to be an act of defiance, continuing the trend seen in his previous conversation with Yahweh (4.9-15). Yet what a petty act of defiance it appears to be! At the time of building his city the only humans in the land of Nod are Cain, his wife, Enoch and Cain's other children, if he had any. This could hardly be called a city of any note—some of his descendants prefer tents (4.20). Jabal comes closer than Cain to living out the curse of a wanderer. Yet ironically, Cain's 'urban' existence removes him from primary involvement with agriculture, and confirms that he has been 'cursed from the ground' (4.11) (see 11.1-9).

Cain's initiative also highlights that human life is now being lived irretrievably away from Eden. Originally, the Lord had planted a marvellous Garden full of delights as the first human dwelling place (2.8-9). All that Cain can provide is a puny 'city'.

Having given us some detail on the first two human generations (2.4–4.16), Genesis moves rapidly to the seventh, with little more than a catalogue of names to fill the gap. In 2.24 the narrator had informed us that the preceding story explained why 'a man leaves his father and his mother and clings to his wife'. Does Lamech's taking two wives indicate a continuation of the spirit of Cain in defying accepted conventions? Regardless, one unambiguous point is made by the listing of Lamech's family. Human multiplication is reckoned only through the male line. All of Lamech's sons become the 'ancestor' (literally 'father') of important advances in civilization. His daughter Naamah is distinguished by being 'the sister of Tubal-cain' (4.22). Unlike Eve (3.20), she is not deemed to be the 'mother' of anything. The patriarchal dominance in society, predicted in 3.16b, is one of Yahweh's curses that seems to meet with little resistance.

The mark Yahweh placed on Cain was devised as a disincentive to murder. Anyone who killed Cain would receive sevenfold vengeance (4.15). On his own initiative, Lamech decided to mete out seventy-sevenfold vengeance—death as a penalty for merely wounding him (4.23-24). He feels no need for a protective mark, and we are not surprised that Yahweh does not offer to him what he offered to Cain. Affairs have declined greatly since Abel was slain, and immeasurably since the forbidden fruit was eaten. Eve could cry 'I have produced a man' (4.1); Lamech exults 'I have killed a man' (4.23) (see Cassuto 1964: I, 242-43). Lamech brags about an act that even Cain would not admit.

The beginning of Cain's genealogy (4.17), was reminiscent of Adam and Eve's procreation in 4.1-2. Verses 4.25-26 provide even more striking parallels. Once again Adam 'knows' his wife; she bears a son; the child is named by his mother; his name is explained by reference to the Lord/God (though much less exultantly than 4.1); Cain and Abel are mentioned by name (cf. Cassuto 1964: I, 245). This reprise announces a new beginning. Eve mentions all three of her sons in one verse. Abel is dead; Cain has been banished; her only hope rests in Seth. This point is enhanced when one realizes that 4.25-26 is chronologically displaced. If Adam is 130 years old at the birth of Seth (5.3), then Seth was born before the seventh generation from Adam. Why place the birth announcement of Seth here? And why in the same verse have Eve remind the reader that Cain killed Abel (4.25), if not to emphasize immediately after Lamech's self-comparison with Cain (4.23-24), that Seth marks a new beginning.

Eve's designation of Seth as a 'seed' (*zera'*) is interesting. It contrasts with Cain's being called a 'man' (*'îš*) at his birth. The previous use of 'seed' was in God's curse on the Serpent, where it was predicted that the Serpent and the Woman's 'seed' would be enemies (3.15). Eve designates Seth as her 'seed', and therefore the line who will engage the Serpent's seed in combat. (See Alexander 1989: 15-16; Hamilton 1990: 242.) The act of giving birth causes Eve to remember the curse on the Serpent (3.15), rather than the curse on herself (3.16). She recognizes that there are still old scores to settle.

After the birth of Seth's son Enosh, 'people began to invoke the name of the Lord' (4.26b), which presumably signifies worship, rather than the preferred name for God (which was already used by Eve in 4.1). Cain has already displayed his inability to worship acceptably. He and his ancestors achieved much in the way of cultural innovations—urbanization (4.17), nomadism, herding, music, metal-working (4.20-22)—but worship comes only with Seth. Cain's line culminates in vengeful Lamech; Seth's line in 'righteous' Noah (6.9). Humanity is diversifying.

Genesis 5

The genealogy of Adam comes immediately after the genealogy of 4.17-26 and takes up the whole of ch. 5. Each genealogy traces its line of descent through one member per generation, until the final generation, when three members are listed (4.20-22 cf. 5.32). The names of several characters in each are either identical: namely Enoch and Lamech, or very similar Cain/Kenan; Irad/Jared; Mehujael/Mahalalel; Methushael/Methuselah. Such similarities in structure and content suggest that human history develops along similar lines in the Cainite and Sethite genealogies. However, each leads to quite different conclusions. While each includes a character called Lamech, who is the only one to speak in the respective genealogies (4.23-24; 5.29), the two characters are clearly distinguished. The Cainite Lamech is arrogant; the Sethite Lamech expresses hope for the future. The Cainite genealogy concludes with Lamech the taker of life; the Sethite genealogy concludes with Noah the preserver of life (as we learn in subsequent chapters).

The structure of ch. 5 is highly schematic. Each generation follows the form: When A had lived x years, he became the father of B. A lived after the birth of B, y years, and he had other sons and daughters. Thus all the days of A were z years, and he died. Such orderliness in the genealogy seems to contrast with the unpredictability of the narratives surrounding it (see Robinson 1986: 598). Yet the symmetry is not absolute (cf. structure of ch. 1). Extra information concerning Adam's son and his naming is provided (5.3b); Lamech gives a short speech (5.29). If A = father and B = son, then the pattern for each generation is ABABA except for the *seventh* generation (see ch. 1; 4.17-26), where the pattern is ABABAA, the additional note A concerning Enoch's 'walking with God' (5.22a). In addition, we read the striking information that God 'took him' (5.24b), rather than 'and he died'. Thus the seventh generation once again deviates from the norm. And the tenth generation names *three* sons and is not concluded until 9.29 where the formula is adapted to take into account the intervening account of the Flood.

Verses 5.1-2 remind the reader of material already presented but also adds to this information. We are told that humankind was 'blessed' (5.2), but we are not told the content of the blessing. The succeeding genealogy is more than enough to remind us that the first element was 'be fruitful and multiply' (1.28). Humans appear to be successfully fulfilling that mandate. However, 5.2 also includes the information that God 'named' human beings. The creation story limits God's naming to the elements of time and space, that is day/night; sky; land/sea (1.5, 8, 10). Verses 5.1-2 therefore, give both reiteration and new detail. The new detail emphasizes the relationship between God and humans. Another item, however, underlines the growing alienation between the two. Adam was created in 'the likeness of God' (5.1), and then fathered a son 'in his likeness, according to his image'. Thus while the 'divine image' is transmitted to the next generation, Seth is further removed than Adam: he is in the image of the image of God.

The concluding refrain of each generation is 'and he died'. Only two deaths have been recorded prior to ch. 5, and both of these were murders (4.8, 23). Here we learn that death is the common human fate, whether through murder or otherwise. The fulfilment of God's prediction 'you shall die' (2.17) may have been delayed, but come it does.

Yet not all die. Enoch, the seventh generation from Adam does not 'die', but is 'taken' by God. It is not entirely clear why Enoch's fate differs from all others. He 'walks with God' (5.22, 24), but so does Noah (6.9), and his life story ends with the stereotyped obituary notice 'and he died' (9.29). Is Enoch's privileged status due more to the fact that he simply fills the favoured spot of seventh generation? (See 4.17-26; ch. 10; 11.10-26; 46.1-27.)

Lamech's statement in 5.29 shows that despite the preoccupations of the genealogy, there is more to human existence than procreation and death. There is the hard toil of working a cursed earth. For some unknown reason, he hopes that his son Noah will alleviate this burden. Why and how are not revealed here. The Flood narrative (6.1-9.27), which constitutes a huge parenthesis in Noah's genealogical entry (beginning in 5.32 but concluding only in 9.28-29), will cast some light on this.

Genesis 6

The Flood account (chs. 6–9), exhibits an interesting tension between its symmetrical form and its chronological content. (See introductory comments to ch. 2 regarding the tensions between the symmetrical ch. 1 and the chronologically incompatible ch. 2.) The Flood narrative's structural symmetry, as it moves from physical order to chaos and back again, can be sketched palistrophically.

> A Noah and his three sons (6.9-10)
>   B Violence in God's creation (6.11-12)
>   C First divine address: resolution to destroy (6.13-22)
>   D Second divine address: command to enter the ark (7.1-10)
>   E Beginning of the flood (7.11-16)
>   F The rising flood waters (7.17-24)
>   GOD'S REMEMBRANCE OF NOAH (8.1a)
>   F' The receding flood waters (8.1b-5)
>   E' The drying of the earth (8.6-14)
>   D' Third divine address: command to leave the ark (8.15-19)
>   C' God's resolution to preserve order (8.20-22)
>   B' Fourth divine address: covenant blessing and peace (9.1-17)
> A' Noah and his three sons (9.18-19)
> (Adapted from Anderson 1978:23-39)

Coupled with this structural symmetry, however, is chronological incoherence. In ch. 1, as the account described the progression away from chaos, time was created, culminating with the sanctified seventh day. Here, as creation reverts to primordial chaos, with waters engulfing the earth (cf. 1.2, 9), the incoherent time references themselves contribute to that chaos. For example, while 7.4, 12 state that rain fell for 40 days, 7.24 and 8.3 say that 150 days covered the same period. Verse 8.2 describes the rain, which began in 7.12 for a period of 40 days, ceasing *after* the period of 150 days (7.24). The two periods of 40 and 150 days seem to be incompatible. (For further detail see Emerton 1987: 402-405). Thus the contrast between palistrophic balance and chronological disarray mirrors the two axes of chaos and order found in the creation and flood accounts.

6.1-8

Rival interpretations of the troublesome 'sons of God' and 'daughters of humans' abound. However, regardless of whether the 'sons of God' are divine beings (cf. similar designations with this connotation in, for example, Job 1.6; 2.1; 38.7; Pss. 291; 89.7; Dan. 3.25), or human descendants of Seth (or possibly Cain, see Eslinger 1979: 71), their offspring borne by the 'daughters of humans' are still judged to be human (6.4). Thus, regardless of their parentage, 6.1-4 underlines the thrust of preceding genealogies: humanity continues to multiply.

The previous genealogies had different forms. Genesis 4.17-26 combined genealogical succession with indications of cultural advancements and human iniquity. Genesis 5.1-32, with the exception of brief observations on Enoch (5.22, 24) and Lamech's statement (5.29), provides genealogical succession only. Only when readers come to 6.1-8 do they realize the more complex issues that have been present from the time 'when people *began* to multiply' (6.1), none of which was divulged in ch. 5. Genesis 6.1-8 explains why 5.3-32 ended with Noah, for with him comes a radical disjunction in human history. The statement that all humanity was corrupt (6.5) causes one to reconsider the seeming distinction between the two genealogies of 4.17-26 and 5.1-32. Verses 4.17-24 implied moral judgment by moving from Cain (bad) to Lamech (worse); ch. 5 assessed only Enoch, and he 'walked with God'. The universal wickedness revealed in 6.5 makes us realize therefore, that lack of condemnation in ch. 5 should not be taken for commendation (see 4.17-26; ch. 5).

Despite the obscurities of 6.1-4, the passage has many details which draw the reader's attention back to the preceding narratives, and help in assessing the significance of the passage. These include the initial statement, 'When people (*'ādām*) began to multiply on the face of the ground (*"dāmâ*)' (6.1), which recalls the previous usages of this wordplay reaching back to the creation of humanity in 2.7. The action of the 'sons of God' recalls that of God himself in ch. 1: 'the sons of God saw (*r'h*) that they were fair (*tôb*)' (6.2) cf. 'and God saw (*r'h*) ... that it was good (*tôb*)' (1.4, 10, 12, etc.). More significantly, 6.1-4 also recalls the offence of ch. 3. In ch. 3 a non-human agent, the Serpent, took the initiative in tempting a human female to become 'like God' (3.5). Similarly, in 6.1-4, non-human agents (as 'sons of God' must surely be), take the initiative in forming relationships with human females whose progeny, while still designated 'men' (NRSV 'warriors'), must inevitably be closer to divinity (cf. 'like God'). The analogies between the crucial acts of the Woman and 'sons of God' can hardly be missed: 'when the woman saw that the tree was good (*tôb*) ... she took (*lqh*)' (3.6); 'the sons of God saw that they were fair (*tôb*), and they took (*lqh*)' (6.2). Such parallels make the reader anticipate God's judgment in 6.3, which like 3.22-24 cuts short human life (see 7.11-16).

God's statement limiting human life to 120 years remains an enigma. Not only is it a reduction from the life spans recorded in previous genealogies, but also in those that succeed. It can hardly refer to a period of grace before judgment, because no mention has yet been made of God's decision to destroy (cf. 6.7), and even when it is there are no indications that God's decision is reversible, which would be necessary for a 'period of grace' to have any meaning.

Elsewhere in the Old Testament, the Nephilim (6.4) and their associates, the Anakim and Rephaim, are distinguished by being wiped out in the Israelite Conquest. (Cf. Num. 13.33; Josh. 11.21-22; 12.4-6; 13.12; 15.14; Judg. 1.20. See Hendel 1987: 13-26). The mention of their name introduces an ominous note confirmed by God's announcement of annihilation (6.7).

Until 6.2 characters see (*r'h*) only that which is good (*tôb*). God with his creation (1.4, 10, etc.); the Woman with the tree (3.6); the 'sons of God' with human women (6.2). That pattern is now broken: 'The Lord *saw* (*r'h*) that the *wickedness* of humankind ...' (6.5). Such a stark contrast presages a radical disruption in God's relation to the world. This is not the first time that God has judged his creation to be less than perfect—in 2.18 he exclaimed, 'it is not good that the man should be alone'. At that time the problem was rectified by creating Woman, but in 6.5 the strong terms expressing the problem of deep-seated universal wickedness, suggests a more drastic solution will be necessary this time.

The echoes of creation in 6.1-3 find their consummation when God announces his regret at having created humanity, and his resolve to blot out his entire creation (6.6-7). The pleasure God previously took in his creation contrasts with his present sorrow and grief. The 'pangs' (*'iṣṣābôn*) and 'pain' (*'eṣeb*) previously laid on the Woman in childbirth (3.16), and on those who 'toil' (*'iṣṣābôn*) with the soil (3.17; 5.29), now find lodgement in the 'grieving' (*'eṣeb*) of God (6.6 cf. 34.7). The narrative conveys the pathos of a disappointed God, rather than the rage of a divine judge (see Brueggemann 1982: 77).

Lamech's prediction (5.29) comes to fruition in the final sentence of this passage which announces that 'Noah found favour in the sight of the Lord', (6.8). Just what such favour might mean unfolds in the ensuing narrative.

6.9-22

The formula, 'These are the descendants of (*tôlᵉdōt*) Noah' (6.9), introduces a major new section of the narrative. The recapitulation of information regarding Noah is not simply repetitive, but allows readers to reflect on their previous knowledge. Genesis 5.28-32 had given largely genealogical information regarding Noah; 6.8 had announced the favour he found with God. Verse 6.9 informs us that in contrast to the rest of humanity (6.5), 'Noah was a righteous man, blameless in his generation.' This assessment suggests a reason why he finds favour with God and a potential confirmation of Lamech's prescience in 5.29. The information that 'Noah walked with God' (6.9) recalls Enoch who did likewise (5.24). In ch. 5, all generations except Enoch died. In ch. 6 we learn that God has 'determined to make an end of all flesh' (6.13), yet there is a man who similarly 'walked with God' (6.9). We might well anticipate that Noah, like Enoch, could escape the common human fate.

The corruption of the earth is manifest, conveyed through the repetition of *šḥt*: 'Now the earth was corrupt (*šḥt*) ... God saw that the earth was corrupt (*šḥt*); for all flesh had corrupted (*šḥt*) its ways' (6.11-12). The same root is employed to show that God's punishment will fit the crime, 'I am going to destroy (*šḥt*) them'

(6.13). (Cf. 9.6; Hamilton 1990: 278.) However, God makes no general announcement of his intentions. The only individual who is told of the impending destruction is the one who will be saved from it (6.13-18).

As with 6.1-8, this section also contains echoes of the creation narrative. Just as ch. 1 prefaces its account of the creation of the earth with a statement of its condition—'a formless void' (1.2), so with the account of its destruction, it is 'corrupt' and 'filled with violence' (6.11). Genesis 1.22, 28 had declared that animals and humans should 'fill the earth', whereas now it is 'violence'. 'God *saw* that the earth was corrupt ...' (6.12), as he had previously 'seen' humanity's wickedness (6.5). This contrasts starkly with the concluding assessment of creation, 'God *saw* everything that he had made, and indeed, it was very good' (1.31). He will now destroy everything that has the breath of life (*rûaḥ ḥayyîm*, 6.17), just as he had previously given it (*nišmat ḥayyîm*, 2.7). The means of destruction—water (6.17), will return the earth to its pre-creation state (1. 2). The animals coming to Noah for sanctuary (6.19-20) recalls their coming to Adam to be named (2.19-20), as their enumeration (6.20) echoes their creation (1.24-25). Noah's unquestioning obedience, 'he did all that God commanded him' (6.22) reveals a quality of obedience matched previously only by creation responding to God's command (ch. 1). Yet the God who in ch. 1 seemed to control everything has by now all but lost control of humanity.

Such a catalogue of allusions to and echoes of the narrative of creation forces the reader to view the ensuing Flood as being more than a destruction, but as a decreation. As such it underlines the extreme seriousness of God's actions.

Genesis 7

7.1-10

The narrative has previously informed us that Noah was a 'righteous' man (6.9). It is now strongly implied that this attribute makes him unique, 'you [singular, that is, 'you alone', NRSV] are righteous before me in this generation' (7.1). If Noah alone is righteous, one may deduce that his family is not. Yet they, together with selected animals will be taken on board the ark (6.18-20). If Noah could save his family because of his righteousness, why, we might well ask, could he not have saved more? The concept of a small number of righteous individuals being sufficient to save a whole community is presented elsewhere in the Genesis narrative in Abraham's dialogue with God (see 18.16-33; 19.1-29).

Noah is told to distinguish between clean and unclean animals, by taking on board seven pairs of the former and one pair of the latter. While we as readers may associate such distinctions primarily with matters regarding dietary taboos (cf. Lev. 11; Deut. 14), this cannot be so for Noah. In Genesis 7 human food is still entirely vegetarian (1.29 cf. 9.1). While God assumes Noah is aware of such distinctions, we are not told how Noah would have known, or why he would need to know. Of more immediate interest to the reader is why clean animals and all kinds of birds (7.3), should outnumber unclean animals seven to one. We are alerted to look for pointers in the ensuing narrative as to why such distinctions are made here (see 8.6-14, 20-22).

God announces that in seven days he will send rain (7.4). The only previous reference to rain had been to inform the reader that its absence had prevented the growth of vegetable life (2.5); its introduction will now exterminate all animal life. Note that as creation was brought from a watery chaos to an ordered conclusion on the seventh day (2.1-3), its obliteration by water will commence on the seventh day (7.4, 10).

Verses 7.6-9 bring to fulfilment the statements made in the previous passage. As predicted, the flood comes on the earth (7.6 cf. 6.17); Noah and his family enter the ark (7.7 cf. 6.18); pairs of animals accompany them (7.8-9 cf. 6.20; 7.2). Whatever God commands is precisely what happens. This recalls the contrast seen earlier, where creation's unquestioning obedience (chs. 1–2) is not matched by humans (ch. 3). If only God could control all human behaviour as he does the natural elements and Noah's family, rather than simply responding to human initiatives, no deluge would be necessary.

7.11-16

This passage, which describes the coming of the flood waters, supplements the similar description of the preceding paragraph, and although it follows the same sequence, is not simply repetitive. The second list, in most instances, provides more precise and supplementary information, as can be seen by comparing the content of the following verses. Together they form an example of 'panel writing' (see McEvenue 1971: 158-59; Wenham 1987: 177).

Date in Noah's life	v. 6a	v. 11a
Flood comes	v. 6b	vv. 11b-12
Noah and family enter	v. 7	v. 13
Animals enter in pairs	vv. 8-9a	vv. 14-15
'As God had commanded'	v. 9b	v. 16

If the 'sons of God' incident (6.1-4) provides one (or the main) reason for God's judgment, there could be a general connection between that offence and this watery punishment. At creation, the waters were divided into two separate spheres of 'above' and 'below' (1.6-8). The cohabitation of the 'sons of God' with human females ignored similar boundaries of above and below. Thus, the punishment takes the form of the disintegration of the divisions between above and below with an inundation emanating from the waters above ('the windows of the heavens') and 'the waters below' ('the fountains of the great deep'). In any case, the description of the inundation recalls that of the undifferentiated chaos that preceded God's creation (1.2), and characterizes the Deluge as an inversion of creation (see 9.8-19).

Noah, to whom all the animals come for sanctuary, recalls Adam to whom all the animals came to be named. The ark represents a 'floating Eden' (cf. Molina 1980: 259), in which one man exercises dominion over the animals. Just as the flood waters produce an inversion of God's creation, so the final statement of the paragraph highlights through assonance the inversion of the expulsion from Eden. In 3.24, God 'drove out (*waygāreš*) the man'; in 7.16b, 'he shut him in (*wayyisgōr*)'. Thus the account combines both positive and negative images, conveying the complex nature of the flood as both punishment for the world and salvation for Noah's family.

7.17-24

The flood waters increase to their climax, covering the mountains (7.20). Consequently all human and animal life, with the exception of that on the ark, is obliterated (7.21-23). Apart from this remnant, the reversal of creation is complete.

Of the two lists that catalogue the victims of the flood, the first begins with birds and concludes with humans (7.21), and the second begins with humans and ends with birds (7.23b). The spatial comprehensiveness of the destruction, moving from heavens (birds) to earth (animals/humans) and back again, reminds the reader of the above/below categories mentioned earlier (see 7.11-16).

v. 21	v. 23b
Birds (*'ôp*)	Humans (*'ādām*)
Domestic Animals (*beḥēmâ*)	Animals (*beḥēmâ*)
Wild Animals (*ḥayyâ*)	and
Swarming Animals (*šereṣ*)	Creepers (*remeś*)
Humans (*'ādām*)	Birds (*'ôp*)

Placed strategically between the two lists is the inescapable fact: 'everything on dry land in whose nostrils was the breath of life died. He blotted out every living thing that was on the face of the ground' (7.22-23a); only the water creatures survive.

When we are told that 'only Noah was left, and those that were with him on the ark', (7.23c), we naturally want to know what *their* fate will be. To be told that 'the waters swelled on the earth for one hundred and fifty days' (7.24), merely adds to the tension. The Flood has reached its peak of destruction. Surely Noah and his companions will not now perish. But what will be their future in a destroyed world?

Genesis 8

8.1-5

The tension which climaxed in 7.17-24 is brought to a swift resolution by the announcement that 'God remembered Noah ...' (8.1a). Just as the flood waters had previously increased, obliterating all human and animal life outside the ark and placing Noah and his companions in jeopardy, so now with God's remembrance of Noah the flood waters decrease and the ark comes to rest on the mountains of Ararat. (Cf. the connotations of 'remember', e.g., Gen. 30.22; 1 Sam. 1.11, and its mirror image 'forget', e.g., Ps. 10.11; Isa. 49.14-15.)

The flood narrative began in an analogous fashion to that of creation, with an observation of the state of the earth (1.2 cf. 6.5, 11). Now at the turning point of the account, the earth has returned to a replica of its pre-creation state, and the preliminary steps of creation are now repeated:

(a) Earth covered by water	1.2a	7.24
(b) Wind/spirit (*rûaḥ*) moves	1.2b	8.1b
(c) Waters recede	1.9a	8.1c-5a
(d) Dry land emerges	1.9b	8.5b

The 'decreation' movement of the Flood is followed by a 'recreation' (see 9.20-29; ch. 10; 31.1-21).

Although there is a sudden shift of mood, there is no immediate return to normality as far as the earth is concerned. While the ark runs aground on the seventeenth day of the seventh month (8.4), it takes another two and a half months for the tops of the mountains to break through the surface of the waters (8.5). This compares with three days for dry land to appear at creation.

8.6-14

Up to this point, all of Noah's actions have been responses to divine commands (cf. 6.22; 7.5). Here, for the first time Noah acts on his own initiative. Yet his motivations for doing so are not clear. While it was a common practice for mariners to release birds as a navigation aid, this is not their function here, with the ark run aground atop Ararat. They seem to be used to determine whether the waters had dried up (8.8, 11). But why does Noah need to use birds to discover this when a simple visual inspection would have been sufficient to tell him the extent of the flood's fall? Equally baffling is the fate of the raven (8.7). It would appear that it never returned but simply 'went to and fro until the waters were dried up from the earth'. If it survived (by eating carrion), then why did it need to be taken into the ark? If it died, then being 'saved' on the ark has a bitter irony (as I will also observe with the 'clean' animals in 8.20). Perhaps Noah's actions are simply confused, serving no useful purpose other than to satisfy his curiosity, for even when he knows that the earth is dry (8.11), he stays put.

8.15-19

True to form, even when he knows that it is safe to disembark, Noah waits almost two months (if 8.12-15 are arranged chronologically), before leaving the ark. Even here, he does not act on his own initiative. He is the epitome of the obedient, righteous person (cf. 6.9). In any matter of consequence he simply responds positively to God's command. This portrayal of obedient Noah, read in the context of the numerous parallels between the creation and flood accounts, raises hopes that this recreation will produce a humanity more successful in obeying God than the original Man and Woman (see 3.1-7; 6.9-22).

8.20-22

Noah's altar is the second structure that he erects. There is a certain irony in the fact that in 6.14-22 he made (*'āśâ*) the ark in order to save life, and in 8.20 he built (*bānâ*) an altar to take life. The sacrificed animals may have escaped God's flood waters, but not Noah's knife. We see now the reason why clean animals outnumbered the unclean aboard the ark. From the next paragraph it would appear that unclean animals also have a purpose— they might not be acceptable for sacrifice to God, but they can be eaten (see 7.1-10; 9.1-7).

God's response to Noah's sacrifice is twofold. First, just as God's original resolution to destroy was his response to the grief in 'his heart' (6.6), so he now resolves in 'his heart' to preserve creation (8.21). Secondly, he pronounces a blessing on Noah and his sons, which God delivers to them (see 9.1-7).

The motivation God gives for not destroying the earth is strange, 'I will never again curse the ground because of human-kind, for the inclination of the human heart is evil from youth; nor will I ever again destroy every living creature as I have done' (8.21b). Noah and his family are the only humans in existence when God says this. His judgment concerning human evil seems therefore to refer to them. Yet this seems incompatible with the previous references to Noah's righteousness. Perhaps God's words should be taken as his realization that Noah's righteousness will not be hereditary. The moral trend of humanity after the flood will be much the same as before. Thus the hopes raised earlier that Noah would mark the beginning of a new obedient humanity, are dashed. The flood may have destroyed a large number of wicked humans, but it has done nothing at all to eradicate the problem of wickedness itself. God's resolve shows, however, that something *has* changed— God's attitude to human wickedness. His tolerance threshold has increased. This is shown graphically in the comparison with 6.5-7. There, the Lord saw evil in human hearts and resolved to destroy. Here, in 8.21 he sees the evil in human hearts and resolves to preserve. Each resolution required a change in *God's* heart. In the first instance towards his creation, and in the second towards the appropriate judgment. Thus while human attitudes to God remain unchanged, God's attitudes to humans have changed.

Genesis 9

9.1-7

This paragraph is introduced and concluded by divine imperatives to Noah and his family to multiply and fill the earth (9.1, 7). These statements recall the original commands to humanity given at creation (1.28). The imperatives in 9.1, 7 enclose a catalogue of statements governing relationships in the renewed creation:

(a) Animals will live in fear of humans (v. 2).
(b) Every animal will be food for humans (v. 3).
(c) Blood must not be consumed (v. 3).
(d) Capital punishment for all humans and animals that take a human life (vv. 5-6).

Thus, we have an envelope of measures that are negative for animals, consumers of blood, and murderers, introduced and concluded by a command to humans to reproduce. Indeed, the structure suggests that human increase will be the cause of the corresponding negative effect on creation.

The introductory and concluding imperatives regarding human reproduction (9.1, 7), underline the continuing importance to Yahweh of this aspect of human activity. Verses 9.1-7 indicate, however, that other aspects of the original announcement in 1.28 have undergone modification.

The relations between humans and animals are brutalized. Not only will all animals fear humans (9.3a), but all animals will be food for humans (9.3a). Thus, animals will be killed not only as sacrifices to God (cf. 8.20), but for everyday food for humans as well. No wonder animals were told 'be fruitful and multiply on the earth'! (8.17). The original 'dominion' granted to humans was in a vegetarian context (1.29-30); human omnivores will inevitably extend that power.

The reader should also not fail to see the omission of the original command to 'subdue' the earth (1.28). The curse of 3.17-19, still in force, countered that original command and makes human subjugation of the earth problematical (see 3.8-19).

Of the original threefold imperative found in 1.28, therefore, one element (human reproduction) has been retained; another (dominion over the animals) has been modified, while subjugation of the earth has been passed over in silence.

Note that the violence envisaged by 9.1-7 is not an innovation. Indeed, violence in creation had been one of the motivations for God sending the flood (6.13). Previously, God had seen the violence and judged it severely. Now, God recognizes that it cannot be eradicated and sets boundaries to it, that is, blood is forbidden as food and there will be retribution for the taking of human life.

The guidelines for the consumption of animals as food are unrestricted (9.3), making no distinction between clean and unclean animals. Thus here, only clean animals may be sacrificed (8.20), but all animals may be eaten. However, as far as Noah and his family are concerned, there is a very practical disincentive to eat unclean animals. The fact that only one pair of unclean animals were taken into the ark means that immediate indulgence in their flesh is likely to be a unique experience!

While the killing of animals is allowed, the killing of humans, whether perpetrated by people or animals, carries the ultimate penalty of death (9.5). That animals should be made accountable for their crimes should not surprise us, given the curses placed on the Serpent in 3.14-15 (cf. Exod. 21.28). The term 'brother' ('every man's brother', *'āḥ* 9.5; NRSV 'each one'), is used here for the first time since ch. 4, where it was similarly used in a context of murder. God's reaction to murder, however, is quite different in ch. 9. In ch. 4 the murderer was protected (4.15b), and the avenger faced execution (4.15a). Here, however, the murderer is not protected and his execution is required, underlined by the chiastic 9.6:

A	B	C
Whoever sheds	the blood of	a human
C'	B'	A'
by a human	shall that person's blood	be shed

The explicit reason for summary execution of murderers is that God made humans in his own image (9.6b). However, this was equally true in ch. 4. This contrast suggests that affairs in the post-flood world are such that stronger disincentives to murder must be applied.

In ch. 1 the image of God was related, in part at least, to human dominion over the animals (see 1.24-31). That also provides part of the context here (9.2-3a, 4). Thus the reaffirmation of humanity as being in the image of God accompanies legislation increasing human dominion over animals. In addition, it is intimated that the fact that a person is in the image of God not only makes murder a crime, but also provides other humans with the authority to avenge the blood of the victim.

9.8-19

Readers have known since 8.21-22 of God's resolution never again to destroy the earth. Now Noah and his family learn of it. The previous passage was bounded by commands to multiply (9.1, 7); this, with the formal establishment of a covenant (9.9, 17a). Not only does God declare his intention never again to destroy, he also provides the recurring sign of the rainbow to remind himself of his undertaking (9.15-16).

The content of the covenant is that God will never again destroy the earth (9.11). The sign of the covenant is the rainbow (9.12-13). But how does the rainbow signify the content of the covenant? Once again, the creation account provides a context for understanding the flood account. Genesis 1.6-8 described the creation of the firmament (*rāqîa*)—a domelike barrier to separate the waters above and below. The flood has vividly illustrated what happens when this function of the firmament is disrupted. God's promise never again to inundate the earth is another way of saying that the firmament will restrain the 'waters above'. The rainbow thus acts as a vivid symbol of the covenant. The arching rainbow mimics the domed firmament restraining the 'waters above', and reminds God to maintain the function of this vital cosmological structure (see Turner 1993: 119-24; 7.11-16).

The establishment of the covenant in this paragraph fulfils God's promise to Noah, 'I will establish my covenant with you', (6.18). Thus, the covenant promised when destruction by water was announced (6.17), turns out to be an undertaking not to destroy by water again (9.15b). As God once saw (*r'h*) human wickedness and determined to destroy (6.5), so now when he sees (*r'h*) the rainbow he undertakes to conserve (9.16). Just as God had previously prefaced his decision to destroy with 'For my part, I ... [*wa*ᵃ*nî hinnî*]' (6.17), so the identical Hebrew formula introduces his covenantal oath to preserve creation in 9.9a. Twice God undertakes to 'remember' (*zkr*) his covenant (9.15-16). Just as

God remembered (*zkr*) Noah in the midst of destruction (8.1a), from now on he will remember never to allow such a judgment (9.16). This paragraph provides a ringing affirmation of God's commitment to his creation, despite the fact that the conditions which induced the Flood will continue to exist. The concluding statement that the whole earth was peopled from Noah's three sons (9.18-19), is confirmation that God was true to his word.

9.20-29
A reasonably long period of time has obviously elapsed between the disembarkation from the ark and events in this episode. Not only has Noah as 'a man of the soil' (9.20) initiated viticulture and enjoyed the fruits of his labour, but he has also become a grandfather. The episode described in this passage is our first glimpse of life under the renewed blessings announced in 9.1-17.

Noah now works 'the ground ['*dāmâ*]' which will never be cursed with another flood (8.21), recalling Lamech's hope that his son would bring relief 'out of the ground ['*dāmâ*]' (5.29). The sequel to the Flood story described here is strikingly similar to the sequel to the creation account, narrated in ch. 3. In each case the offence is connected with the consumption of a certain fruit: the fruit of the knowledge of good and evil (3.3-6) and grapes from Noah's vineyard (9.20-21). Both offences have 'nakedness' as a central motif (though the terms differ: '*ārôm* in 3.7, 10 and '*erwâ* in 9.22-23). Both are followed by the offended party issuing curses in poetic form: God in 3.14-19; Noah in 9.25-27 (the only poetic curses in Genesis 1–11). Both stories involve the covering of the naked party by another: by God with animal skins in 3.21; by Shem and Japheth with a garment in 9.23.

These connections are reinforced by the Edenic allusions earlier in the Flood narrative. For example, in certain respects Noah was another Adam: on the ark he was in charge of all the animals (1.26; 2.19-20; 7.15; 8.16-17); and had a special rapport with the earth (2.5, 8; 3.19; cf. 9.20).

Thus life after the recreation of the flood follows a similar path to that after the original creation of chs. 1–2. These parallels confirm God's assessment of post-flood humanity: 'the inclination of the human heart is evil from youth' (8.21b).

Just how similar pre- and post-flood humanity is can be seen by comparing this passage with 6.1-4. Both passages have taxed exegetes' ingenuity over the years. Nevertheless, even a cursory reading of the two passages reveals instructive connections. Verses 6.1-4, whatever else they might convey, are concerned with illicit sexual liaisons that occurred immediately before the flood and provide (at least part of) the motivation for God's sending the Flood. Verses 9.20-27 narrate an episode that occurred after the Flood and is also probably concerned with sexual matters. In fact, whether the passage refers to homosexual rape, castration, incest or Ham's simple viewing of Noah exposed in his tent (and all have at various times been suggested), the story carries sexual connotations to a greater or lesser degree. The semantic range of *'erwâ* (nakedness) contains significant sexual connotations, so that 'to see nakedness' is used as a euphemism for sexual offences (e.g., Lev. 20.17). Just as the 'sons of God' take the initiative, but humanity is punished (6.3), so Ham committed the offence but his offspring (Canaan) is cursed (9.25-27). I would suggest that the underlying connotations of sexual offence in these two (admittedly enigmatic) passages reinforce an important theological statement regarding chs. 6–9. The Flood changed nothing. Unacceptable human behaviour leads up to the Flood and is demonstrated immediately afterwards. This correspondence allows an expansion at the beginning and end of the palistrophe suggested by Anderson (see introductory comments to chs. 6–9).

Noah's genealogy A (5.32)
   Offence: Judgment on offenders; 'grace' to Noah (6.1-8)
      A Noah and his three sons (6.9-10)
        B Violence to God's creation (6.11-12)
          C First divine address: resolution to destroy (6.13-22)
            D Second divine address: command to enter the ark (7.1-10)
              E Beginning of the flood (7.11-16)
                F The rising flood waters (7.17-24)
                   GOD'S REMEMBRANCE OF NOAH (8.1a)
                F' The receding flood waters (8.1b-5)
              E' The drying of the earth (8.6-14)
            D' Third divine address: command to leave the ark (8.15-19)
          C' God's resolution to preserve older (8.20-22)
        B' Fourth divine address: covenant blessing and peace (9.1-17)
      A' Noah and his three sons (9.18-19)
   Offence: Judgment on Canaan; blessing on Shem, Japheth (9.20-27)
Noah's genealogy B (9.28)

Thus not only the character of Noah, but more importantly entrenched human wickedness, bracket the entire Flood story.

In fact, matters seem to be worse. On eating the fruit, the Man and Woman have their eyes opened and they *know* that they are naked (3.7). However, when Noah partakes of the fruit, he becomes naked, but has no idea of his true state (9.21, 24). In ch. 3, nakedness was a state not even a husband and wife could tolerate before each other. They take the appropriate action of clothing themselves (3.7); Ham's actions form a stark contrast (9.22).

Noah's curse of Ham's youngest son (cf. 10.6), is one of the few places in Genesis where the youngest fares worse than the oldest: 'lowest of slaves shall he be to his brothers' (9.25b). A feature of the Genesis narratives is the inversion of primogeniture, for example, Cain/Abel, Ishmael/Isaac, Esau/Jacob and Joseph/brothers. This incident, however, raises a further question. Why does Noah curse Canaan when it was his father Ham who committed the offence? Perhaps Noah cannot curse Ham because he has already been blessed by God (9.1), or possibly because Ham, Noah's youngest son (9.24), had committed the offence. Ham's youngest son (10.6) is cursed (see Wenham 1987: 201). Regardless of his motives, Noah's curse potentially affects all future human society. If 'from these [Shem, Ham and Japheth] the whole earth was peopled' (9.19b), and if Canaan becomes the slave of Shem and Japheth (9.26b, 27c), future international relations are being determined here. The reader might well question, however, the efficacy of Noah's words. Do they have the same force as the words of God? And in any case, how confident can we be that seemingly authoritative divine words, let alone human pronouncements, will actually be fulfilled? The sequel to the creation account saw God's will overturned. Perhaps Noah's words will likewise become unrealized hopes. (See, e.g., 10.15-20; 25.1-18, 19-34; 29.15-30; 30.1-20.)

The final genealogical note (9.28-29), completes the information initiated in 5.32. The intervening material has been a huge parenthetical block introduced and concluded by Noah's genealogy. Noah's demise may have been delayed for 350 years after the Flood (9.28), but eventually, like all the victims of God's watery judgment, he too dies (9.29).

Genesis 10

The conclusion of Noah's personal genealogy in 9.28-29 is followed by the extended genealogy of his sons (10.1-32). The account in ch. 10 of the dispersal of the nations, however, would fit better chronologically after the Tower of Babel episode (11.1-9). Chronological sequence has been sacrificed for thematic connections between chs. 9 and 10. One obvious point of contact is between God's previous commands to multiply and fill the earth (9.1, 7), and the catalogue of offspring and geographical dispersal presented here. But perhaps a more important link is achieved when ch. 10 is read immediately after Noah's speech in 9.25-27. That announcement by Noah consisted of a curse on Canaan (and Ham?) and a blessing on Shem and Japheth. Canaan's fate is to be the slave of Shem (9.26c) and Japheth (9.27c). Thus the genealogy of these three descendants of Noah that follows maps the world in which those hierarchical relationships will potentially be played out (see 12.4-9).

As well as containing important linkages with previous material in the primaeval history, ch. 10 also marks an important new departure. For almost the first time in the primaeval history we are able to visualize the geographical locations of individuals. This chapter introduces readers to the world they know. Specific geographical details have been sparse before this, for example, the information that the ark came to rest on the mountains of Ararat (8.4). The only relatively detailed account to occur before this is the description of the rivers that flowed out of Eden (2.10-14), with which ch. 10 has a number of similarities. For example, the same locations occur in both passages: Havilah (2.11; 10.7); Cush (2.13; 10.6); Asshur/Assyria (2.14; 10.11, 22). The negative connotations of Assyria noted in 2.10-14 are confirmed here by its association with Nimrod (see 10.6-20 below). The motif of division, using the same verb *prd*, occurs in both (2.10; 10.5, 25, 32). Just as after creation the rivers spread out across the world, so after the flood do the descendants of Noah's sons. These parallels once again illustrate the narrative's presentation of the flood as a recreation (see 8.1-5, 15-19; 9.20-29).

Previous genealogies have shown a preoccupation with the number seven (see 2.1-4a; 4.17-26; ch. 5; 46.1-27), and ch. 10 might well provide another example. While the seventh element in genealogies has previously been highlighted, ch. 10 contains 71 elements. This is tantalisingly close to an exact 70 (7 x 10), and several suggestions have been made for deleting one member to produce the 'correct' total. The reference to Nimrod has all the indications of being a parenthetical note in the genealogy. Interestingly there are six genealogical lists in 10.2-7 (Japheth,

Gomer, Javan, Ham, Cush and Raamah). Verse 8 begins the seventh list. However, it reverts to Cush, who has already been mentioned (10.7a), and concerns the exploits of Nimrod, son of Cush who was omitted from the previous list. The deletion of Nimrod, highlighted and distinguished in this way from the other genealogical elements, would reduce the actual total to 70.

As with previous Genesis genealogies, ch. 10 focuses on three groups—in this case, Shem, Ham and Japheth. The genealogy of Cain concluded with Jabal, Jubal and Tubalcain (4.19-22). Adam's genealogy ends with Noah and his three sons (5.32), while that of Noah will end with Terah and his three sons Abram, Nahor and Haran (11.27) (see Ross 1980: 340-53).

Strangely, from a presumed Israelite reader's perspective, there would seem to be one nation too few rather than one too many. Where is Israel? The closest that the Table of Nations comes is the mention of Eber, traditional ancestor of the Hebrews. Is Israel of such insignificance that it can be ignored in a comprehensive ethnographical list? Or is it so important that what is presented here is the 'rest of the world', a 'clearing of the decks', with the detailed story of Israel to be anticipated as coming later? A hint that Israel's importance is in the background might be seen in the genealogy's reversal of the usual Shem, Ham, Japheth sequence (found in the *tōlᵉdōt* heading, 10.1), so that the listing concludes with Shem, 'the father of all the children of Eber' (10.21).

The comparative importance of the progeny of each of Noah's sons can be judged by the disproportionate amount of space devoted to Ham. Most of the extra space is taken up by the parenthetical note on Nimrod, which forms the seventh paragraph of the genealogy. Nimrod is described as being a *gibbōr* ('mighty warrior', 10.8). The last time we read of *gibbōrîm* (6.4, probably the progeny of the 'sons of God' and 'daughters of humans'), God's judgment followed soon afterwards (6.5-7). Does another *gibbōr* presage a similar divine judgment? The comment that 'the beginning of his kingdom was Babel ...' (10.10) awaits expansion later (see 11.1-9). But the fact that his name may be translated 'we shall rebel' suggests that Nimrod is a bad omen of things to come.

In this section dealing with Ham, note the amount of space devoted to Canaan, who was cursed in 9.25-27. Verses 10.15-20 indicate that even one who has been cursed by Noah can participate in fulfilling God's blessing to be fruitful, multiply and fill the earth (9.1, 7; see Cassuto 1964: II, 167-68). The emphasis on Canaan alerts the reader to look out for future developments.

The final section detailing the descendants of Shem contains an even more enigmatic reference to Peleg, in whose days 'the earth was divided' (10.25). When read in the context of the previous statement regarding Nimrod, the division of the earth suggests an ominous event (see 11.1-9).

Verse 10.32 forms an inclusion with 10.1, reminding us that this procreation took place 'after the flood' (cf. 9.28). It is another indicator that events after the flood are very similar to those before. Nimrod, like the Nephilim of 6.4 belongs to the *gibbōrîm*, and in the days of Peleg, as in the days of Noah, an as yet undefined but ominous event with worldwide consequences occurs.

Genesis 11.1-26

11.1-9

The creation narrative, which had echoes in the flood story, resounds also in the story of Babel. Whereas ch. 1 moved from chaos (*tōhû wābōhû*, 1.2) to order and rest (*šābat*, 2.1-3), Babel reverses the move, beginning with order ('the whole earth had one language and the same words', 11.1) and ending with chaos ('therefore it was called Babel, because there the Lord confused the language of all the earth', 11.9a). The story line of the primaeval history is thus enveloped by chaos. But there is a significant transition from physical chaos (ch. 1) to moral chaos (ch. 11).

Verses 11.1-2 inform us that a linguistically uniform humanity migrated until it arrived at Shinar. This location has already been mentioned in the previous chapter (10.10), in the extended parenthesis on Nimrod that forms the seventh paragraph of the Table of Nations. The significance of this branch of the Noachic family, telegraphed in ch. 10, is taken up here.

The term *miqqedem* (11.2a) can be translated either 'from the east' (NRSV) or 'eastward' (ASV, NAS). Since this passage describes human movements after the Flood which saw the grounding of the ark on the mountains of Ararat, the latter option is more likely (though Shinar/Babylon is actually south-east from this location). If humanity is indeed migrating towards the east, ominous connotations arise. I have already noted the associations of the flow of the Tigris 'east of Assyria' (2.14). The Man and the Woman were banished from Eden (planted in the east, 2.8), and the cherubim prevented their return 'at the east of the garden' (3.24). Cain becomes a vagabond in the land of Nod 'east of Eden' (4.16). Thus while settling down in the east (11.2) might suggest a revivified

Eden for human habitation, we also know that it is the destination of the dispossessed and judged. As readers we anticipate disaster rather than blessing.

It is almost as if the characters in the story share the readers' foreboding. Unlike Cain's paltry efforts to counter his sentence of wandering with an urban development (see 4.17-26), they resolve to build a city of note with a skyscraper-tower because 'otherwise we shall be scattered abroad upon the face of the whole earth' (11.4). This statement brings us to the heart of the story. What is their resolve and why does Yahweh react as he does? Note that they wish to 'make a name' for themselves (11.4). This ambition marks a new departure. Previously, names have been given by superiors to inferiors (1.5, 8, 10; 2.20, 23; 3.20; 4.17, 25-26; 5.1, 3, 29). Read against this background, the human desire to make a name for themselves suggests not only a desire for a reputation, but also for autonomy. That, of course, was the original human offence (see 3.1-7, 20-24).

I have already noted that the chaos/order dynamic links this story to ch. 1, and in the people's ambition we find another connection. One of God's desires for humanity at creation was that they 'fill the earth' (1.28), and this command was repeated to Noah and his family after the Flood (9.1). They decide, however, to settle in Shinar. As they state quite clearly they do not want to be scattered over all the earth (11.4). Note that their use of the cohortative, 'Come, let us ...' echoes God's use of the same construction at creation (1.26), when he created humanity and commanded it to 'fill the earth' (1.28). Here humanity repeats God's 'let us ...' but refuses to fill the earth. Seen in this light, God's punishment of dispersal fits the people's crime. We have been forewarned by the chronologically displaced ch. 10 that humanity spread over the whole earth. We now learn that was achieved by confusing human language. The fact that God does not merely destroy the tower indicates that its construction is not the main issue. Thus the judgment at Babel has a more far-reaching impact than did the Flood. As I noted above, the Flood changed little. Whereas the Flood 'blotted out' humans from the surface of the earth (6.7), Babel 'scatters' them across the face of the earth (11.8-9). Babel's fragmentation of society is still with us. With exquisite irony those who wanted to make a name for themselves do indeed receive a name—Babel (11.9). They had wanted to make a name by settling down in their city, but the name they receive through the Babel/*bālal* ('confuse') wordplay (11.9) actually describes their scattering.

Despite many parallels between 11.1-9 and previous episodes it also forms a contrast. All previous acts of divine punishment have been mitigated with some measure of divine grace. Thus Adam and Eve, though expelled from the garden, do not receive an immediate death penalty (cf. 2.17) but do receive garments to cover their nakedness (3.21). Cain is expelled to live the life of a vagabond (4.12), but is given a mark to protect him from vengeance (4.15). The earth is destroyed by water (7.21-23), but 'God remembered Noah' (8.1a). Such ameliorization of punishment, however, is not present at Babel. While such an omission might mean that the Babel episode is a particularly harsh example of divine displeasure, it also alerts the reader to look out for a possible response of grace in the ensuing narrative (see 12.1-3).

11.10-26

The dimensions of this passage are indicated by 11.27 where Terah's *tôlᵉdōt* formula ('Now these are the descendants of Terah'), introduces a major new section of the book. Verse 11.26 therefore, with its announcement of Terah and his three sons (cf. 5.32), brings the primaeval history to a close. From Adam to Enoch was seven generations; Enoch to the sons of Terah is another 14 generations. The preoccupation of previous genealogies with multiples of seven causes us to expect something special from Terah's offspring, especially as he fathers them at the age of 70 (see 2.1-4a; 4.17-26; ch. 5; ch. 10; 46.1-27). It might also make us wonder about the significance of Eber (father of the Hebrews), who comes seven generations after Enoch (11.14). It is not surprising to learn that the total ages in 11.10-26 (2,996) is divisible by seven, as is the total of ages from Adam to Noah (8,575), and obviously the grand total of ages in the primaeval history (11,571).

Shem's line is reckoned through Arpachshad. We have already been informed that Shem had more sons than Arpachshad (10.22), and that he was not the firstborn. Why is the line of Arpachshad singled out and his eldest brother Elam ignored? Here is an indication that the laws of primogeniture do not always pertain in Genesis and that the predictable nature of the form of the genealogy belies hidden complications in the larger narrative. What is only hinted at in the primaeval history becomes a feature in the ancestral history.

Genesis 11.27–25.18:
The Abraham Story

11.27-32

The primaeval history was introduced with the generations (*tôlᵉdōt*) of the 'heavens and the earth' (2.4a); the ancestral history with the generations (*tôlᵉdōt*) of Terah (11.27). The present *tôlᵉdōt* takes account of events that have transpired since ch. 1 by noting the frustrations of human existence. We have become used to death notices punctuating the Genesis genealogies. But here we are told that Haran died before his father Terah did. The genealogy of ch. 5 contained only one such example of father outliving son—and the son in question was Enoch, marked out as being exceptional in more than one way. In 11.10-26, no fewer than three sons (Arpachshad, Peleg and Nahor) die before their fathers. To these three is now added Haran. In addition we are informed that 'Sarai was barren; she had no child' (11.30). Not only do all humans die, but some do so prematurely and others fail to reproduce. The human imperative to reproduce and fill the earth (1.28; 9.1, 7) is being threatened on more than one front. Read in this context, the inability to procreate is a greater problem than the curse of pain in childbirth (3.16). Thus while the primaeval history ended with understated optimism, noting that Terah fathered three sons at the propitious age of 70 (11.26), the ancestral history commences with a pessimistic reminder of the human condition. This gloomy scenario is embodied in the deprivation experienced by two characters. Lot has no father while Abram has no child. As readers we await the resolution of these complications.

Terah emigrates from Ur of the Chaldaeans, taking with him his childless son and daughter-in-law and his fatherless grandson. While they set off in the direction of Canaan they settle in Haran. We are given no motivation for this move. However, this little group do form a contrast with the people of Babel. This former group had wanted to settle down in one place, refusing to fill the earth. Terah's family need no persuasion to move on, but Sarai's barrenness complicates their ability to fill the earth.

Genesis 12

12.1-3

This paragraph underpins the entire Abram story. While it forms
a link with preceding material, its major function is to provide a
foundation for the ensuing plot of the Abram story.

First, looking back to the previous chapter, we see that God's
command to Abram to leave his present locale and move on
amounts to a continuation of the trek already begun by his father
Terah. The people of Babel also emigrated and 'came upon a
plain in the land of Shinar' (11.2). In contrast to their fortuitous
discovery, Abram is told, 'Go ... to the land that I will show you'
(12.1). Thus the end of the primaeval history and the beginning
of the ancestral history present pictures of sundry migrations
(see 31.1-21). However, while the scattering of the Babelites
across the earth was a divine judgment (11.9), Yahweh's command
to Abram to move on is bound up with his blessing (12.1-3). An
element of this blessing is that 'all the families of the earth shall
be blessed' (12.3b). Babel had seen the judgment and utter confusion of these selfsame 'families of the earth'. In addition, the
Babelites had desired to 'make a *name*' for themselves (11.4),
which ironically they did—'Babel'. In contrast to their stated
ambition, Yahweh promises Abram, 'I will make your *name*
great' (12.2b). Thus the formulation of the opening command to
Abram suggests that his destiny will be to reverse the effects of
God's judgment on Babel.

A pivotal element in the promise is Yahweh's statement, 'I will
make of you a great nation' (12.2a). All of the other nations of
the earth have already been catalogued in ch. 10. The great
nation promised to Abram is an addition to their number, and
will be a source of blessing for all of them (12.3b). This announcement creates dissonance with a previous statement. The stark
words, 'Now Sarai was barren; she had no child' (11.30), are
recalled. This inability of his wife to procreate does not negate
the possibility of Abram's becoming a great nation. But in the
absence of any indication to the contrary it demonstrates that
the route to nationhood will not be through Sarai. And no matter
how it might come about, this promise can surely not be fulfilled
in Abram's lifetime. The narrative thus intimates a future for
this element beyond the confines of Genesis.

The enigmatic nature of Yahweh's command to Abram to go to
the land 'that I will show you' should be noted. Abram is given no

indication of the land to which he should go. Nor is he informed of what he should do once he gets there or why he is going there. There is no suggestion that Abram will be given this land, wherever it is. It could simply be another land like Haran, in which he is to live as a sojourner. Nevertheless, the importance of land has been established in this introductory statement, and will generate our interest as we continue our reading of the narrative.

Note the correspondence between the increasing specificity of the command in 12.1 and the increasing universality of the promise. The injunction to leave moves from the general to the specific, 'your country ... your kindred ... your father's house'. This narrowing focus of the imperative is matched by a widening focus of promise, moving from Abram (12.2) to his associates (12.3a) to all the families of the earth (12.3b).

There are two problems in translating this paragraph. The first concerns the last clause of 12.2, 'so that you will be a blessing'. The Hebrew actually contains an imperative, and a growing number of scholars favour retaining that sense here: 'be a blessing!' So Abram is not simply being informed that he will become a blessing, but is commanded to be a blessing. If the force of the imperative is retained then the following Hebrew clauses should be rendered as consequences of that imperative: 'Be a blessing, so that I may bless those ...'

In other words, the promises of 12.3 depend upon Abram being a blessing. Just as clearly, the promises of 12.2a (great nation, blessing and great name), depend upon Abram obeying God's command in 12.1, 'Go!' (See, e.g., 12.10-20; 20.1-7; 26.1-11; ch. 34.)

The second problem is the last clause of 12.3, 'and in you all the families of the earth shall be blessed'. The connotation of the verbal form is unclear, and an alternative translation is possible, 'by you all the families of the earth shall bless themselves' (NRSV footnote). So is Abram being promised that he will become a blessing to the nations, or simply that the nations will use Abram's name when blessing themselves (whatever that means)? I favour the former possibility, especially in light of the imperative in 12.2 which commands Abram to be a blessing. (For more detail see Turner 1990a: 53-61.)

Genesis 12.1-3, therefore, contains three main elements: a promise of becoming a great nation; a command to go to an unnamed land; a command to be a blessing. These elements of nationhood, land and blessing provide the context for the plot of the whole Abram story.

12.4-9

While Abram's response to the divine imperative is immediate and positive, it also creates some tensions with the previous paragraph. Abram certainly leaves his country. He also emphatically leaves his 'father's house'. A cursory glance at the ages ascribed to Terah in 11.26, 32 and the information that Abram was 75 when he set out, reveal that Abram left his father in Haran (according to MT but not LXX). In fact his father lived on for another 60 years. But does Abram obey the command to leave his kindred? The narrator's comment that 'Lot went with him ... Abram took ... his brother's son Lot' (12.4a, 5a), clearly demonstrates that he did not. If his nephew is not his kindred, then who is? Since God's call came to Abram at Haran, most of his kindred have already been left behind at Ur. When we consider, however, that despite the injunction to leave his kindred, the childless Abram takes the fatherless Lot, the possibility is raised that from Abram's perspective, Lot is not simply kindred. Sarai has not provided a son through whom the promised nation will come; but his dead brother has.

With Abram's arrival in Canaan the narrative comments laconically, 'at that time the Canaanites were in the land' (12.6b cf. 10.15-20). This information comes hard on the heels of the promise that all the world's nations will be blessed through Abram. How might this be true of the Canaanites? The phrase 'at that time' indicates that the Canaanites are no longer in the land. The next verse provides the reason why: Yahweh promises, 'to your offspring I will give this land' (12.7a). This seems to contradict the announcement that all nations will be blessed through Abram. It also raises the question of why *this* land? Why are the Canaanites to be dispossessed? Why could not God dispossess the inhabitants of Ur or Haran and give *that* land to Abram's descendants? We are aware, however, that the destiny of Canaan has been broached before. In 9.25 Canaan was cursed with slavery to his brothers, and Abram is descended from Shem. So Yahweh's statement in 12.7a suggests that as far as relationships with Canaanites are concerned, Noah's curse (9.25) overrides the divine blessing (12.3b).

Yahweh's promise to Abram in 12.7 recalls the initial command in which he was told to go 'to the land that I will show you'. No explicit indication is given to Abram that he has arrived at that land. And the promise of 12.7 applies to Abram's descendants, not to him personally, so there is no indication that Abram himself will possess or even live in this land. Consequently, 'Abram journeyed on ...' (12.9), continuing his southerly trek.

12.10-20

In fact the famine renders the whole land of Canaan unpromising territory for Abram. As a consequence, Abram continues his journey southward through the Negeb and on to Egypt.

While in Egypt the fate of the promises given in 12.1-3 becomes particularly acute. Abram has taken with him his wife, who is barren, and his nephew Lot, who is Abram's only link with the next generation. Sarai though barren is beautiful. Abram surmises that this will place his life in danger with the unscrupulous Egyptians, though why he should think so is a mystery; he had travelled unmolested through Canaan. Thus he requests Sarai to tell the Egyptians that she is his sister. This is without doubt a bare-faced lie. Not only is it intrinsically improbable, but 11.29 which told us of Abram's marriage also told us that his brother Nahor married his niece. If Sarai had also been a blood relative we would surely have been informed (see 20.8-18). If the Egyptians think Sarai is his wife they will need to kill him to get her. If she is only his sister, Abram can preserve his life (and get a handsome bride price into the bargain, 12.16 cf. 24.53). True to form, the Egyptians are agog at the ravishing Sarai, and she is recruited to join the bevy of beauties at Pharaoh's court. Abram is unlikely to see Sarai again, but God has previously said nothing about Sarai being essential for the fulfilment of the divine promises. She can therefore be sacrificed without endangering the promises. But he must ensure the safety of himself and Lot if the catalogue of commands, blessings and promises of 12.1-3 are to see the light of day (see 14.13-16; 20.1-7; 26.6-11).

However, it is precisely that programmatic paragraph (12.1-3), which raises some problems in the mind of the reader. The climactic promise was that all the nations would be blessed through Abram. We have already had occasion to adjust our expectations with the news that the Canaanites will lose their land to Abram's descendants. Now Abram meets the Egyptians. Far from blessing them, Abram's lies and instigation of adultery places the Pharaoh under the curse of God (12.17). This contrasts sharply with the material blessing Abram derived from the Pharaoh (12.16).

A further contrast is created by the characterization of Pharaoh. Whereas Abram is presented as being morally compromised in this incident, the Pharaoh is an honourable man. His questions to Abram are pregnant accusations. 'What is this you have done to me?' (12.18b), registers his outrage, using the same construction as God when condemning the Woman in the garden (3.13; cf. 29.15-30). 'Why did you not tell me that she was your wife?' (12.18c), indicates that if Abram had told the truth, he would have had nothing to fear. For if adultery was unthinkable, then so would be murder. We look in vain for any blessing on the nations in this episode.

The moral standing of Abram and the Pharaoh are clearly set out (see 19.1-29). But the stance of Sarai is more enigmatic. She is silent throughout the episode. Does her silence indicate her complicity in Abram's ruse? Or is she portrayed as a powerless victim, a pawn in her husband's hand? Future episodes will illustrate the kind of character Sarai really is (see 16.1-6, 7-16; 18.1-15; 20.8-18; 21.1-7, 8-21).

Pharaoh's brusque expulsion of the party from Egypt echoes Yahweh's initial commission. Yahweh had said, 'Go! (*lek*) ... So Abram went' (12.1a, 4a). Pharaoh says, 'Go! (*lek*) ... so Abram went' (12.19; 13.1). The same words contrast the initial divine promises with the subsequent human condemnation. The story of Abram, it seems, might be a complicated affair.

Genesis 13

Abram and his party return to Canaan. The episode in Egypt had highlighted Abram's relationship with his wife. This chapter reveals more about his relationship to Lot.

13.1-7

Just as Abram previously 'went down to Egypt' (12.10), he now 'went up from Egypt' (13.1), thus bringing his journey full circle. A similar balance is created by the Pharaoh's largesse which makes Abram 'very rich (*kābēd*) in livestock' (13.2), reminding the reader that his reason for leaving Canaan had been because 'the famine was severe (*kābēd*) in the land' (12.10). To such subtle reminders of previous narrative is added an explicit and detailed statement that Abram returned to the exact spot in Canaan where he had built an altar and called on Yahweh (13.3 cf. 12.8).

These allusions emphasize that the story has returned to its beginning. Abram is back where he started from. The episode in Egypt had been a dead end; the story must now progress within Canaan.

Yet life within Canaan is threatened. Their return had been due to their forcible expulsion from Egypt, not because the famine had abated. If the land had been unable to support them before, what are they to do now, laden down with livestock and servants given to Abram as a bride price for Sarai?

13.8-13

Abram's suggestion that he and Lot should separate in order to reduce tension between their herders is obvious common sense. Abram does not, however, suggest a complete breaking of their relationship. His proposal is simply that they each choose pasturage *within Canaan*. When giving directions Hebrews faced eastward. Thus Abram's offer of either the 'left' or 'right' to Lot corresponds to either the north or the south of Canaan. Lot's eyes, however, wander in neither direction; his attention is riveted on the *east*—that part of the Jordan valley which includes the cities of the plain (see Helyer 1983: 79). Genesis 10.19 had placed these cities within Canaanite territory, but at its extreme limits. This is reflected in 13.12, which contrasts Abram's remaining in Canaan with Lot's sojourning among the cities. Abram lives in the heart of Canaan while Lot lives at its furthest boundary, vulnerable to attack from outside or open to the temptation to migrate beyond its frontiers. The irony of this should not be missed. The overabundance of possessions Abram acquired from Pharaoh when he was willing to separate himself from his wife actually causes the separation from Lot, whom Abram considered to be more crucial to the fulfilments of the promises than Sarai (see 12.10-20).

Several details in this paragraph produce ominous overtones. Lot observes that the Jordan plain is 'like the garden of the Lord, like the land of Egypt' (13.10). While this provides a positive assessment of its appearance, we know that both of these locations have been scenes of judgment and expulsion (3.23-24; 12.19-20). This connection is underlined by further details. 'Lot journeyed eastward' (13.11), continuing the eastward movements of the dispossessed: the Man and Woman (3.24); Cain (4.16); the people of Babel (11.2). What, we might well ask, will Lot's eastward journey result in? While the statement that Lot 'saw that (*r'h kî*) ...' (13.10a), recalls God's assessment of his good creation (1.4, 10), it also reminds us of the action of the Woman contemplating the forbidden tree (3.6); the sons of God assessing the daughters of humans (6.2) and Yahweh's appraisal of the flood generation (6.5). The information that Lot's destination was wicked Sodom (13.13), strongly implies the negative connotation of the construction here.

The insight that these events took place before the destruction of the cities of the plain provides a rare anticipation of later plot development. This explicit telegraphing of future doom confirms the implicit details mentioned above. Verse 13, with its assessment of Sodom's great wickedness, is obviously to be taken as the motivation for God's destruction. Its use of the term 'wicked' (*ra'*) recalls the victims of the flood (6.5; 8.21). These specific details divulged to the reader create dramatic irony. We know what Abram and Lot do not know. We now anticipate the events foreshadowed by the text while the characters must await their destiny in ignorance (see 18.16-33).

The offer confirms Lot's importance to Abram. Yahweh had promised Abram that his descendants would possess Canaan (12.7). While Abram is not yet in possession of the land he offers part of it to Lot, an act consistent with his assessment that Lot is his heir. Lot's choice is obviously motivated by self-interest, taking the best for himself. While he stands in some contrast to Abram in this chapter, he seems to have learned something from his uncle's antics down in Egypt. Just as Abram had abandoned Sarai to preserve his own interests, now Lot gives his uncle a taste of his own medicine. Yet in choosing to distance himself from Abram, he ironically facilitates the letter of Yahweh's initial command to Abram that he should abandon his kindred (12.1).

13.14-18

Yahweh had previously commanded Abram to go to the land that he would 'show' (*r'h*) him (12.1). While the importance of Canaan for Abram's descendants has already been announced (12.7), Yahweh's 'showing' Abram the land is now formalized with another command to Abram, this time to 'look' (*r'h*, 13.14) over all Canaan together with a promise that Yahweh will give not only to his descendants but also to him 'all the land that you see (*r'h*)' (13.15).

The fulsome blessing of land and progeny given to Abram here stands in stark contrast to the ominous tones of anticipated judgment and destruction in the previous paragraph. If what Yahweh says to Abram is true, and if the position taken by this commentary on 13.8-13 is correct, then a tension is created. If Lot meets his expected fate how will the progeny promise to Abram ever be fulfilled? Either Lot must be spared his doom or Abram must look for progeny from another source. Hints of both possibilities will engage the reader's interest as the plot unfolds (see 14.13-16; 15.1-6; 18.16-33; 17.15-22; 19.30-38).

The chapter begins and ends with Abram living in tents (13.3 cf. 13.18) and worshipping at altars (13.4 cf. 13.18). Thus the narrative contrasts Abram with Lot, who similarly 'moved his tent' (13.12), but built no altars; he lives among the wicked of Sodom. Lot's journey has been more than geographical.

Genesis 14

The anticipated dangers of Lot's going to the edges of Canaanite territory come to fruition in this chapter. Chapter 13 saw Lot separating from Abram in order to avoid strife. It is ironic therefore that his move actually involves him in the greater strife of inter-city warfare. A family squabble with Abram would have been preferable to the problems they both experience in this chapter.

14.1-12

What made the cities of the plain attractive to Lot also appealed to foreign kings. The detailed listing of the protagonists reminds us of the larger world in which this story takes place. Amraphel, the first king cited, is king of Shinar, the location of Babel. From here the nations were scattered across the earth. Tidal, the last foreign interloper mentioned, is king of Goiim (Hebrew for 'nations'). Thus Babel, which formed the backdrop for the call of Abram, is now intruding into the story itself. In addition, the names of the kings of Sodom and Gomorrah carry negative connotations: Bera is compounded on *ra'* ('evil'); Birsha on *rāšha'* ('wicked'). Their names reinforce the negative assessment of these cities given in ch. 13.

The incursions of these Mesopotamian kings raise again the divine promises to Abram. Just as the aim of these kings is to subjugate Canaan, Abram has been promised that [he and] his descendants will be given this same land (12.7; 13.15). Thus Abram and the kings are opponents. The end result of Abram's obedience to Yahweh's initial command (12.1-3) is that all nations will be blessed. The arrival of Tidal king of Goiim/ Nations provides Abram with an opportunity to live up to this expectation.

Previously we learned that not only are the Canaanites still in the land (12.6; 13.7), but also that famine conditions cannot support Abram's entourage (12.10; 13.6). Now we discover that other outsiders have an eye on the region. All in all, Abram's possession of Canaan seems to be neither a readily achievable goal nor an attractive proposition.

Not only does Chedorlaomer's coalition complicate the land promise, but also the promise of nationhood. The most important point is left to the final climactic statement, 'they also took Lot' (14.12a). In ch. 13, Lot had chosen to separate from Abram. Here, he is forcibly removed even further. The same question arises here as in ch. 13, but this time with more immediacy. Will Lot be spared, or will Abram need to look for an heir from a different source?

14.13-16

Abram's response is immediate. He musters his men, inflicts a crushing defeat on Lot's abductors and returns home triumphant. The succinct account emphasizes Abram's victory and the return of Lot. On reflection, however, we realize that Abram's action on the battlefield was a desperate ploy that put his life in danger. This forms a strong contrast with his adventures in Egypt. There, Abram had felt his life to be in danger when he anticipated the abduction of Sarai. Yet on that occasion he avoided all temptations to be heroic, concocting a ruse that guaranteed his safety but condemned his wife to an adulterous relationship (12.11-15). In the present episode, however, Abram willingly risks his life when Lot is abducted. The relationship between the narratives is underlined by verbal similarities. Both Sarai and Lot are 'taken' (*lqḥ* 12.15; 14.12). Kinship terms are used to describe both, 'Say you are my *sister* (*'āḥôt*)' (12.13); 'When Abram heard that his *brother* (*'āḥ*), NRSV 'nephew') ...' (14.14). In each narrative Abram emerges with the riches of foreign kings, through the indirect agency of a family member (12.16; 14.16). The two accounts confirm Abram's comparative assessment of Sarai and Lot. If necessary Sarai can be discarded, but Lot must be preserved. As far as Abram can understand the will of God, the future great nation must come through the potential of Lot rather than the proven barrenness of Sarai (see 12.10-20).

This incident provides Abram with an opportunity to mix with yet more of the nations. It is true that Canaanite kings benefit incidentally from his actions. But if we add his present routing of the Mesopotamian kings to his previous deception of the Egyptians one might well wonder how Abram will become a blessing to the nations. One more opportunity presents itself in the next episode.

14.17-24

On returning from battle Abram is met by two Canaanite kings. The first is the king of Sodom. We have already been informed that the inhabitants of Sodom 'were wicked, great sinners against the Lord' (13.13), and this king must hold ultimate responsibility for that. Melchizedek, king of Salem, also a Canaanite, then comes on the scene, but forms a great contrast. He blesses Abram effusively and Abram responds positively. By comparison the king of Sodom is churlish toward Abram who responds curtly. One thing is clear from this passage: one cannot generalize about Canaanites nor about Abram's relationship to them.

Melchizedek's blessing recalls Yahweh's promise, 'I will bless those who bless you' (12.3a). Here, however, Melchizedek uses the name of El Elyon ('God Most High'), rather than Yahweh. Thus his blessing affirms his positive assessment of Abram yet at the same time registers the fact that they are devotees of different gods. Yet Abram's response strikes a surprisingly ecumenical note by equating the two deities, 'I have sworn to the Lord, God Most High' (14.22). Abram seems to be learning the art of diplomacy.

The Hebrew text is ambiguous over the matter of the payment of tithe, reading literally, 'and he gave to him a tenth of everything' (14.20). Did Abram pay tithe to Melchizedek or vice-versa? Since Melchizedek is a priest, though not of Yahweh, then in the light of later Pentateuchal law it would seem more likely that Abram paid tithe to him (e.g., Num. 18.21; Neh. 10.38; Mal. 3.10). The general context also supports this (see 14.23). In fact the brusque interjection by the king of Sodom, 'Give me the people, but take the goods for yourself' (14.21), can be read as his alarmed response to Abram's dispersing of Sodom's riches in tithe payments of people and booty to Melchizedek. One would have thought that he was in no position to be negotiating terms. Abraham's response conveys thinly disguised annoyance at the king's command. Abram will not withhold anything other than the provisions used by his servants and an equitable settlement for his Amorite allies who accompanied him (14.23-24). In light of this assurance Abram's tithe to Melchizedek must have been confined to the recaptured goods of Sodom's neighbours (or at least Gomorrah's, see 14.11). By implication therefore, Abram shows more generosity to Sodom, where Lot will continue to live, than he does to its neighbours, to whom he gives no such generous treatment. The incident is complex, with generosity and self-centredness being exhibited in turn by both Canaanite kings and Abram. This is not a simple account of how Abram is a blessing to the nations.

Abram's relationship to the nations is given another ironic twist by the final statement of the chapter. For the first time we learn that Aner, Eshcol and Mamre the Amorite, inhabitants of the land, assisted Abram in the rescue of Lot. So the people who are instrumental in rescuing Lot are the very ones Abram believes will be dispossessed of their ancestral real estate by his descendants through Lot. These representatives of the nations have been a blessing to Abram in the short term, but will he bless them in the long term? (See 15.16.)

Genesis 15

The introductory words of this chapter, 'After these things ...' (15.1a), are more than an indication of temporal succession. They are an invitation to read the following episode in the light of the preceding. When this is done the reader observes a number of points of contact, some of which make an immediate impact on one's reading, others are tantalising while yet others remain enigmatic.

On the large scale we note how elements in ch. 14 are now developed by the revelations of ch. 15. In the previous chapter foreign kings plundered the Canaanites; in this chapter Abram is reminded that his descendants will dispossess the Canaanites of their land. There, Abram plundered Lot's captors; here he is told that his enslaved descendants will be enriched at the expense of their oppressors (recalling in part Abram's enrichment when in Egypt, 12.10-20). Whereas in ch. 14 some Canaanites (Abram's Amorite allies and Melchizedek), were portrayed positively, here their descendants are judged more negatively and more in line with previous assessments (13.10, 13).

There are also verbal echoes between the chapters in a number of details. Damascus (14.15; 15.2) is mentioned here and nowhere else in Genesis; 'covenant' in 14.13 (literally 'possessors of the covenant of Abram') and 15.18; 'Amorite' in 14.13 and 15.16, 21. These two accounts share an interest in giving (*ntn*) and taking (*lqḥ*), the verbs occurring seven times each in both chapters, almost one-third of all uses in Genesis. One wonders with the rabbis about the troublesome 'Eliezer' (see below on 15.2), the numerical value of whose name just happens to equal 318, the exact number of Abram's trained men (14.14). The significance of some of these details will be addressed in the following commentary.

15.1-6

The dialogue between Abram and Yahweh, the first between them in the story, allows Abram to express his views on the development of the nationhood promise. Previously his actions and words have given indirect indicators of his perceptions. His words here provide a clearer revelation of his psychology. Abram's concern for Lot in ch. 14 had once again illustrated how important to Abram his nephew was for the establishment of the promised great nation. Therefore, the rendering of 15.2-3 in modern translations takes us by surprise. In response to Yahweh's announcement that his 'reward shall be very great' (15.1b), Abram counters that he still has no offspring and that 'the heir of my house is Eliezer of Damascus' (15.2b), adding 'a slave born in my house is to be my heir' (15.3b). Such translations (here NRSV) seem to leave Lot entirely out of the picture by introducing an unknown character, Eliezer.

Such conventional renderings of the verses, however, are misleading. First, the Hebrew of 15.2b is unintelligible, with the footnotes of most versions acknowledging the fact. The phrase 'the heir of my house' is an attempt to render *ben mešeq bêtî*. Nobody has a clue what *mešeq* means and all attempts to translate are shots in the dark. Also, as some scholars acknowledge, not even 'Eliezer of Damascus' is certain. (See Skinner 1930: 279, and my discussion in Turner 1990a: 69-72.) Secondly, the Hebrew of 15.3b reads literally 'a son of my house' (*ben bêtî*); there is no reference to 'slave'. Conventional translations attempt to identify the 'slave' of 15.3b with Eliezer of 15.2b (often on the basis of now discredited evidence from Nuzi). This seems to produce a cohesive translation but is at best problematical. I would suggest that the usual assumption that 15.2b and 3b are synonymous is misguided. While 15.2b is not understandable, perhaps the best construction we can put on it is that there possibly was a character in Abram's entourage called Eliezer who was a *ben mešeq bêtî*, whatever that was. The term might well refer to a position of authority within the family normally held by a child of the head of the household. Abram's words in 15.3b should not be taken as a redundant repetition of the sense of 15.2b. Here Abram says that his heir will be 'a son of my house'. The individual he refers to is anonymous, but there is no better candidate to fit this description than Lot, his dead brother's son.

If Abram still has Lot in mind as his heir, why does he complain to Yahweh? Yahweh's announcement had promised 'your reward will be very great'. Abram takes this to refer to his progeny, which is anything but 'great'. He has no children of his own and all of his hopes are vested in one individual—Lot. Abram does not complain that Yahweh has given him nothing, but that in contrast to Yahweh's affirmation of a 'very great reward' he has in fact very little. And Yahweh's initial statement, 'Do not be afraid' (15.1b), suggests that Abram has been exercised over this issue for some time. Yahweh's reply addresses this problem. He does not simply affirm that Abram will have progeny, but that he will have a huge number of descendants (15.5).

Despite the problems of translation and thus interpretation posed by this paragraph, one aspect is unambiguously clear. Abram will father a son (15.4), and the numerous progeny promised in 15.5 will come through him. Lot, and anyone else, is thus eliminated from contention. Yahweh's announcement necessitates a major adjustment in Abram's thinking. It is now required not only that he believe in many progeny, but more importantly, that these will come through his own biological son. The story has had a number of surprises, but none of these has equalled the statement here that Abram 'believed the Lord' (15.6a). Abram moves from exasperated contention to absolute conviction in next to no time, with only the stars of heaven by way of proof (15.5). This warns us that whatever we might expect from Abram in the rest of the story, transformation of perspective should not surprise us.

We have already seen how the dialogue in this paragraph reveals Abram's emotions at a deeper level than previously by allowing him to articulate his thoughts about the promise. In 15.6 the narrator divulges Yahweh's assessment of Abram. This also reveals Yahweh's attitude to Abram at a deeper level than has been done before. When Abram believes, Yahweh considers him to be 'righteous'. So this paragraph marks a milestone in the narrative's presentation of both Abram's and Yahweh's relationship to the promise and to each other. Will Abram continue to believe Yahweh? And what will be Yahweh's assessment of Abram if he does not?

15.7-21

The narrative's attention moves away from progeny to land. This provides Yahweh with the opportunity to reveal that his leading goes back to Terah's initial move from Ur and not simply Abram's from Haran (15.7). A different aspect of the divine promise might be in focus but the structure of the passage is very similar. A divine announcement 'I am the Lord' (15.7a, cf. 15.1b) elicits a question from Abram, 'how am I to know ...?' (15.8, cf. 15.2a), to which God responds with a sign, 'Bring me a heifer' (15.9a, cf. 15.5a). One thing that these similarities show is that not all questions have been answered or problems solved in 15.1-6.

Just as the previous passage revealed Abram's doubts concerning the fulfilment of the nationhood promise, here he registers his concerns about the land. Now that Yahweh has removed Lot as his heir, Abram has no tangible foothold on nationhood other than Yahweh's promise. This has always been the case with the land promise. Abram's response to Yahweh's repetition of the promise, 'O Lord God, how am I to know that I shall possess it?' (15.8), confirms that he still does not possess it, and the rest of the passage details just how far away its possible fulfilment lies. It will not come in Abram's lifetime; only in that of his descendants—and fairly distant ones at that, regardless of how one understands 'four hundred years' or 'fourth generation' (15.13-16, 18).

Yahweh's 'proof' to Abram that he would have a son of his own had amounted to an inspection of the heavens (15.5). Confirmation of the land promise to Abram's descendants through that child is achieved by the ceremonial slaughter of assorted animals. While formally sealing the covenant promise between the two parties, the act provides no more hard evidence to Abram than had the celestial bodies previously. If he is to believe, then he must simply believe the word of Yahweh. And this he finds hard to do consistently. No sooner has he accepted by faith alone God's promise of progeny (15.6), than he requests hard evidence for the land promise (15.8).

The progeny promise had been clarified in 15.1-6, when Yahweh revealed that only a biological son would suffice. Here the land promise is clarified further. The boundaries of the land of promise are specified in greater detail than before. Yahweh leaves no room for ambiguity as to which land Abram's descendants will possess, the one from whom they will be descended, and the approximate time scale involved. The delay in possessing the land is entirely in the hands of the Amorites/Canaanites, whose wickedness has not yet reached the required level. Abram can do something about the progeny promise, in fact *will have to do* something about it. But he can do nothing about the land promise, other than having progeny to possess Canaan.

The fact that the Amorites are not yet ripe for judgment confirms the preceding chapter. While the king of Sodom rules over 'great sinners against the Lord' (13.13), and has a sharp exchange with Abram (14.21-24), Abram's Amorite allies and Melchizedek king of Salem present the positive side of the people of the land. The important role of these ethnic groups in future events is further suggested by the list in 15.19-21. The Amorites are listed seventh and the Jebusites (Jebus equals Salem) tenth, positions which as we have seen in previous genealogies are occupied by the major players (see 2.1-4a; 4.17-26; ch. 5; ch. 10; Rendsburg 1992: 266-72).

The promised fulfilments of posterity and land will impact on the third element of the initial divine promise, that of Abram being a blessing (12.2b). The oppression of Abram's descendants might well be as unjustified as the dispossession of the Canaanite's land is justified. Neither action, however, can be construed as a blessing on these particular nations.

In the description of oppression in a foreign land (15.13-14), the villains remain anonymous. The catalogue of nations with which the chapter ends shows that the narrative has no prejudice about identifying other nations. So why the omission here? Not divulging the name of the oppressors means that *Abram* does not know their identity. Second-time readers, however, must know that Egypt will be the culprit. This provides the possibility for dramatic irony in the rest of the Genesis narrative. For example, the promised land will extend to 'the river of Egypt' (15.18). For Abram, this is simply part of a geographical listing; for the second-time reader, however, apprised by 15.13-14 and wider knowledge brought to the text, it strikes a chord. It is a reminder that Abram's descendant might well possess the land, but they will be hemmed in by antagonistic nations. Similarly, the irony for the reader in recalling how Abram himself previously came out of Egypt with great possessions is lost on Abram. And anticipating briefly, a major character in the next chapter is Hagar the Egyptian. The reader might therefore see ironies in Abram's relationship with her which again are entirely lost on the patriarch.

Genesis 16

When Abram had visited Egypt he took the initiative for his own personal ends and Sarai passively complied (12.10-20). This resulted in Sarai's (probable) sexual liaison with the Egyptian king and God's intervention to rescue her. The passage ends with animosity and expulsion (12.18-20). In this present incident intial roles are reversed. For her own personal ends Sarai takes the initiative, speaking for the first time in the narrative (16.2), and Abram passively complies. This entails Abram having sexual relations with an Egyptian slave-girl (part of the booty from Pharaoh?), and in the aftermath God has to intervene to rescue Hagar. Animosity and expulsion feature here also. The similar structures of the two stories are obvious. As a consequence the questions previously asked about Abram, Sarai and Egyptians inevitably arise again here (see 12.10-20; 21.8-21).

The divine pronouncement in 15.13-16 had similarly recalled 12.10-20. In turn, it also anticipated the incident here. Abram had been informed that his descendants would be aliens in a foreign land (i.e., Egypt), where they would be oppressed as slaves. In ch. 16 we meet an Egyptian who is an alien in a foreign land; she is a slave who is oppressed. As that previous episode was concerned with the fulfilment of Yahweh's promises, the similarities posed by ch. 16 invite us to read it from the same perspective.

16.1-6

From the beginning of the story we have known that Sarai is barren (11.30). What we have not known until the previous chapter is that Abram will father his own heir. Yahweh had announced that Abram would have a child (15.4); with unconscious irony Sarai announces that 'the Lord has prevented me from bearing children' (16.2). The reminder of Sarai's infertility with which the chapter starts is, therefore, not a redundant repetition. It underlines the difficulty of fulfilling the promise and Sarai's words raise the question of divine causality. Sarai's barrenness had previously forced Abram to look to Lot, but now his nephew has been explicitly eliminated as a candidate. Sarai's continuing barrenness is now resurrected as a problem for Abram's fathering a child. Since Yahweh has not included Sarai in any of his pronouncements, if Abram is to father a child presumably he must find a fertile woman to act as a mother.

For the first time in the narrative Sarai asserts herself. Having simply accompanied and obeyed her husband passively before this, her initiative here indicates how burdensome she views the curse of childlessness. Her intensely personal tragedy is shown in her omission of any reference to Abram's posterity promise; her aim is to obtain children for herself (16.2b). If Abram had been able to 'adopt' Lot, the son of his dead brother, why can not she 'adopt' the child of her slave? (see 12.4-9, 10-20; 13.8-13, 14-18; 14.13-16). Her words underline the differing perspectives of the characters and the reader. For Sarai, Hagar's pregnancy will herald the end to her years of childlessness. For Abram and the reader, it ushers on to the scene Abram's heir and the fulfilment of Yahweh's promise. Thus Abram's willingness to embrace Hagar is not simply an act of compassion to end his wife's misery. Yet Abram has fathered a child by an Egyptian—which the second-time readers knows is the very nation alluded to in 15.13-14 that will later oppress Abram's descendants. Thus the reader's unease is in tension with Abram's presumed emotions.

Abram's success in impregnating Hagar confirms what all know: 'Now Sarai was barren' (11.30). Yet strangely, Abram's demonstration of manhood is limited to this one act. In other matters he weakly acquiesces to his wife's demands. He not only unquestioningly slips into Hagar's bed but abandons the woman to her fate, 'Your slave-girl is in your power; do to her as you please' (16.6a). Obeying his wife's command had opened up the possibility of fulfilling the posterity promise; giving pregnant Hagar over to her now seriously threatens it. Previously, Abram's cowardice was understandable (see 12.10-20); here, it defies rational explanation.

If Abram's actions are irrational then so is Sarai's accusation. Sarai's complaint is that because she told Abram to get Hagar pregnant, Hagar's subsequent contempt for her is Abram's fault (16.5)! The incoherence of the argument illustrates how deep-seated is the emotional trauma of Sarai's barrenness. Yet our sympathy for Sarai is tempered by the knowledge that she mistreats Hagar because Hagar 'looked with contempt on her mistress' (16.4b). She had hoped to 'obtain children (lit 'be built up' [*bnh*]) by her', 16.2b). Instead of being built up she is disdained. Her response to Hagar when her ploy backfires reveals a rather mean-spirited woman whose status in the household is of even more concern to her than her childlessness. Sarai had asked for God to judge between herself and Abram but her appeal for justice rings hollow in light of her treatment of Hagar.

Both the narrator and Sarai say that Hagar looked with 'contempt' (*qll*) on her mistress (16.4-5). The same verb was used in Yahweh's original promise to Abram: 'the one who curses (*qll*) you I will curse (*'rr*)' (12.3). This prediction does not bode well for Hagar as the narrative continues.

16.7-16

Having fled into the wilderness from Sarai's persecution, Hagar meets the angel of Yahweh. Her response to his two questions, 'Where have you come from and where are you going?' (16.8), reveals how desperate she is. She answers only the first. Escaping from Sarai is her only aim; she does not know where she is going. He announces that her descendants through the son in her womb will become so numerous 'that they cannot be counted for multitude' (16.10). This recalls Yahweh's previous promise to Abram that his son will be the source of innumerable progeny (13.16; 15.5). The conclusion seems clear: Ishmael, born of Hagar, is the son of promise. This seems confirmed by the command to return to her mistress Sarai, and thereby to Abram's household. While Hagar's return might be good news for Abram, it was likely to be bad news for the women involved. Hagar was returning to an oppressive situation where no guarantee had been given of any change of attitude on Sarai's part. Sarai, having removed the woman who irked her when pregnant, is unlikely to welcome her back to give birth.

The prediction that Ishmael will be at loggerheads with everyone, does make us wonder how this line of descent will result in the blessing of the nations (12.3). However, with the plot having been so convoluted up to this point, this is hardly a major problem. While Ishmael's future strife (16.12) might seem to perpetuate the disharmony within Abram's household, it actually shows a role change. This is emphasized by the motif of 'hand' (*yād*). Abram told Sarai that Hagar 'is in your hand (*yād*, NRSV 'power')' (16.6); the angel told Hagar to return to Sarai and 'submit under her hand (*yād*, NRSV 'submit to her')' (16.9). Of Ishmael the angel predicted, 'with his hand (*yād*) against everyone and everyone's hand (*yād*) against him' (16.12). Ishmael's destiny shows that Hagar's present position—under another's hand—will not be perpetuated in her son.

In the previous passage we had looked with anticipation to see whether Yahweh would fulfil the promise of 12.1-3 by cursing Hagar because she had looked with 'contempt' (*qll*) on Sarai. We note, however, that this prediction was contingent on obedience to a divine imperative, 'be a blessing!' (12.2; see 12.1-3; 16.1-6). As Abram and Sarai have not been a blessing to Hagar, we should not be surprised by the inversion of our expectations in 16.7-16, where blessing rather than curse comes on Hagar.

The final line of 16.12 is enigmatic: 'and he shall live at odds with all his kin (lit. brothers)'. Who will be Ishmael's brothers/kin? Other children of Hagar or of Abram by Hagar or other women? If Hagar becomes pregnant again, what will Sarai do about *that*? Surely children of Sarai could not be meant? Also, the phrase 'at odds with' ('*al p°nê*) could be translated 'to the east of'. The juxtaposition of 'brother' and 'east' recalls the story of Cain, who rose up against his brother and settled in the east (*qedem*, 4.16). With these connotations, how much of the angel's words is blessing and how much curse?

A great deal of naming occurs at the end of the chapter. The angel of Yahweh tells Hagar to name her child Ishmael, 'God has given heed' (16.11). The name reveals Yahweh's self-perception; he is a God who hears. Hagar names Yahweh El Roi, 'God who sees' (16.13). This is the sole example in Genesis of a human naming God and reveals Hagar's perception of God. Thus the first two namings reveal the point of view of the namers. Two more namings occur: the anonymous naming of the well Beer-lahoi-roi, 'well of the living one who sees me' (16.14) and Abram's naming the child Ishmael (16.15). These are second-hand namings, however, revealing nothing of the namers other than that they have heard of Hagar's experience. Will the affirmations of the first two namings, that God 'sees' and 'hears', be confirmed by subsequent developments in the plot? (See 21.8-21.)

In Hebrew, the first word of the chapter is Sarai; its last is Abram. This summarizes the shift of focus in the story. Sarai's motivation for giving Hagar to Abram was so that 'I shall obtain children by her' (16.2). The concluding statement goes out of its way to stress Abram's paternity at the expense of Sarai's maternity, 'Hagar bore Abram a son; and Abram named his son, whom Hagar bore, Ishmael. Abram was eighty-six years old when Hagar bore him Ishmael' (16.15). *Abram* has a son and *Hagar* bore him.

None of the characters emerges from this chapter entirely positively. Abram's passivity in giving his wife free rein is as disastrous here for Hagar as his initiative in Egypt was for Sarai. Any sympathies for Sarai in her predicament of barrenness are dissipated by her harsh treatment of Hagar. Even sympathy for Hagar over her ill treatment is tempered by knowledge that her haughty attitude toward Sarai was uncalled for. Characters' motivations and readers' judgments are rarely straightforward in Genesis (see Trible 1984: 9-35).

Genesis 17

Coming after a silence of 13 years, the content of ch. 17 is marked out as significant. With no communication from Yahweh between Ishmael's birth and adolescence, the child's growth towards maturity would have reinforced Abram's expectations that this was the child of promise. When God breaks the silence he does so with a lengthy monologue, with just one brief response from Abram (17.18). The only human action of any note in the chapter is Abram's circumcision of his household. Yahweh's lengthy speech does more than provide a break in the narrative action. It also gives a summary reminder of the covenant promises while developing them further in significant ways.

The similarities with ch. 15 are obvious: God introduces himself (17.1 cf. 15.7); expands on the covenant (17.2-7 cf. 15.9-18); promises numerous descendants (17.8 cf. 15.5), land (17.8 cf. 15.18), and a son (17.19, 21 cf. 15.4); and Abram questions Yahweh (17.17 cf. 15.3, 8; see Skinner 1930: 290). These similarities actually highlight the significant development that takes place here. In ch. 15, believing the promises is righteousness (15.6); in ch. 17 being righteous is the condition for the fulfilment of the promises (17.1-2; see 22.1-19).

17.1-8

God's command to Abram utilizes the same construction as that in 12.2d-3a (see 12.1-3). Just as there God's blessing of Abram was contingent on Abram's obedience, so here God's promise to make his covenant with Abram (17.2) depends on Abram's obedience to his imperatives in 17.1. God's intent can be seen more clearly if we translate 'walk before me, and be blameless *so that [in order that]* I will make my covenant between me and you'. The reader has had occasion to query Abram's actions in previous episodes, but here is an explicit indication that at least some plot developments from now on will be moulded by his behaviour. Just as God will be assessing whether Abram 'walks before' him in a blameless manner, so will the reader. The magnitude of the ethical challenge facing Abram is indicated by the echoes of former passages recalled by the phrase 'walk before'. Enoch and Noah both 'walked with' God (5.22, 24; 6.9). In addition, Noah was judged to be 'blameless' (*tāmîm*), which is also Abram's challenge. Abram must emulate Noah if, like him, Yahweh is to make his covenant with him.

The covenant that Yahweh will eventually make with Abram is an expansion of the covenantal promises made in previous chapters. Abram has already been promised a great nation and numerous descendants. Here, nations (i.e., plural) and kings are promised to him, together with a promise of divine presence with these descendants in perpetuity (17.7). Presumably this will be one way in which through Abram 'all the families of the earth shall be blessed' (12.3). These promises supplement the angel's speech to Hagar regarding the future greatness of Ishmael (16.11-12). In particular, the element of land promise missing from that previous speech is included here. Thus all the elements of the divine promises first announced in 12.1-3 and supplemented and illuminated by developments since, congregate around the character of Ishmael.

The announcement of Abram's destiny is accompanied by a change of name. This feature continues the motif of naming from ch. 16. With the exception of Hagar's naming of God (16.13), only unnamed entities have received names. Here, a character is renamed. The new name 'Abraham' (interpreted to mean 'father of a multitude'), advertises to all what up to this point had been private knowledge between a man and God. For the name to be descriptive of reality, however, Abraham must rise to the ethical challenge which Yahweh has set him (see also 35.1-15).

17.9-14

NRSV captures nicely the emphasis of Yahweh's continued speech to Abraham, 'As for you ...' (17.9). The previous passage had started with Abraham's obligation but had continued with a catalogue of what Yahweh would do (17.2, 4-8). Yahweh now returns to his previous starting point in 17.1 by reminding Abraham of his obligation: 'You shall keep my covenant.'

But what exactly is the covenant? Yahweh's words 'This is my covenant ...' (17.10), outline only the obligation to observe circumcision. The next verse, however, refers to circumcision as the *sign* of the covenant, indicating that the covenant is something larger to which this sign points. If we look ahead slightly to 17.19-21 we discover that Yahweh will establish his covenant only with Isaac. Since Ishmael is later circumcised but lives outside of this covenant, we must conclude that the covenant is something much greater. Therefore, Abraham's moral obligations (17.1) must exceed the perfunctory performance of a physical sign.

Just as Noah walked with God, was deemed to be 'blameless' and was given the covenantal sign of the rainbow (6.9; 9.13-16), so Abraham is called on to walk before God, be blameless and to observe the covenantal sign of circumcision. The universally observed rainbow was a sign to remind God of his obligations (9.13-15); the hidden and personal circumcision seems to operate as a reminder to Abraham and his descendants.

17.15-27

Nothing in the chapter so far has prepared Abraham for the bombshell dropped by Yahweh here. Sarai is to have a name change just like her husband, but this is a minor detail. For the first time Abraham is told that Sarai, to be known henceforth as Sarah, will give birth to a son. Indeed this son will be the one through whom the nations mentioned as Abraham's descendants in 17.4-6 will be traced. Abraham had learned in ch. 15 that he would father the child of promise; now he is told that Sarah will be the mother. The conclusion is stark: Ishmael is not the son of promise. Abraham's passionate doubting of whether a couple of their age could possibly procreate (17.17), constitutes a plea for Ishmael, 'O that Ishmael might live in your sight!' (17.18). Yahweh informs him that this will not be possible and continues by differentiating between Abraham's current son by Hagar and future son by Sarah. Ishmael will be blessed and become a great nation (17.20), but the future son is the one with whom Yahweh will 'establish' his covenant. That is to say, the covenant promises first outlined in 12.1-3 will be traced through Isaac. Note how these developments echo earlier ones. Abraham had previously trusted in Lot (see 12.4-9, 10-20; 13.8-13,

14-18; 14.1-12, 13-16.). As a result of strife he left Abraham's household (13.8-13). When in danger Abraham had brought him back (14.13-16), but Lot was then eliminated from contention (15.1-6). In ch. 16 Hagar, pregnant with Ishmael, left Abraham's household because of strife. She returns and gives birth, but then Ishmael is eliminated from contention (17.15-21).

Abraham's initial reaction on hearing that Sarah will be a mother is to fall on his face. He has done this once already when God first approached him (17.3). That previous action was an act of reverence in response to promises he has heard before (17.2). He assumes that they will be fulfilled through Ishmael. The second time that he throws himself on the ground, however, he does so with a laugh of exasperation and words of incredulity. The first action shows his comfort with Ishmael as the focus, reinforced by 13 years of non-communication from Yahweh. The second registers just how resistant to change he is. Notice also that unlike ch. 15, where the last major adjustment to the posterity promise was made, the narrator does not add 'and he believed the Lord' (15.6). Thus as readers we will have to assess whether Abraham's subsequent actions indicate belief on his part. This is no idle pursuit, for the promises of this chapter are predicated on Abraham's walking before God and being blameless (17.1-2).

The chapter concludes with Abraham's circumcision of his entire household. The repetitive style leaves no doubt that both he and Ishmael undergo that rite, obeying the covenantal conditions commanded in 17.9-14. It tells us nothing, however, about his attitude to the developments detailed in 17.15-22. Circumcising Ishmael does not mean that he believes Sarah will have a son.

Genesis 18

Chapters 18–19 form the longest sustained episode in Genesis, with many issues in the former chapter only being clarified by the latter. They explore in depth not only the complex characters of Abraham, Sarah and particularly Lot, but also the ambiguities of God's ways with human beings.

18.1-15

There is nothing unusual in Abraham encountering Yahweh (18.1), though no previous cases are as physically concrete as here (cf. 12.1; 13.14; 15.1; 17.1). Indeed, the intimacy with God experienced by Abraham recalls that of the Man and Woman with the Lord God in the garden (cf. 3.8-21). Given that precedent, this encounter might well be disturbing. There is some ambiguity initially, as to whether all three visitors are a manifestation of Yahweh, or whether he is only one of them, with two heavenly accomplices. Nevertheless, while for the narrator, and hence the reader, it is Yahweh who visits Abraham (18.1), from Abraham's perspective, it is three *men* (18.2). This explains Abraham's actions. In his encounter with God in the previous chapter, Abraham 'fell on his face' (17.3). So it is not likely that he knowingly scrambles about his encampment hastily putting together a meal to serve to Yahweh. He has not yet seen through the *in cognito* of his visitors.

The opening verses of the chapter dwell over the details of Abraham's activity in order to stress his hospitality. Previously, he has not been shown in the best light when encountering strangers (12.10-20; cf. 20.1-18). But here, Abraham acts as the ideal host. He 'ran', 'bowed' to the earth (18.2), 'hastened', (18.6), and so on. The contrast between the understatement of his speech, 'a little water ... a little bread' (18.4-5), and the lavishness of the feast he prepares which includes cakes, curds, milk and meat in abundance (18.6-8), also underlines his generosity. Abraham's hospitality, like Job's, demonstrates his righteousness (Job 31.31-32; cf. Ps. 37.21, 25-26; Prov. 21.26).

The visitors do more than indulge in small talk while enjoying this feast. Their visit, it transpires, is more than a chance encounter. They have a message concerning Sarah, repeating God's previous confidential promise to Abraham (17.15-16). Sarah will soon have a child (18.10). When Abraham had first heard this preposterous announcement, he had laughed out loud and then protested (17.17-18). When Sarah overhears the same, she too laughs and expresses obvious objections. The repetition here of the prediction concerning Sarah's impending pregnancy is not redundant. Not only does it provide an insight into Sarah's attitude to the promise, but also underlines Abraham's reaction. Sarah's spontaneous laugh, like Abraham's previous outburst, has all the characteristics of a response to unbelievable news. She has not heard of such a thing before. Yet Abraham has known of it for some time. His wife's reaction reveals that he has never told her. Why bother her with such unbelievable nonsense? Sarah's objection to the whole notion is also revealing, 'After I have grown old, and my husband is old, shall I have *pleasure* (*'ednâ*)?' (18.12). The term used, while unique to this verse, is thought to convey the sense of sexual pleasure. If Abraham and Sarah are experiencing no sexual pleasure, then they are no longer having sexual relations. What better way to demonstrate disbelief in the hope of a child?

The dialogue between host and guests also begins to clarify for Abraham and Sarah the identity of the visitors. They start to exhibit more than human characteristics. Despite not having been introduced to her, they know Sarah's name (18.9). One of their number predicts that Sarah will have a son, claiming an insight into the divine will (18.14). Despite Sarah's laugh being a private matter, and her protestations of innocence, the visitors know what she has done in the privacy of the tent (18.13, 15). As the narrator divulged from the outset, these are heavenly visitors.

18.16-33

The visitors depart and Abraham accompanies them 'to set them on their way' (18.16). The narrative allows the reader to be privy to Yahweh's intentions regarding Sodom and Gomorrah (18.17-21), which leads to the crucial discussion between Abraham and Yahweh concerning the fate of the cities (18.22-33). They are going to discover just how wicked the city is and whether the outcry which has come to Yahweh is justified or not (18.20-21). Prior to the angelic visit to Sodom, Yahweh does not know how wicked the city is and has not decided whether he will destroy it or not. Their superhuman knowledge of 18.9-15 does not extend to omniscience. What Yahweh is 'about to do' (18.17), is to investigate the degree of Sodom's sinfulness (18.20-21). Abraham *assumes* that the purpose of such an investigation is to decide whether to destroy or not, and his dialogue with Yahweh in 18.22-33 shows his assumption to be correct.

Some obvious questions arise. Why should Yahweh feel it necessary to divulge to Abraham on this particular occasion what he is about to do (18.17)? The reason cannot simply be Abraham's importance in the narrative, otherwise Yahweh could well consult Abraham all the time. A clue is given when Yahweh draws a connection between divulging his intentions concerning Sodom on the one hand, with Abraham's destiny of becoming a great nation on the other (18.17-19). Earlier in the narrative Abraham had put his (partial) trust in Lot as his descendant (see 12.4-9, 10-20; 13.8-13, 14-18; 14.13-16). In Abraham's eyes therefore, there could well be a very specific and important connection between the possible destruction of Lot's dwelling place and Abraham's destiny as a great nation. This is not the first time that Abraham has intervened on Sodom's behalf. His overriding motivation before was to rescue Lot (14.14). Just prior to the present episode, Ishmael was dismissed by Yahweh as the son of promise, much to Abraham's displeasure (17.18-19). The child promised to Abraham and Sarah has not yet been born. It is true that Lot has already been eliminated as a possible heir (with Yahweh's promise of a biological son in 15.4), but if he should die in the destruction of Sodom it would leave Abraham feeling exposed. Before the birth of his promised son—should he ever be born—Abraham has two 'half-chances' for a descendant in Ishmael and Lot, and he wishes to preserve their candidature at all costs. This explains why he willingly circumcised Ishmael (17.25-26) and pleads for Sodom. Abraham's plea to save the whole city on ethical grounds is motivated largely by a desire to save his nephew and potential heir and with him Abraham's destiny.

Note that Abraham does not plead for the salvation of a righteous remnant from the destruction of Sodom. Abraham knows his nephew better than that (see 13.8-13). In addition, Abraham has met the Sodomites first hand (ch. 14), which has surely made him aware of the information divulged to the reader in 13.13, 'Now the people of Sodom were wicked, great sinners against the Lord'. Knowing this, he may well wonder what corrupting effect they have had on Lot. As a result, Abraham pleads for the salvation of the whole city, on the basis of the vicarious righteousness of a minority of 10. In his pleading, Abraham divides the inhabitants of Sodom into two mutually exclusive groups: the righteous and the wicked (18.23, 25). Abraham's plea for the vicarious salvation of the whole city means that regardless of whether Lot is deemed to be righteous or wicked, he will be saved along with the rest of the city—if there are 10 righteous Sodomites (see 7.1-10; 19.30-38).

Abraham's presumed motives, however, clash with the reader's privileged knowledge. Since 13.10b, all readers of this story have known that the Lord destroyed Sodom and Gomorrah. So one is left with the uneasy feeling that Abraham's efforts to dissuade Yahweh will be in vain. If so, then what of Lot's fate? (See 13.8-13.)

Genesis 19

19.1-29

The scene now moves to Sodom, and immediately conjures up parallels with the opening of ch. 18. There, Abraham had been sitting at the opening of his tent in the heat of the day when three visitors approached, to whom he offered hospitality (18.1-5). Here, Lot is sitting at the gate of Sodom at evening time when two visitors approach to whom he offers hospitality (19.1-3).

The angels visited Sodom to discover the extent of its wickedness (18.21). This precise motivation for the angel's visit to Sodom suggests a reason for their initial refusal of Lot's hospitality. It is a test to discover whether his offer is purely perfunctory or genuine. Lot's insistence on opening his home to them shows him to be a true host, no less than Abraham. Since giving hospitality to strangers is a feature of righteousness (cf. 18.1-5), then Lot has demonstrated that, on this particular point, there is at least one righteous person in Sodom. He reproduces the same righteous hospitality as his uncle Abraham.

No sooner has Lot served his evening meal than the visitors discover that the rest of the Sodomites are not so kindly disposed to strangers. The piling up of epithets in 19.4 emphasizes that the entire city surrounded Lot's house. This one act reveals that there are not even 10 righteous people to be found in Sodom. Lot, as the righteous host, however, comes to the aid of his guests. Leaving his house to speak to the townspeople reinforces his positive portrayal in 19.1-3, and contrasts him explicitly with the crazed mob. The righteous host condemns the wickedness of the entire city (19.7).

However, from now on the narrative makes significant modifications to this initial presentation of Lot. Lot's offer to the mob, giving them license to do to his daughters whatever they please (19.8), is quite shocking. Lot's initial gentlemanly behaviour must not blind us to the real horror he proposes for his daughters. To have offered *himself* to be homosexually abused in place of his guests would have maintained his role as a righteous host. It would also have been a more logical offer, given the apparent sexual predilections of his lust-crazed neighbours. But, rather than self-sacrifice, he chooses to offer his virgin daughters. Surely Lot's offer of his daughters is an act of wickedness.

The analogies between Abraham's and Lot's acts of hospitality were noted above, but Lot's offer here also compares with

Abraham's charade in Egypt (12.10-20). Abraham, feeling himself to be in a life and death situation, had been willing to surrender Sarah to the Pharaoh's bed. This was not recorded to Abraham's credit. The same judgment must be passed on Lot, who in a desperate situation was likewise willing to offer members of his own family to satisfy the lusts of strangers.

The increasingly complex nature of Lot's character is confirmed in the next development, where the angels, convinced of the depravity of the whole city (19.13), tell Lot to give the news of the city's destruction to his relatives so that they too might be saved. At first sight Lot seems to stand in contrast to his debauched sons-in-law, who in response to Lot's words, think their father-in-law is joking (19.14). However, they might well think so because they fail to hear the ring of conviction in Lot's voice; for in the morning Lot shows that he himself does not take the angels' word seriously. He 'lingered' in Sodom (19.16), even while the warning of imminent destruction was on the angels' lips. He feels comfortably at home and, like his sons-in-law, cannot be persuaded to leave. He has to be dragged outside the city. His lingering hardens into outright disagreement with his saviours over his place of sanctuary (19.18). His pleading for Zoar shows his extraordinary attraction to the cities of the Jordan valley. (For 19.27-29, see next section.)

19.30-38

Lot cuts a rather paranoid figure. Previously, he went to Zoar because he was afraid to live in the hills (19.17-19). Now he moves to the hills because he is afraid to stay in Zoar (19.30). Somewhat like Cain, banished to the land of Nod (4.16), he lives a restless, wandering existence.

If one judges Lot negatively when he offers his daughters to the mob, one can hardly do otherwise than pass the same judgment on this sordid episode with his daughters in the cave. In fact, there seems little to choose between those who escaped from the city and those who perished in the flames. The daughters might well feel that they face some problems in finding husbands, but surely overstate their case (19.31). They had found potential husbands in Sodom, so why not in Zoar which they have just left? Their action might tell us something about their inventiveness, but what does it say about their father? How exactly, does one make another person drunk? Lot was old enough to know when enough was enough. But he no longer has any control over his life. He is easy prey for his daughters. It is difficult not to see in their seduction an ironic comment on Lot's previous attempt to sacrifice them (19.8). Lot receives due recompense for his previous actions. At the beginning of the story Lot offered food to two angels; at its conclusion he is plied with wine by his two daughters. The stark contrast symbolizes the contradictions that are Lot.

As we look back on this chapter it can be seen that the characterization of Lot goes through several stages of development. At first he is presented as being righteous—he is the ideal host (19.1-3). This assessment has to be modified when we see him attempting to protect his guests (admirable in itself) by offering his daughters (19.8). The reader's assessment of Lot becomes increasingly critical as he procrastinates in his exit (19.16-19), names his own refuge just a short distance away (19.20), and is finally seduced into an incestuous union with his daughters.

The story of Sodom's destruction has certain basic similarities with the Flood narrative (chs. 6–9). Both narratives describe the destruction of a wicked human community (although ch. 19 is not so broad in scope), and in each a remnant is saved. A comparison between the central characters in each narrative, Noah and Lot, yields interesting results. From the start Noah is portrayed positively. He finds favour in God's eyes (6.8), is deemed to be righteous, walks with God (6.9b), and is contrasted with the corruption of his world. In the Flood narrative as a whole, with the possible exception of 9.20-27, Noah is the ideal righteous man. Despite his limited characterization, we see that Noah always takes the right initiative (e.g., 8.20-22). Noah is the one who leads; others accompany him (e.g., 7.7-9, 13, 15, 23b; 8.1a, 18).

By contrast, in the Abraham story, Lot is either the passive, used individual or when he does take the initiative, invariably makes the wrong choice. At the beginning of the story other people take Lot, or he merely accompanies them (11.31; 12.4, 5; 13.1, 5); the kings take Lot (14.12), while Abraham brings him back (14.16). In Sodom the angels drag him indoors (19.10); his procrastination results in his being taken again by the angels (19.16). Finally, it is appropriate that passive Lot's final appearance is an act of utter passivity: 'he did not know when she lay down or when she rose' (19.33, 35). With the one exception of his offer of hospitality (19.1-3), Lot makes the wrong choices; in ch. 13 he decides to move toward wicked Sodom, and when there offers his virgin daughters to the mob.

Throughout the Flood narrative Noah is entirely silent. He does not speak until immediately before his obituary notice (9.25-27). In contrast, Lot is almost verbose in his speech to the angels, the townspeople and his sons-in-law. Yet in the final episode of his drunken stupor in a cave (19.30-38), he becomes silent. The contrast between Lot's speech and Noah's silence is suggestive. Even the silent Noah speaks out against the outrage of his son's (sexual?) offence (see 9.20-29). Lot's silence in 19.30-38, in contrast to his previous speech and protests, demonstrates how far he has moved from his position at the beginning of the story, where he resolutely objected to the wickedness of attempted gang rape (19.6-7). By the end of the story, he not only raises no objections to incest, but is totally unaware of what has happened. His ignorance does not absolve him of blame, but again suggests a contrast to Noah. On awaking, Noah *knows* what has taken place (9.24); Lot never does.

At almost every step of the way, Lot is an inversion of Noah. In contrast to Noah's obedience (6.22; cf. 7.5), we read of Lot's procrastination and objections (19.17-18). It is understandable why Noah 'found favour in the sight of the Lord' (6.8). Lot's behaviour, apart from his initial act of hospitality, recommends him to no one, and the reader is tempted to hear a tone of incredulity in Lot's voice when he says to the heavenly visitors, 'your servant has found favour in your sight' (NRSV 'with you', 19.19).

One additional comparison crystallizes the chapter's presentation of Lot. At the structural centre of chs. 6–9 we read the salvific statement, 'God remembered Noah' (8.1). By comparison, God's act at Sodom is summarized in 19.29, 'God remembered *Abraham,* and sent Lot out of the midst of the overthrow'. The contrast could hardly be greater. Noah preserved humanity and his family because of his righteousness. Poor Lot cannot even save himself. He has to be dragged out of the city by the angels, and is saved through his association with Abraham. He is certainly not saved because of his righteousness.

Lot is a complex character. He is both righteous (e.g., in his offer of hospitality) and wicked (e.g., in his offer of his daughters). Lot's characterization has implications for reading, this time from hindsight, the crucial dialogue between Abraham and Yahweh (18.22-33). When Abraham starts to plead with Yahweh he asks, 'Will you indeed sweep away the *righteous* with the *wicked?*' (18.23). The distinction between these two categories forms the basis for their whole dialogue, in which Abraham succeeds in getting Yahweh to agree to a remnant of 10 righteous being sufficient to save the whole city. Abraham assumes that each inhabitant of Sodom belongs to one of two mutually exclusive groups. However, the way in which Lot is presented in ch. 19 shows that the moral world of Genesis is more complicated than Abraham assumes. One character at least, Lot, will not fit entirely into either category. The depiction of Lot in ch. 19 shows how flawed Abraham's assumption was, that a person is either righteous or wicked.

Contrasts also emerge between the agreement hammered out between Yahweh and Abraham (18.22-33), and the subsequent turn of events in ch. 19. Yahweh had agreed to spare the entire city if 10 righteous could be found. The investigation carried out by the angels revealed that not even this minimal righteous remnant was present. In keeping with the previous conditions, Yahweh destroyed the city. He did, however, rescue Lot and his daughters. But according to the agreed terms, Lot and his family should have perished in the flames. This should have been their fate even if one judges them to be righteous, for Abraham did not plead for the rescue of the righteous, but for the rescue of the entire city (including Lot), if 10 righteous could be found. The story suggests quite strongly that Yahweh was not hoodwinked by Abraham's pious posturing and gave him what he really wanted—Lot—when he consigned Sodom to the flames: '*God remembered Abraham,* and sent Lot out of the midst of the overthrow' (19.29). One wonders whether Abraham would have pleaded for the salvation of Sodom at all if he had known that this would be the result.

One is also left wondering, however, whether Lot's rescue was a better fate than that which would otherwise have overtaken him. To have perished in the flames of judgment that visited his wicked neighbours, or to have died a heroic death defending his guests from their hands, is arguably preferable to losing one's dignity and moral sense as one is dragged reluctantly to some refuge and alcohol-induced incest. Further, the rescue of Lot is not unmitigated good news for Abraham. His rescued nephew fathers the progenitors of two nations, the Moabites and Ammonites, who will subsequently harass Abraham's descendants (e.g., Josh. 24.9; Judg. 3.12-13; 10.7; 11.4). As Abraham discovered, human beings may certainly question and accuse Yahweh, and cause him to alter his course of action (18.22-33). But there is a price to pay.

Genesis 20

Chapter 19 ended with Lot's daughters treating their father as though he were their husband. Chapter 20 begins with Abraham treating his wife as though she were his sister. The comparison does not flatter Abraham. There is also a contrast with the previous episode. In ch. 19 a foreign community's lack of hospitality contrasted with Abraham's hospitality in ch. 18. In ch. 20 the obverse of this is seen: Abraham's lack of integrity contrasts with the principled behaviour of a foreign king. Once again, we are reminded that the characterization of neither Abraham nor foreigners is a straightforward matter.

The visitors who came to Abraham's tent in ch. 18 brought with them more information concerning the promise of Sarah's motherhood (18.9-15). Sarah's laughing response showed how difficult it was for her to believe this (18.12). The intervening episode of the angelic visit to Sodom, its destruction and Lot's deliverance has deflected our attention from the fulfilment of this promise. We return to it now.

20.1-7

The parallels with 12.10-20 are immediately obvious. Travelling southwards Abraham sojourns in alien territory (12.10 cf. 20.1). He passes his wife off as his sister (12.13 cf. 20.2a), and Sarah is taken into the king's household (12.15 cf. 20.2b). The terse account of 20.1-2 reveals a great deal about Abraham's attitude to the divine promise that Sarah will have a son. We have already been suspicious about his previous claim that Sarah is his sister (see 12.10-20). And Abraham knows what happened when he claimed that his wife was his sister—a foreign king found her irresistible. On that previous occasion our sympathies lay with Sarah as she was the pawn in Abraham's strategy. But at least in Egypt Abraham could claim that Sarah's part in the progeny promise had not been mentioned. He can claim no such alibi here. Sarah's indispensable part in the story has been revealed to both Abraham (17.15-16) and to the couple together (18.9-15). The passage of time, however, has not changed their disbelief. While both of them willingly conspire to dupe Abimelech, it underlines Abraham's conviction that Sarah will never get pregnant. As in Egypt, she is expendable (see 12.10-20; 26.6-11). Ironically, depending on how one translates the difficult Hebrew of 18.10, 14 (i.e., will Sarah bear the child 'in the spring', RSV, or 'in due season' NRSV?), the couple could assume that Sarah is already pregnant. Initially at least, this could only be affirmed by faith, since the cessation of Sarah's menstrual cycle long before this (18.11) would mask the fact. But faith is conspicuous by its absence in this chapter.

The text is unambiguous in its presentation of Abraham's actions. The stratagem perpetrated on Abimelech could have resulted in the king's sinning against Yahweh (20.6). Quite apart from the initial command that Abraham is to be a blessing to the nations (12.2), he is also bound to live a righteous life and to instruct others in ethical behaviour as preconditions for receiving his promised blessings (see 17.1; 18.19). Chapter 20 is a conspicuous example of his failure to do so, and thus casts doubt on how God will be able to ratify his covenant with him. In fact it is Abimelech, rather than Abraham, who can rightly claim to be 'innocent' (*saddîq*, 'righteous', 20.4; *tōm*, 'blameless', 20.5). As an 'innocent/righteous people' he belongs to that group Abraham was so solicitous about in 18.22-35. He stands in contrast not only to Sodom and Lot in the previous chapter, but also to Abraham in this chapter.

All of this makes Yahweh's assessment of Abraham being a 'prophet' who will intercede for Abimelech (20.7), all the more amazing. Given Abraham's record in his relationship with foreigners (e.g., 12.10-20), how likely is he to do this? And if Yahweh now speaks directly in a dream to Abimelech, why does he need a prophetic intercessor? One thing, at least, is clear. The drastic actions threatened by Yahweh in response to Abimelech's taking of Sarah, confirm that she is just as crucial as Abraham for the production of an heir (20.7b).

20.8-18

Rather than Abraham instructing others in righteousness (18.19), he receives a lecture on the same subject from Abimelech. 'What have you done to us? ... You have done things to me that ought not to be done' (20.9; see 29.15-30). His following question echoes the thoughts of the reader, 'What were you thinking of, that you did this thing?' Abraham's answer damns himself, regardless of whether he is telling the truth or lying through his teeth. He claims (as he did in Egypt), that he felt his life was in danger, and this prompted him to act as he did. He asserts, however, that this is his regular practice, 'at every place to which we come' (20.13). So he would have had Sarah masquerade as his sister regardless of whether there was any 'fear of God' (20.11) in Gerar or not. Is it really credible that Abraham thought his life was in danger everywhere (which is what his statement implies)? There is no evidence in the narrative that his life has ever been threatened, other than when he voluntarily risked his life for Lot (14.14-16). We have every right to be as suspicious of this claim as we are of his insistence that he and Sarah are siblings. On the other hand, if he does tell the truth, just how many beds has Sarah warmed over the years, and how many other individuals has he seduced into sinning against Yahweh (see 20.6, 9)? If he tells the truth, his life has been characterized by deception and unrighteousness—the very opposite of Yahweh's demand, 'walk before me and be blameless' (17.1).

The contrast between Abraham and Abimelech is emphasized by Abraham's statement that he considered Gerar to be bereft of 'the fear of God'. Yet the basis for his haggling with God in 18.22-33 was based on the very premise that there was a righteous remnant even in Sodom. Abimelech's dignified behaviour and principled response to Abraham shows just how wrong Abraham's assessment of Gerar had been, or perhaps simply confirms suspicions that Abraham's excuses in this paragraph are pure fictions. If there is no 'fear of God' in Gerar, just how much is there in forcing one's wife to commit adultery, an act which even the 'godless' Abimelech knows to be wrong?

Abimelech would have been justified if he had sent Abraham packing (cf. 12.19b-20). Instead, he makes the generous offer that Abraham may live wherever he likes within his territory. Abraham had previously made a similar offer to Lot (13.9). His action then had indicated his understanding of the divine promises and Lot's place within them. Abimelech's action, by contrast, is one of sheer generosity.

Both God and the narrator have consistently referred to Sarah as Abraham's wife (20.2, 3, 7, 14, 18). The whole incident revolves around the fact that this is her true role. It is therefore ironic that Abimelech, in his parting speech to Sarah should refer to Abraham as her brother (20.16). Rather than confirming the truth of Abraham's claims it simply registers Abimelech's belief that he was. Or is his statement laden with sarcasm? His speech also confirms that great wrong has been done not only to himself, but to Sarah. 'It is your exoneration (lit. 'a covering of the eyes') ... you are completely vindicated' (20.16). Sarah might have complied with Abraham's deception; but Abimelech sees her along with himself as Abraham's victim.

Abraham's final action in this episode raises hopes that he might be capable of more than self-interest in relation to the nations—or anyone else for that matter. As Yahweh had said, Abraham prayed for Abimelech. The result is that the curse wrought by Abraham's actions is reversed. This is certainly an improvement on his behaviour in Egypt (12.10-20). But does it really amount to being a blessing to the nations (12.2-3)?

Genesis 21
The chapter begins with the long-awaited birth of the son of promise. However, rather than his arrival bringing equilibrium to Abraham's household, it sparks off another crisis. The narrative presents a classic portrayal of the interplay between the major characters and their respective points of view.

21.1-7
The extended narrative that detailed the progress of the progeny promise is finally cut short. The child of promise is conceived, born, named and circumcised in the space of four verses. While his arrival has been anticipated by the reader for a long time, his actual advent takes one by surprise. Since 17.1 the fulfilment of the promises has been contingent on Abraham's being 'blameless' (cf. 18.19). Yet the son arrives immediately after the shenanigans of ch. 20. On reflection, however, we recall how the previous chapter ended. 'Abraham prayed to God' on behalf of Abimelech (20.17). This is a rare example of Abraham doing something for somebody else that was not linked to furthering his own ends (cf. rescuing Lot, 14.14-16; pleading for Sodom, 18.22-33). The chapter division tends to obscure the connection between the last act of ch. 20 and the first of ch. 21. Chapter 20 ends with fertility being restored to Abimelech's household; ch. 21 begins with fertility being granted to Sarah. The juxtaposition of these two events suggests that if Abraham's prayer produced the first, it might well have produced the second. Indeed, Abraham's turning from his own selfish interests for once could well be an act of 'doing righteousness' (18.19), which Yahweh had made the condition for fulfilling the promise.

Sarah's speech, with its reference to laughter, recalls the mirth that accompanied Yahweh's previous promises of a son. Genesis 17.17 recounted Abraham's laugh of frustration; 18.12 presented Sarah's laugh of unbelief. Here we have the laughter of delight (20.6). Thus laughter at the birth of the child not only

recalls the promise, and how difficult it was to believe, but also
transforms doubting anticipation into joyful realization.

Sarah's rhetorical question in 21.7 asks, 'Who would ever have
said to Abraham that Sarah would nurse children?' Both Sarah
and we know, of course, that God has said it (17.16; 18.10). The
incredulity in her voice underlines both the inherent implausi-
bility of the event and confirms the difficulty she has had in
trusting that God could do what he said he would do.

The description of the conception and birth of Isaac is remarkably concise (20.2), especially in light of the significance of the
event in the plot. Ishmael's account took up far more space (16.4-
16). As we shall see, the summary nature of Isaac's birth account
is not done to discount its significance, rather the narrative has
its eye on the conflict that his birth introduces into the story.
Despite Sarah's statement that 'God has brought laughter for
me', it is a rather different emotion that characterizes most of
the rest of the chapter.

21.8-21

The mood of celebration surrounding the birth of Isaac continues
through to the feast at his weaning. However, his mother soon
changes the festive atmosphere. The Hebrew text says simply
that Sarah saw Ishmael playing, with no reference to Isaac
(21.9). That was sufficient. As far as Sarah is concerned, Ishmael
has served his purpose. Just as Abraham had previously had a
surrogate son in the person of Lot (see e.g., 12.4-9; 15.1-6), Sarah
had achieved this though Ishmael (see 16.2). He had also been
the obvious family heir, a fact conceded by Sarah in her cruel
outburst demanding Ishmael's expulsion (21.10). In fact, it is
possible that the text contains a play on words which points to
the role conflict between the two boys. Sarah saw Ishmael
m^eṣaḥēq, that is, 'playing the role of Isaac' (Coats 1983:153; see
26.8).

This episode centres on the fate of rival sons. The word 'son'
(*ben*) occurs 12 times in the first 13 verses (used seven times of
Isaac and five times of Ishmael). The various points of view of
the characters regarding the two sons are clearly delineated.
Sarah's point of view is that Ishmael is 'the son of Hagar' (21.9),
not *Abraham's* son as in 16.15-16. Isaac is 'my son' (21.10).
Abraham's point of view is conveyed via the narrator. Ishmael is
'his son' (21.11) just as Isaac is 'his son' (see 21.3-5). God's point
of view regarding Ishmael combines the perspectives of Sarah

and Abraham. He is both the 'son of the slave woman' (Sarah's point of view) and 'your offspring' (Abraham's point of view). Standing outside this circle the narrator, Hagar and the angel of God use neutral language to describe Ishmael in 21.14-17. Here be becomes simply 'the child' (e.g., 21.14-15) or 'the boy' (21.17). This careful presentation of diverse points of view highlights the cause of the dispute in this episode. The problem is not personally precipitated by either Ishmael or Isaac, but by Sarah's, Abraham's and God's varying perceptions of what those sons actually are.

Even though Sarah's treatment of Ishmael is callous, her assertion that he will 'not inherit along with my son Isaac' (21.10) accurately foreshadows God's declaration, 'it is through Isaac that offspring shall be named after you' (21.12). And upon reflection we realize that such an outcome has been on the cards since 17.21, 'but my covenant I will establish with Isaac'. One only wishes that the woman who declared 'God has brought laughter for me' (21.6), could have been less vindictive in her triumph.

Echoes of previous episodes underline how earlier decisions have come home to roost. Previously Abraham had 'listened to the voice of Sarai' (16.2), when she had suggested the sexual liaison with Hagar. Now Sarah demands the expulsion of Hagar and her child and God tells Abraham to 'do as she tells you' (21.12). Sarah's initial easy suggestion contrasts with her current bitter demand. This shift finds its corollary in Abraham's previous acceptance of the dalliance with Hagar and his present distress at the thought of expelling his son. Both Sarah and Abraham, however, are at one in their dismissive attitude to Hagar. Sarah's only desire for Hagar is that she should be rid of her. Abraham's concern on hearing Sarah's demand is confined to 'his son' (21.11, though cf. 21.12a). Neither expresses any anxiety over *Hagar's* fate.

Just as Abraham expels his Egyptian slave and son, so Abraham himself had once been expelled by an Egyptian (12.18-20). The reversal of roles cannot hide the fact that in both incidents Egyptians were the victims. And we have far more sympathy for Hagar and Ishmael here than we did for Abraham in Egypt (see introductory comments to ch. 16). Hagar finds herself expelled for the second time. On the first occasion because Sarah made her life unbearable and on the second because of Sarah's express demand. This incident, however, places her in far greater danger. In ch. 16 she arrives at a spring of water (16.7); in ch. 21 she is left with no water and the life of mother and son is threatened (21.15-16). In ch. 16 she was met by the angel of Yahweh who told her to return, to name her son Ishmael and who also promised a great future for his descendants. In ch. 21 the angel of God appears with another promise of future greatness (21.18), but with no command to return to Sarah. The narrative does, however, remind the reader of the significance of that earlier incident when her son was named Ishmael ('God hears', 16.11), by telling us that 'God heard the voice of the boy' (21.17). Significant he might be, but not as significant as Isaac. The parting of the ways has come (cf. 21.12-13; see 22.1-19).

21.22-34

The issue of the progeny promise seems to have been settled. Isaac and Ishmael have had their respective destinies mapped out and live in their own space. We now move on to more mundane matters—relationships between neighbours and disputes over wells. As we shall see, however, other aspects of the divine promises are still in view.

Abimelech's approach to Abraham shows that he still has misgivings about him. He links two matters: God's obvious presence with Abraham, and a suspicion that Abraham might 'deal falsely' with him (21.22-23). This speech suggests that Abraham has not demonstrated beyond question the necessary correlation between ethical behaviour and relationship with Yahweh that Yahweh himself has demanded (see 17.1-2; 18.19).

The dispute over wells and the covenant that ensues recalls other issues that have been running through the Abraham story. Abimelech's speech reminds Abraham that he has 'resided as an alien' in Abimelech's land (21.23), and this point is repeated by the narrator at the end, (21.34). Thus while the progeny promise seems to have come to a final resolution, the promise of land is as far away now as ever. The dispute over wells and its resolution also illustrates how much stuttering progress is being made in the area of Abraham's becoming a blessing to the nations. His presence in foreign territory does not fill its inhabitants with unqualified happiness.

Genesis 22

The previous chapter had seemed to close the door decisively on any further developments in the progeny promise. Now, with

God's command to Abraham to sacrifice Isaac, it is abruptly thrown back into chaos.

22.1-19

The bombshell of 22.1-2 returns the reader to the beginning of the Abraham story. God commands Abraham to 'Go!' (*lek-lᵉkā*). This is the second time that God has used those exact words. In 12.1 he had commanded Abraham to 'Go!' (*lek-lᵉkā*) from his country and family. That imperative initiated the entire enterprise that has sustained the reader's interest up to this point. Its repetition here seems to bring it to a shattering conclusion. The original command had been difficult enough. Despite ambiguity over *where* he was to go and *how* he was to become a great nation, it had clearly called on Abraham to cut himself off from his past, but had at least included the promise of a glorious future. But its repetition in 22.2, with its demand to slay Isaac, presents no ambiguity or uncertainty and demands that Abraham cut himself off from that future. All future hope rests on Isaac.

This command must rank as the least comprehensible in a series of divine amendments to the progeny promise. We have come to expect Abraham to put up stiff resistance to such innovations. His acceptance of God's revision of the plan in 15.6 is the exception. Subsequently, he has pleaded with God on behalf of Ishmael when he was eliminated from contention (17.18), and argued with God face to face over Sodom in order to preserve Lot (18.22-33). Thus, given the fact that God's present command would demolish the entire enterprise that started back in 12.1-3, it is nothing short of amazing that Abraham obeys unquestioningly, setting off for Moriah without a word of complaint. This is one of those rare instances in the narrative where Abraham does indeed rise to the divine challenge, 'walk before me, and be blameless' (17.1). The echo of 12.1-3 passes a comment on Abraham's exercise of faith. There at the outset Abraham responded with unquestioning faith (12.4), just as he does here. As we review Abraham's career with God, however, we realize that his life has been lived largely between these two extreme responses. The fact that ch. 22 returns to the beginning suggests that the story has now come full circle and will soon be at rest. But with so many previous misleading indicators of plot development we as first-time readers cannot be sure.

The action of ch. 22 occurs 'after these things' (22.1). This formula could well indicate more than simply the events of ch. 21, but with the echoes of ch. 12 imply *all* 'these things'—that is ch. 22 needs to be read with the entire Abraham story as its backdrop.

In a passage as terse as this, repetitions stand out all the more. Yahweh's command, 'Take your son, your only son Isaac, whom you love' (22.2) would be needlessly verbose if it served only to convey information. Each phrase, however, is weighted to convey the poignancy of the act. Previously Abraham had thought he had a son on a number of occasions (see, e.g., 12.4-9; 16.7-16.). All have been dismissed; only Isaac is left. He is Abraham's *only* son because he is his *last* son. The moving intimacy between father and son as they walk to the place of execution is conveyed by another repetition, 'So the two of them walked on together' (22.6, 8).

A number of reminders of the expulsion of Ishmael impacts on our reading. The first is when 'Abraham rose early in the morning' (22.3), exactly as he had when he had disposed of his other 'son' (21.14). The correspondence is unsettling, carrying both negative and positive connotations. It reminds us that once again the life of a son is at risk (cf. 21.16), but raises the possibility that if Ishmael had been saved from death, might Isaac also? The narrative drops tantalizing clues that Abraham might be thinking along similar lines. He tells his young men that he and Isaac will return to them after they have worshipped (22.5). Is this simply bravado, or does he recall Ishmael's rescue (assuming that he knows about it)? Similarly, Abraham's response to Isaac's question (22.7-8), makes us wonder what exactly might be going through his mind. The dialogue is an exquisite example of dramatic irony. Isaac's question regarding the whereabouts of the sacrificial lamb makes explicit that Isaac does not know what Abraham and the reader knows. But Abraham's response, 'God himself will provide the lamb', while possibly being only bluster, or at worst deception, might suggest that Abraham knows something that the reader does not know.

Once they have arrived at the appointed place, the pace of the narrative slows. More than three days journey have been compressed into 22.1-8, with room given mostly to broad description and significant dialogue. Now, in 22.9-10 each action is described in minute detail. We see Abraham going through each of the necessary preparations for the death of Isaac, delaying the inevitable to the very last moment. The normal sequence was to bind and kill the sacrifice before placing it on the altar (cf. Lev. 1.3-9, 10-13, etc.). But here, Isaac lies bound upon the altar, still alive. His despatch can no longer be postponed. Abraham raises the knife.

The hopes that were raised earlier by the parallels with ch. 21 seem to have been vain. Yet as soon as the narrator mentions 'the angel of the Lord' (22.11), readers may guess what he will say before he opens his mouth. The expulsion and rescue of Ishmael was a dress rehearsal for the 'sacrifice' and deliverance of Isaac. Just as Hagar 'saw a well of water' (21.19) which saved Ishmael's life, so Abraham 'saw a ram' (22.13) and substituted it for his son.

The narrator prefaces these events with the words, 'God tested Abraham' (22.1). As readers we know that the command is a test. But without any indication to the contrary the test would seem to be whether Abraham will indeed kill Isaac. Thus the reader's anxiety level is raised, especially when Abraham sets off giving every indication that that is precisely what he will do. But why should God want to test Abraham? While it is true that many previous incidents could be labelled 'tests' (e.g., the initial call in 12.1-3), this is the only one explicitly labelled as such, so it must have some particular significance. The answer to this question is provided by the angel's words in 22.12, 'Do not lay your hand on the boy or do anything to him; *for now I know that you fear God,* since you have not withheld your son, your only son, from me'. In other words the incident is a test to discover whether Abraham is committed to Yahweh. Before Abraham stood with dagger raised atop Mt Moriah, Yahweh obviously queried Abraham's loyalty. And even a cursory review of preceding episodes reveals how justified that doubt was. God's command is an absolute test of faith. Will Abraham obey God regardless of the consequences? The curious passivity of Isaac at the 'sacrifice' and its sequel underlines that this is a test of *Abraham's* faith in Yahweh, not of Isaac's obedience or compliance to his father. Once placed on the altar, Isaac takes no part in the action at all. Isaac's possible responses or protests are of no importance. Abraham returns to his young men; what Isaac does we are left to guess at. The focus throughout is on Abraham.

I have had occasion to mention several times the crucial nature of the statement in 17.1-2, which links the making of the covenant between God and Abraham dependent upon Abraham's 'walking before' God and being 'blameless'. Abraham's subsequent behaviour was anything but blameless—for example, questioning God's removal of Ishmael, passing off Sarah as his sister and so on. Chapter 22 brings us to the crisis—Abraham's last chance to demonstrate whether he is capable of fearing and presenting himself 'blameless'. Because Abraham does obey unquestioningly, then the covenant promises can be ratified: 'Because you have done this ... I will indeed bless you, and I will make your offspring as numerous as the stars of heaven ...' (22.16b-17a; see Alexander 1983: 21).

This chapter started with an echo of 12.1-3. The paradox contained in that original command is confirmed and expanded here. When God first spoke, Abraham had to give up his present land in order to be shown the land of promise; he had to give up his current family in order to become the father of a great nation. On Mt Moriah, he had to be willing to give up his only son in order to become the father of a multitude.

22.20-24

The positioning at this point of the news concerning the family of Abraham's brother is significant. Over the years Abraham has struggled to perceive the exact focus of the progeny promise. Its fulfilment has teetered on a knife-edge as several individuals have recommended themselves as the avenue of fulfilment (see, e.g., 12.4-9; 17.15-27). And the true son of promise has just escaped death by a whisker. Abraham now hears news that his brother Nahor has been reproducing at an amazing rate—12 sons by his wife and a concubine, plus untold numbers of daughters. The picture is one of domestic bliss in Haran. Nahor has not had to go through the torture of Abraham's family life, with its infertility, intrigues and divine amendments. But then again, through none of his sons will all the nations of the earth be blessed.

Genesis 23

23.1-20

A series of characters has narrowly escaped death: Lot (ch. 19); Abimelech (20.7); Ishmael (21.15); Isaac (ch. 22). The sequence is brought to a close with the announcement of Sarah's death. Just as the incident on Mt Moriah had underlined the ultimate significance of Isaac, so with Sarah's death the promise that she would 'give rise to nations; kings of peoples shall come from her' (17.16), can now be fulfilled only through Isaac, her only son.

The brevity of Sarah's death notice contrasts with the detail provided for Abraham's acquisition of a grave. It is with the latter that the chapter is chiefly concerned. If Sarah's death reminds us of the faltering fulfilment of the progeny promise, Abraham's negotiations over a grave confirm how far away the land promise is from fulfilment. Abraham's lack of possession of the land is underlined by the fact that he must buy something as basic as a grave for his wife. His acquisition (23.17) is depressingly insignificant when compared to the tract of land 'from the river of Egypt to the great river, the river Euphrates', promised to his descendants (15.18). Abraham is well aware of this discrepancy, introducing himself to the Hittites as 'a stranger and an alien residing among you' (23.4). Their reply, in which they refer to him as 'a mighty prince' (23.6), is not simply oriental etiquette, for despite his lack of land Abraham has enormous resources. He simply accepts Ephron's asking price of four hundred silver shekels for the property. While it is difficult to compare prices at different periods, Jeremiah paid only 17 shekels in a comparable transaction (Jer. 32.9), and Omri paid only six thousand shekels (i.e., two talents, Exod. 38.25-26) for the entire site of Samaria (1 Kgs. 16.24). It would appear that Abraham paid well over the odds. One might have expected him to haggle for a better deal, as his 'auction' with God (18.22-33) shows him to be well aware of the custom! At the beginning of the Abraham story Abraham received great wealth from an Egyptian because of Sarah (12.16), and again from the Philistine King of Gerar for the same reason (20.14). Now, towards the end of the story he gives much of that wealth to a Hittite because of Sarah. *Paying* such a huge amount for such a small property emphasizes that the divine promise of *giving* the whole land to Abraham's descendants is still a long way off (cf., e.g., 12.7).

Genesis 24
The style of this chapter is the most expansive in the Abraham story, with lengthy repetitions and verbose speeches. This shift from the generally terse style indicates that the narrative has arrived at a major transition point where it wishes to dwell for a while. Not surprisingly, the matter which calls for such treatment is the major concern of the Abraham story: the next generation.

24.1-9

No sooner is Sarah dead and buried than we are informed that Abraham 'was old, well advanced in years' (24.1); that is to say, Abraham's own death and burial cannot be too far off. His story is winding down to its inevitable resting place, but there remains one crucial task. Yahweh might well have 'blessed Abraham in all things' (24.1), but not all promises have been fulfilled. Abraham has a son through whom his descendants will potentially come. But in order for this to become reality, Isaac must find a wife.

Marrying a Canaanite, however, is not an option. Abraham has just shown in his purchase of Machpelah from Ephron that he can be on friendly terms with other inhabitants of the land. But there are limits to such liaisons. While we are not told explicitly, Abraham's refusal to consider a Canaanite bride for his son could well be that such a union would blur the family lines and he would not then become the father of a distinct nation. Therefore Isaac must marry one of his own kin. But this proposal itself causes problems. If Isaac were to return 'home' to marry a relative, he might not return. This would place in jeopardy the promise of possessing the land of Canaan (24.6-8). Therefore Isaac must remain in Canaan. The double problem of maintaining purity of lineage and ultimately possessing the land is to be solved by remaining *here* but marrying from *there*.

Events at the end of the Abraham story recall those at the beginning. In 12.1-3 God told Abraham to leave his country and kindred so that he could become a great nation. Now, in order to maintain that hope through Isaac, there must be a return to that same country and kindred. Thus the possibility of a great nation arose by leaving; the continuity of that hope is achieved by returning—but only by proxy; the dangers of geographical dislocation are as great as absorption into Canaanite culture.

Abraham's first and last words in the whole narrative of chs. 12–25 constitute an intriguing inclusion regarding the divine promises, wives and foreigners. His first words (12.11-13) showed his desire to maintain the momentum of the divine promises (see 12.10-20). So do his last words in the entire narrative recorded here. In ch. 12 his words justified the ploy of giving his wife to a foreigner. His speech here shows his refusal to take his son's wife from foreigners in order to retain hope of the promises. The inclusion illustrates not only the importance of those initial promises throughout the Abraham story, but also the fact that fulfilment is still a long way off.

24.10-27

Abraham's servant set off for 'the city of Nahor' (24.10). The narrative has already indicated what he might find there, with its news about Nahor's family that came to Abraham just after the aborted sacrifice of Isaac (see 22.20-24). With such evidence of family fertility, what better place to go to find an array of possible brides for Isaac? So the servant, on arrival, positions himself at the well at a time 'when women go out to draw water' (24.11). He obviously does not anticipate having immediate success, for in his prayer he proposes a sign which will indicate which young woman is God's choice (24.12-14). His scrutiny of potential brides is rather like the parade of potential partners filing past Adam (2.19-20). While general hospitality was a social obligation (cf. Abraham, 18.1-8 and Lot, 19.1-3), presumably it was not usual for an unmarried girl to water strangers' camels, otherwise the test lacks force. Immediately the first candidate arrives, and the narrator divulges her name. She is none other than Rebekah. Her significance had already been telegraphed back in ch. 22, when Abraham had been told about Nahor's family. In what was otherwise a mere catalogue of names, it was noted that 'Bethuel became the father of Rebekah' (22.23). The reader now learns the reason for that expansion. The servant, however, is still in the dark. It is only when the young woman has demonstrated hospitality which goes beyond the cultural norm, and then told him that she is a member of Abraham's kindred, that the pious servant can acknowledge Yahweh's immediate answer to his prayer.

24.28-67

The domestic scenes recounted here, where Rebekah's family entertain Abraham's servant and Rebekah meets Isaac, convey, despite their prolix language, the essential characteristics of Laban, Abraham's servant, Rebekah and Isaac.

Laban is first on the scene. We have already seen his sister's hospitality, and Laban does not hold back in giving the servant an extravagant welcome. There is, however, just a hint of opportunistic self-interest in his hospitality. His warm reception is offered 'as soon as he had seen' Rebekah's lavish jewellery (24.30). If indeed he had run out to meet the man immediately he had heard the news (24.30), then he did not have time to prepare the house for his guest and provision for his camels, as be claims. He might simply be showing oriental etiquette. He might just as easily be trying to ingratiate himself with a wealthy benefactor. He is a character worth keeping an eye on as the story moves on (see 29.1-14).

Abraham's servant has been a model of faithful service and piety so far in the story. This portrayal is continued in his lengthy speech to Rebekah's family. He opens his presentation by referring to Yahweh's blessings (24.34), and concludes by blessing Yahweh (24.48). His piety is not so otherworldly, however, that he fails to see the need for diplomacy when he repeats the instructions that Abraham had given him. He explains his presence with them by saying, correctly, that Abraham insisted on getting Isaac's bride from his own kin. He studiously avoids, however, telling them that Abraham demanded that Isaac not accompany him under any circumstances (24.6). That might well have seemed insulting, especially considering the warm welcome he has received.

Rebekah's first sight of Isaac is of his evening stroll out in the field. What he is doing there is not clear. While most versions translate as 'went out to meditate,' NRSV suggests 'to walk' (24.63). All translations are guesses, the Hebrew verb being unique to this verse. Whatever he was doing in the fields around home simply reinforces one of the striking aspects of Isaac. He is the least active and least travelled of all the patriarchs. Generations either side of him traverse the ancient east, but the furthest abroad Isaac gets is to be out in the Negeb. While it was Abraham who prevented Isaac from accompanying his servant, he seems to be excessively tied to home, and in particular to his mother. Sarah would have been dead for three to four years by now (23.1 cf. 25.20), and even granting an extreme closeness between mother and son, this seems an excessively long mourning period. Only the arrival of the fair Rebekah, it seems, can provide the comfort he needs (24.67). In this light, perhaps it was melancholy or depression that caused him to be out in the fields when Rebekah arrived. For Abraham, the getting of a wife for Isaac is bound up with the divine promises (24.7); Isaac's horizons are not so broad—Rebekah provides comfort after his mother's death. His lack of reference to the divine promises is all the more striking given Abraham's and Rebekah's family's statements (24.7, 60).

Rebekah is much more robust. At home she has already exhibited fitting behaviour for a patriarch's bride, responding graciously when first meeting the servant (24.17-20), offering him hospitality (24.25), and willingly accompanying him back to Canaan (24.57-58). On arriving in Canaan she veils herself on first meeting her future husband. She is not only from the correct family, but is the ideal wife. Her attractive impetuosity in setting off into the unknown contrasts with Isaac's passive drabness.

Yet one detail is omitted. Rebekah's emotions, unlike Isaac's, are never conveyed. We know that he was comforted by Rebekah's arrival (24.67b), but more importantly 'he loved her' (24.67a). But what Rebekah thinks of Isaac we are not told. This matter will become important as we move into the Jacob story (see 25.19-34.)

Genesis 25

25.1-18

No sooner has Isaac taken Rebekah as his wife 'after his mother's death' (24.67), than 'Abraham took another wife, whose name was Keturah' (25.1). While Isaac's liaison brought him comfort after Sarah's death, Abraham's new wife Keturah brings not comfort, but children. The succinct way in which the six sons of this union are catalogued stands in stark contrast to the narrative's account of the tortuous route leading to the birth of Isaac. In light of this contrast, we are not surprised at Abraham's bestowal of 'all things' to Isaac, and his dismissal 'with gifts' of all other sons. (Gen. 25.6 presumably includes Keturah's children, even though it refers only to concubines' children.) To have tolerated the presence of so many others would have undermined the uniqueness of Isaac. Yet this policy means that the east country is becoming thickly populated with Abraham's progeny (cf. 13.11; 16.12). For how long can the physical distance of this group from Isaac be maintained?

And finally, Abraham dies. From the narrative's point of view he could have died as soon as Isaac had been born. But he lingers on through the 'offering' of Isaac, the death of Sarah, the getting of Rebekah, marriage to Keturah and begetting of sons through her and untold numbers of concubines. His burial by both Isaac and Ishmael (25.9), encapsulates the complexity of genealogical succession at the heart of the narrative. Denied his role as first-born and exiled eastward, Ishmael nevertheless registers that like Isaac, he is just as much his father's son.

Abraham rests at Machpelah within the land, while Ishmael's progeny increase outside the land (25.12-18). He might have been exiled from the land of promise, but the final paragraph of the Abraham story provides the genealogy of *Ishmael*. While this could be construed as the narrative's way of summarily dismissing Ishmael before it turns its attention to Isaac's future, it also recalls previous promises given regarding Ishmael. In 17.20 Yahweh had promised Abraham that Ishmael would father 12 princes and become a great nation. Here, 25.12-16 confirms the promise fulfilled. We now ask, will the predictions regarding Isaac also be fulfilled? Will nations and kings rise from him (cf. 17.16)? Will the promise of 22.17-18 concerning offspring, victory over enemies and blessing the nations be fulfilled rapidly through Isaac, or will as many narrative complications intervene in his future as they did in his past? More ominously, we might recall God's promise to Hagar that her son's antagonism will be directed against his brothers (16.12). That prediction is darkly hinted at by the ambiguity of 25.18b. Does Ishmael live 'in the presence of/alongside' his brothers (KJV, NRSV), or 'over against/in defiance of them' (ASV, RSV, NAS)? That the last line of the Abraham story hints at strife and contention does not augur well for the next major block of the book.

Genesis 25.19–36.43: The Jacob Story

The announcement in 25.19, 'These are the descendants of (*tôlᵉdōt*) Isaac', commences a major new section of the book. But it begins by looking over its shoulder to the Abraham story by adding laconically, '... Abraham's son: Abraham was the father of Isaac'. Only those who have followed the twists and turns of the story since ch. 12 will recognize how condensed and selective that statement is. While it records the outcome of the progeny promise in chs. 12–25, it says nothing of the questions which consumed the ongoing story: Who will be Abraham's heir and when will he arrive?

Just as before, here is a narrative containing barrenness (25.21 cf. 11.30; 16.1), two sons (25.22-23; cf. e.g., 17.18-19), and two nations (25.23; cf. 17.16, 20), engaged in conflict and struggle (25.22-23; cf. e.g., 16.12). The Abraham story ends and the Jacob story begins with *tôlᵉdōt* statements in which are embedded allusions to conflict and struggle (25.12, 19). While the last words of the Abraham story are ambiguous (see 25.18), it is certainly in keeping with the thrust of the previous narrative to interpret them as predicting fraternal strife. The divine oracle in 25.23, however, unambiguously announces contention between brothers. These notes of conflict at the end of the Abraham and beginning of the Jacob narratives set up a major thematic link between them. However, while conflict developed and grew throughout chs. 12–25, here it is present from the outset and defines the relationship between the brothers, suggesting that it will be even more dominant in this story than it was in the previous one.

25.19-34
Rebekah's barrenness obviously recalls Sarah's. But Rebekah's problem is announced and resolved in one verse (25.21). Only when we read 25.26 are we informed that her barrenness lasted 20 years. The narrative has no desire to detail these two decades of waiting, indicating that this story will not emphasize

barrenness and delayed births of heirs. It will again, however, be centred on the firstborn. This is made clear by the inversion of primogeniture announced in the divine oracle, which sets the agenda for the entire narrative (25.23). Whereas Ishmael and Isaac appeared only after detailed narrative developments, here, Esau and the younger heir-apparent Jacob are present at the beginning of the plot. The questions here therefore, regarding heirship, are not who? or when? but how? and why?

The reader of Genesis will have learned by now that very little is straightforward in this book. The genealogy that concluded the previous section (25.12-18), indicated the fulfilment of promises made to Ishmael. The question of whether promises made regarding Isaac will be fulfilled begins to be answered in 25.21— and true to form, it appears to be as complicated as it was in the previous generation (see 25.12-18).

Rebekah's initial actions confirm her portrayal in ch. 24. There she showed generous hospitality to Abraham's servant, was beautiful and willing to go to Isaac, was blessed, demure and modest (24.18-67). To these she now adds evidence of piety, consulting the Lord regarding her pregnancy just as Isaac had prayed when she was barren (25.21-22). This pious domestic scene is somewhat disturbed, however, by the partiality of the parental love (25.28), especially as her love for Jacob (and thus her implied shunning of Esau), is given no motivation. This is the beginning of the narrative's portrayal of her metamorphosis from dutiful bride to scheming mother.

The details of the divine oracle in 25.23 need to be noted carefully. It functions as a thematic preface to the whole of the Jacob story, just as 1.28 did for the primaeval history, and 12.1-3 for the Abraham story. Additionally, its very nature as a word from Yahweh makes it significant in a narrative where divine speech is much less frequent than in chs. 12–25.

The oracle predicts a strife-torn future for the twins in Rebekah's womb; it will be an unequal struggle, ('one shall be stronger than the other'); primogeniture will be overturned, ('the elder shall serve the younger'); and the struggle will continue through future generations, ('two nations are in your womb'). Later, 27.27-29, 39-40 will expand on these motifs, but at the outset we are prepared for a story of fraternal division, conflict and service in which the younger will usurp the elder's rights. The successive *tôlᵉdōt* of Ishmael (25.12-18) and Isaac (beginning in 25.19), remind us that Abraham fathered two contending sons, the progenitors of two nations in which the younger was dominant. Now, Yahweh announces that Isaac has done the same, but unlike Abraham his two sons share the same womb in dual conception, suggesting that their struggle will be more radical than that between Isaac and Ishmael. The division motif is not limited to the brothers in Rebekah's womb, but is taken up by the parents. Isaac loves both Rebekah (24.67) and Esau (25.28); the narrative states only that Rebekah loves Jacob (25.28). Isaac loves Rebekah because she comforts him in his bereavement, and Esau because he provides food for his cultured palate. Rebekah's favouritism of Jacob, just like Yahweh's, is merely noted, not explained. As the narrative develops, husband and wife contend with one another, but by proxy through their twins. It is a contention in which opposite poles attract. Esau the active hunter is favoured by the passive, senile father, and Jacob, the 'quiet man' (25.27), is favoured by his mother, whom we will soon discover, does not hesitate to take the initiative.

Esau's actions and speech as well as the explicit judgment of the narrator provide fairly detailed characterization. The muscular Esau's skill lies in hunting (25.27), and he is favoured by Isaac because he provides him with gourmet fare. Yet Esau himself squanders his birthright for common lentil stew. Here is no man of sophisticated taste or speech. He cares not what he consumes—'some of that red stuff' (25.30) will do. His agreement to Jacob's demand to sell him his birthright before he can eat the stew reveals a person governed by the needs of the moment rather than long-term considerations. The quick succession of verbs, 'he ate and drank, and rose and went his way' (25.34), completes the picture of an unsophisticated, unthinking (and vulnerable?) oaf. In case the reader misses the thrust of the narrator's presentation we are told explicitly, 'Thus Esau despised his birthright' (25.34). In other words, a moment's reflection would have revealed to Esau that he was getting a raw deal. But he never stopped to think.

The characterization of Jacob is more opaque. He is described as being *tām* (25.27), rendered by NRSV as 'quiet', but elsewhere signifying 'blameless' or 'innocent' (e.g., 2 Sam. 15.11; 1 Kgs. 9.4; Job 1.1). The latter benign connotation seems impossible here in light of his heartless treatment of Esau in 25.29-34, hence all versions opt for this accommodated understanding, suggesting perhaps 'brooding' or 'calculating'. Does he drive a hard bargain with Esau on the spur of the moment or is it a premeditated act?

If Esau's actions show that he 'despised his birthright', what does Jacob's stratagem reveal about *his* attitude to the birthright? Has he been lusting after it? Is he merely after the material gain of a double share of the family inheritance (cf. Deut. 21.17), or is his move part of a larger plan? If so, has his mother told him of the oracle with its promise of more than material advantage? The narrative provides no unambiguous answers to these questions, being content to intrigue the reader with possibilities. What it does not leave to chance, however, is the depiction of Jacob's ruthlessness, regardless of his motive.

Genesis 26

Chapter 26 continues the motif of conflict raised by the previous passage. Here, however, conflict within the patriarchal family extends to embrace foreigners.

Genesis deals with Isaac more perfunctorily than any other patriarch, his role being confined largely to this chapter and the next. He fails to emerge from Abraham's shadow. We have already seen in 25.19-34 a number of motifs familiar from the story of Abraham. Several more which were developed at length in chs. 12–25, such as divine blessing, human deception, moral superiority of and conflict with the nations, covenant-making at Beer-Sheba, and so on, occur here once again in a single chapter relating to Isaac. Even the general thrust of the Abraham story, which moved from infertility to progeny, is reflected in this chapter's journey from famine (26.1) to wells of water (26.33). The points of contact and manner of narration project an Isaac who can do no more than relive his father's life.

26.1-5

The opening verse is so closely reminiscent of 12.10 that the narrator kindly informs us not to confuse the two incidents. Yet another famine hits the land of promise and Isaac moves on to greener pastures in Gerar, where his father had previously wandered (20.1). The same king Abimelech (and army commander Phicol, 26.26), presides as before (20.2; 21.22, 32). In case Isaac considers duplicating Abraham's even earlier trek to Egypt in order to escape starvation (12.10), Yahweh prohibits him from doing so. Isaac's seeking refuge in foreign parts demonstrates once again that the chosen land is not always the most attractive (cf. 13.10-11; 12.10). This chapter confirms that the chosen people are not always the most attractive either.

Chosenness is prominent from the outset. Yahweh's speech in 26.2-5 repeats the basic elements of his previous blessings on Abraham, but also expands slightly on the land promise. The lands which Isaac and his descendants are promised include his present location in Gerar, which is part of Philistine territory, not explicitly included in God's previous land promise to Abraham (13.15-17; 15.18-21; 17.8). Gerar's incorporation into Yahweh's future gift means Isaac has actually not left the land of promise. Indeed, Isaac never leaves the land of promise, regardless of famine or the need to get a wife. He is the least travelled of all the patriarchs; rooted to the land. Excitement is the lot of other characters.

I noted before that the fulfilment of the covenant promises to Abraham was often made conditional upon Abraham's obedience (see 12.1-3; 17.1-2; 22.15-17). And here with Isaac we see the same phenomenon. The promises of divine presence and blessing, gift of the land, numerous offspring and blessing for nations rest upon Isaac's response to the divine command to 'Reside in this land as an alien' (26.3a). Isaac's obedience here will not only guarantee the land promise (26.3), but also enable the granting of the promises of progeny, nationhood and blessing previously guaranteed to Abraham (26.3b, 5a; cf. 22.16-17). The depth of obedience potentially demanded by Yahweh is chillingly alluded to with the observation 'because Abraham *obeyed my voice*' (26.5a), a phrase taken from 22.18, where obedience to Yahweh's voice had required a willingness to sacrifice Isaac himself.

26.6-11
Not surprisingly, in light of the conditional promises outlined in 26.2-5, 'Isaac settled in Gerar' (26.6). While living there he meets Abimelech, and there is no clearer example of Isaac walking in his father's footsteps than this encounter.

Echoes of earlier incidents in chs. 12 and 20 have prepared us for what happens next. The famine is explicitly connected with that in 12.10, which with the prohibition on going to Egypt recalls the 'wife-sister' episode there. Isaac finds himself in Gerar, in King Abimelech's domain—the same territory and ruler as Abraham's second 'wife-sister' ruse (20.1-18). Thus the resumé of the covenant promises in 26.2-5 has only delayed the inevitable. Isaac introduces Rebekah by saying, 'She is my sister' (26.7). Isaac might only have been in Sarah's womb on the last occasion he visited Gerar, but he acts as if he had been an eye witness. He is willing to trust God to be with him while he dwells in the land (cf. 26.3), but apparently does not trust him to give protection from those whom he believes will lust after his wife.

At the outset Abraham was informed of Yahweh's desire that he and his descendants be a blessing to the nations (12.2b-3). Yet the foreigners who encountered Abraham would not have deduced this from his actions, and Isaac here continues the family tradition. No sooner has the promise of being a blessing to the nations been repeated (26.4b), than Isaac re-enacts his father's deception with the possibility of bringing guilt upon Abimelech and his people (26.10 cf. 20.9).

Unless one assumes that ch. 26 is chronologically displaced, Isaac's act is even more audacious than Abraham's, for by this time Rebekah would have already borne Esau and Jacob. We might previously have wondered about the credulity of foreigners who believed Abraham's lies, but at least Sarah had been childless and with some imagination might be seen as an unmarried and desirable woman. Isaac must have been a consummate liar to have convinced the Philistines that the mother of the two children in his party was his eligible sister. Yet even he realized the ruse was wearing rather thin and once the game was up did not attempt Abraham's desperate ploy of claiming that she really was his sister (20.12). Perhaps more intriguing to consider is Isaac's motivation here. While this is the third 'wife-sister' episode, none is simply the repetition of any other, and each serves a particular purpose in its narrative context. In ch. 12 Sarah was expendable because, as Abraham understood matters, she had no role to play in the fulfilment of the divine promise of nationhood. In ch. 20 likewise, she may be disposed of because although Abraham has now been told that she will have a child, he doubts that she ever will. But for Isaac, Rebekah has already fulfilled her role. She has given birth and the next generation is guaranteed. Having played her part she may now be set to one side. The Genesis narratives give us little hope for anything other than pragmatic patriarchal chauvinism from its male characters. Women are dispensable for all kinds of reasons.

Isaac had no more reason to fear for his life than his father had 60 years previously. Yet, like Abraham, Isaac thinks the worst of foreigners (cf. 20.11). He interprets their questions concerning Rebekah as veiled announcements of sexual interest. He lies to save his life. Yet even after living in the country for 'a long time' (26.8), not a soul has made any move for Rebekah.

While this might be because Rebekah has not preserved her physical allure as well as the geriatric Sarah, more importantly it suggests that the men of Gerar's questioning concerning Rebekah had been simple curiosity, making conversation with a stranger, and not evidence of lechery as Isaac had mistakenly thought. While Abimelech's statement in 26.10 indicates that Rebekah might conceivably have ended up in someone's bed, the fact is she did not. Isaac had needlessly feared the Philistines, for if adultery was abhorrent (26.10), surely murder (Isaac's concern in 26.7), was equally so. The incidents in chs. 12, 20 and 26 show that the ploy of proffering the matriarch's sexual charms becomes increasingly less successful. In ch. 12 it is likely that Sarai did end up in Pharaoh's bed; in ch. 20 she is taken, but is rescued before Abimelech can approach her; in ch. 26, Rebekah is not even taken (see Exum 1993: 102).

Abimelech uncovers the charade when he sees Isaac 'fondling' Rebekah (26.8). The Hebrew expresses this through a wordplay on the root *ṣḥq*. Isaac (*yiṣḥāq*) fondles (*mᵉṣaḥēq*) Rebekah. While the root occurs a number of times in the Genesis narrative, the particular form found here (piel participle), occurs in only one other place in the Old Testament. In 21.9 Sarah had seen Ishmael 'playing' (*mᵉṣaḥēq*). So both sons of Abraham are joined together in the use of this verbal form. In both incidents it introduces conflict: in ch. 21 between Sarah on the one hand and Hagar, Ishmael and Abraham on the other, and in ch. 26 between Abimelech and Isaac. Here is just one more example of the way in which Isaac repeats previous history. Not content to mimic his father, he re-enacts his brother's role too. Through all of this, Rebekah just like Sarah before her, says not a word; her thoughts are never revealed. By contrast, Isaac here acts like Abraham from precisely the same motives (26.7 cf. 12.12; 20.11). While all three episodes are usually subsumed under the title of 'Wife-Sister' stories, they tell us far more about the 'Husband-Brother'.

Yet again the patriarchal family comes off second best in comparison to the nations that they and their offspring are called to bless. Abimelech's heated exchanges with both Abraham (20.9-10) and Isaac (26.9-10), show him to be a man of higher principles (see 29.1-14). While it would be too much to argue that like Abraham he has kept Yahweh's 'charge, commandments, statutes and laws' (26.5), one is inclined to think that he would have needed less prompting to do so had he been asked. He certainly seems to learn more quickly from experience. His announcement of capital punishment for any who interfered with Isaac and Rebekah is understandable in light of his previous experience in ch. 20, where Yahweh pronounced death for him should he transgress (20.7). He would also be eager to avoid a repetition of infertility in his household which had resulted from Abraham's previous visit (20.18). Barrenness is no more desired in the royal house of Gerar than it is in the patriarchal family.

26.12-33

In 26.3 Yahweh had promised to bless Isaac if he remained in Gerar. Isaac had obeyed, and true to his word 'the Lord blessed him' (26.12). Such simple conditions and uncomplicated human response have been rare in Genesis so far (cf. 22.1-3). The content of the blessing is outlined in a catalogue of material prosperity in 26.13-14. In addition the former promise of blessing is hinted at more subtly in 26.12 with its use of the root zr'. Yahweh had promised 'I will make your offspring [zr' as noun] as numerous as the stars of heaven' (26.4). In 26.12, 'Isaac sowed seed [zr' as verb] ... and ... reaped a hundredfold'. The root carries different connotations in each context, but the wordplay means that Isaac's agricultural success reminds the reader of greater blessings to come. Yet the fact that we observe plays on words rather than multiple births underlines that here as previously, the fulfilment of much in the patriarchal promises will not occur just yet. Isaac does have two sons, but this is no improvement on Abraham, who also had two sons, only one of whom was 'his only son' (22.2, 12, 16). Similarly, division between Isaac's sons has already been predicted.

The trend to postpone the fulfilment of promises continues in the strained relations between Isaac and Abimelech in 26.15-33. Isaac's blessing only evokes envy from his hosts. We still await the blessing on the nations. In the meantime it seems the best we can hope for is controlled animosity.

The conflict rages around the precious commodity of water. The Philistines had filled up Abraham's wells with earth. No motivation for this act of sabotage is stated explicitly, but it had been done some time before, 'after the death of Abraham' (26.18). In 21.25-33, in a previous dispute over wells, Abimelech had covenanted with Abraham to guarantee him access to the wells he had dug. No mention had been made of Abraham's progeny, and once Abraham was dead the wells were blocked. Why anyone should want to deplete water resources makes no sense, unless it

was Abimelech's petulant way of obliterating the memory of
Abraham. Isaac's redigging of wells not only provides scope for
him to compete with the herders of Gerar, but for them it also
brings back unhappy memories of his father. For the reader it
also brings back memories of the conflict in ch. 13, where similarly the servants of Abraham and Lot were at loggerheads over
pasturage. These echoes of previous incidents confirm the basic
motif that dominates chs. 25–36—conflict. The patriarchal
family are in conflict not only between themselves but also with
their neighbours. This strife is memorialized in the names given
to the wells, 'Esek' (Contention) and 'Sitnah' (Enmity) (26.20-21).
The one well which causes no dispute, 'Reheboth' (Room), does
not completely counterbalance the others. Its name does not
connote Peace or Harmony, simply space to exist separately. The
oracular prediction of conflict between brothers in 25.23 casts its
shadow further still.

Just as 26.6-11 has striking parallels in the Abraham story
(chs. 12 and 20), so does 26.12-33. The covenant-making scene in
21.22-24, already alluded to above, makes its impact on a reading
of this passage. Some major points of contact can be concisely
listed. Abimelech and Phicol meet the patriarch (21.22 cf. 26.26),
and the king records his recognition of God's presence with him
(21.22 cf. 26.28). He calls on the patriarch to take an oath not to
harm him (21.23 cf. 26.29), stating that he himself has acted
honourably (21.24 cf. 26.29). As a consequence oaths are made
(21.24 cf. 26.31), and the place is named Beer-sheba (21.31 cf.
26.33 [anticipated also in 26.23]). Both episodes take place in the
context of digging wells (21.25 cf. 26.17-22). The close relationship between the two incidents, together with the repetition of the
patriarchal promises and 'wife-sister' episode also found in this
chapter, raise once again the fundamental elements of the patriarchal promises: land, blessing, progeny and relationship to the
nations. Issac does not carry any of them any further forward.
We read, 'Isaac dug again the wells of water that had been dug in
the days of his father Abraham' (26.18). His labour here is a meta-
phor for his actions throughout this chapter. He simply ploughs
the same furrow as Abraham, hardly deviating to left or right.

There are, of course, one or two points of difference. For
example, the implied etymological derivation of Beer-sheba is
different in the two passages (21.30-31; 26.32-33). But more tellingly, the motivations for making the covenant in each passage
are quite different. In ch. 21 Abraham protests that Abimelech's

servants have done him harm (21.25). Abimelech protests his ignorance and we have no reason to disbelieve him (21.26). The two then make a covenant that recognizes Abraham's rights over the well (21.27-32). In ch. 26, however, the initiative is reversed. Abimelech fears that Isaac will harm him (because Yahweh is on Isaac's side?, 26.28-29). Thus they form a mutual non-aggression treaty (26.29-31). Whether Abimelech's fears are justified or not, the fact that in this passage the roles are reversed and a foreign king approaches a patriarch with fears that necessitate a covenant makes one thing clear. This nation's perception of the patriarchal family has not stood still with Isaac, it has worsened. How Abraham's descendants will be a blessing to the nations remains a mystery.

26.34-35

The bulk of ch. 26 explored the tense relations between Isaac and the inhabitants of the land. Since Hittites are included in the generic term 'Canaanite' (see 23.2-3; 27.46–28.1), Esau's Hittite wives reveal his remarkably open-minded spirit when compared to his grandfather and father. While Abraham was not above buying land from Canaanites/Hittites (23.16), he was implacably opposed to intermarriage with them (24.3). Isaac resurrects the old animosities with foreigners at Gerar. Esau is far more accommodating. Yet his foreign liaisons 'made life bitter for Isaac and Rebekah' (26.35), just as life in Gerar had produced contention and enmity (26.20-21). It is one thing for Isaac to offer his wife to foreigners, quite another for Esau to take his wives from foreigners. If sharing wells with Philistines had caused so much strife, one can only imagine the bitterness of the domestic scene with Canaanites as permanent fixtures in Esau's tents. That the name of one of Esau's fathers-in-law, Beeri, apparently means 'my well', is ominous.

Genesis 27.1-40

27.1-17

In the Jacob story, ch. 27 proves to be as crucial for the transmission of the promises to the next generation as ch. 22 was in the Abraham story. While in ch. 22 the question was 'Will the chosen son survive?', here the reader asks, 'Will the chosen son gain the blessing?' Note the following points of contact between the two chapters.

Each episode presents a father and son alone in which one party is at best economical with the truth (cf. 22.8). Yet in both incidents, whether as son or father, Isaac is the victim. The terms 'my son' (*beni*) and 'here I am' (*hinnenni*) occur several times in Genesis (e.g., 21.10; 6.17), but the only uses of these terms in the same verse in Genesis are confined to 22.7; 27.1, 18. '[Isaac] said to him, "My son"; and he answered, "Here I am' (27.1; cf. 27.18). During the ascent of Moriah Abraham's reply to his son's inquiry was, 'Here I am, my son' (22.7). The similar dialogue in both episodes highlights the central role of sonship which is threatened in both passages, though in different ways. In addition, just as Abraham 'went (*hlk*) and took (*lqh*) the ram' (22.13), so Jacob 'went (*hlk*) and got (*lqh*) [the kids]' (27.14). While not an uncommon word pair, it occurs four times in ch. 22 (22.2, 3, 6, 13), and three times in this chapter (27.9, 13-14). The going, taking and killing of these animals provides in each story the means to evade the seemingly inevitable—the death of Isaac and the blessing of Esau.

This episode is clearly one concerning the respective fates of elder and younger sons, but it also reveals much about the parents. The implied tension between Rebekah and Isaac noted already surfaces again in their direct address to the twins. Isaac calls Esau 'my son' (27.1, 21, 24, 37); Rebekah calls Jacob 'my son' (27.8, 13, 43). Isaac does call Jacob 'my son' (27.18, 20-21, 25-27), but only when Jacob masquerades as Esau. Rebekah never calls Esau 'my son'. Indeed, nowhere does she ever speak to him. It is left to the narrator to remind us that the brothers are 'her elder son Esau' and 'her younger son Jacob' (27.15). Nowhere is either child called 'their son', even when it would be appropriate to do so (e.g., 27.5). The narrator's choice of words largely reflects the perception of the characters themselves: Esau is '*his* son' (27.5), Jacob is '*her* son' (27:6 17). Taken as a whole, the narrative expounds parental division and favouritism.

The oracle of 25.23 casts its shadow over the entire chapter. The future for the two sons outlined there is threatened by Isaac's dying wish to bless Esau (cf. Jacob's similar blessing in chs. 48–49, especially 49.29). Jacob has already received the birthright, but his ambitions require its formal ratification through the blessing. The significance of achieving both is highlighted by the wordplay between *berākâ* (blessing) and *bekōrâ* (birthright).

Esau's wives might be irritants to Isaac but they do not prevent his giving Esau the blessing. The narrative does not divulge

whether Rebekah told Isaac of the oracle of 25.23, or whether he
is aware of the transfer of birthright from Esau to Jacob in
25.29-34. (After all, the reversal of primogeniture should not be
a novel idea to *him*.) If he does know, then his action here is
similar to Abraham's when he remonstrated 'O that Ishmael
might live in your sight!' (17.18). Like Abraham he protests that
the firstborn should retain his pre-eminence. And he does seem
to break with the usual protocol of deathbed blessings by calling
only one son before him (cf. chs. 48–49; 50.24-25; Deut. 31–34;
Josh. 23–24; 1 Kgs. 2.1-9). On the other hand, he might be totally
unaware of the developments in the story so far. Certainly it
would take little imagination to see Rebekah orchestrating
events for the benefit of her younger son, not worrying her
husband with details he would be better off not knowing. Jacob's
silence would also be understandable, while Esau would not
wish to advertise what a fool he had made of himself. This latter
scenario, which seems more likely to me, would present the old
patriarch as a pathetic figure, a duped, senile, passive character,
unaware of what is taking place outside his tent, and as we shall
soon see, confused about what takes place within it (27.18-33).

Rebekah forms a stark contrast to her blind, uncomprehending
and vulnerable husband. Her hoodwinking of Isaac sits uncom-
fortably with the previous observation that Isaac loved Rebekah
(24.67), though his treatment of her at Gerar indicates that this
should not be romanticized. And if Isaac can lie about *her* identity to Abimelech, why can't her son Jacob give Isaac a taste of
his own medicine? She is aware, scheming and in control. Isaac
is the dormant character for whom things must be done—Esau
must hunt his game, prepare his food, and so on. Rebekah is the
active character who initiates proceedings—persuades Jacob,
instructs him, prepares the food, and so on. While the ancestral
line is traditionally presented as, Abraham-Isaac-Jacob, one
begins to wonder in this story whether this should be revised to
Abraham-Rebekah-Jacob. She certainly outperforms both her
husband and mother-in-law. Sarah too had overheard plans for
the firstborn, but her response had been simply to laugh (18.10-
12). By contrast, when Rebekah overhears Isaac's plan she strikes
immediately with a cunning strategy (27.5-13). Her instruction
to Jacob, 'obey my word as I command you' (27.8), expresses
authority more at home on the lips of the dominant male in these
patriarchal texts, than of a wife. Isaac had passed her off for a
while as his sister, but she passes off kid disguised as game and

Jacob disguised as Esau with aplomb. She is not only confident, but quite ruthless, as her reassurance to Jacob reveals: 'Let your curse be on me, my son' (27.13). Win or lose, she is committed to her course of action (see 35.8). The fact that she concedes the possibility of receiving a divine curse suggests that she is motivated more by her personal bias for Jacob (25.28) than by a desire to facilitate God's will decreed in 25.23.

27.18-29
This crucial paragraph is introduced by a precise verbal echo from ch. 22. Verse 18 repeats a sequence of 5 Hebrew words from 22.7, but with a telling twist at the end. Previously we read, '... his father and he said 'My father', and he said, 'Here I am *my son.*' Now we read, '... his father and he said 'My father', and he said 'Here I am, *who are you my son?*' The parallel with ch. 22 underlines yet again that this passage like the former is pivotal for the ongoing patriarchal promises. But the shift from declarative (22.7) to interrogative (27.18) in the father's answer subtly emphasizes that deception and intrigue is much more at the heart of this story than of the former.

The tension built up by the dialogue between Isaac and Jacob is almost a match for that raised by the conversation between Abraham and Isaac on Moriah. But whereas Isaac's question shows him to be only dimly comprehending of his fate in 22.7, suspense builds immediately in ch. 27 as he shows that his suspicions have been aroused. Just one syllable of Hebrew from Jacob is enough to make Isaac suspicious. Having been addressed as 'My father' the force of Isaac's question must be '*Which* son are you?' (27.18). Jacob tells a quick lie, 'I am Esau *your firstborn*' (27.19). Characters and readers alike already know Esau's status, but in the drama being played out we must be reminded of what is at stake, just as Abraham was when commanded, 'Take your son, your only son Isaac, whom you love' (22.2). However, Jacob's attempt to hurry on to the blessing ceremony is thwarted. For the first time in his life Isaac puts up resistance. He questions the speed of 'Esau's' return (27.20a). Jacob must now steel himself to lie more convincingly. But even his pious reply (27.20b), does not deflect Isaac's suspicions. The danger to Jacob is increased as Isaac moves his investigation from sight (which we know is impaired), and hearing, to touch and smell (which his love for savoury food suggests is quite well preserved). The old man must decide between the conflicting messages that his senses are communicating to him. His hearing tells him it is Jacob; his touch that it is Esau. Isaac's indecision, indicated in 27.23, is obscured by traditional translations. 'So he blessed him' (NRSV), presents Isaac as completing the blessing, then resuming his interrogation (27.24), when it is obviously too late to change anything. The clause should in fact be translated 'as he was about to bless him' (Speiser 1964: 209; cf. JPSV; TEV. Though cf. Ska 1992: 520). That is to say, the tension is not resolved but heightened as Isaac moves towards blessing Jacob but then backs away to continue questioning. Jacob's mettle as a liar is tested further; he comes through with flying colours. But even after affirming his identity as Esau, Jacob must wait. He must now serve up the food to his father which might once again arouse the old man's suspicions. What Jacob's response would have been to the obvious question, 'Is this really game, my son?', we are left to ponder, for the cravings of Isaac's stomach silence any lingering doubts. Only after he has been wined and dined by his son do we come to the climax of the scene. Jacob's treachery is sealed with a kiss (27.27). An act between intimates, showing kinship and trust, becomes the consummate deception when Isaac inhales with Jacob's breath the smell of Esau's clothes (27.27).

Isaac might be fooled, but for the reader most of Jacob's statements are transparent lies: 'I am Esau your firstborn'; 'I have done as you told me'; 'now sit up and eat of my game'; 'I am [your son Esau]'. But one more statement encapsulates the moral ambiguity of this tale. Jacob tells his father that he caught the game so quickly 'Because the Lord your God granted me success' (27.20). Is this just one more untruth, or could Jacob be saying more than he realized? I can not help but feel that Jacob's words here, which reproduce the same idiom as that expressed by Abraham's servant in 24.12, should be pondered more deeply on this occasion. For the Lord had indeed predicted pre-eminence for Jacob over Esau. Is Jacob taking God's name in vain or not? And just how involved is God himself in this scene? (See, e.g., 27.30-40; 28.10-22.)

Chapter 25 divulged that Esau was a hunter, a man of the field, while Jacob was a quiet man, living in tents. True to form, while Esau is out in the field, Jacob is in his father's tent. In fact, ch. 25 anticipated a large number of events in ch. 27. Jacob prepared stew and gave it to his brother (25.29a); Rebekah prepares kid and Jacob serves to his father (27.14, 19). Esau came in from the field (25.29b); Esau is sent out to the field and returns from the field (27.3, 30). Esau made a request to eat (25.30); Isaac requests a meal (27.4, 25). The birthright's sale was sealed with stew (25.31); the blessing is sealed with savoury food (27.25). Esau ate (*'kl*) and drank (*šth*, 25.34); Isaac eats (*'kl*) and drinks (*šth*, 27.25). Important plot developments revolve around food. It is Jacob and Rebekah who do the preparing and Esau and Issac who (until 27.31), do the eating. The preparing serves the needs of the schemers and the eating satisfies the victims.

Finally, after surviving a welter of questions, physical examination, tasting of food and smelling, Jacob receives the blessing he craves. It supplements the programmatic divine oracle received by Rebekah in 25.23 and has three main elements. The motif of service introduced then is repeated, this time predicting universal lordship over both 'peoples' and 'brothers'—that is those within and outside the patriarchal family (27.29a). To these are now added the blessings of fertility and prosperity (27.28), and reciprocal blessings and curses (27.29b). And still Isaac does not realize that from his perspective he has blessed the *wrong son*.

27.30-40

In a movingly poignant scene, Esau enters with the meal his father had ordered. But he is too late. This point is emphasized by the dialogue which reproduces almost exactly key elements from the previous scene:

Jacob:	Now sit up and eat of my game, so that you may bless me (v. 19)
Esau:	Let my father sit up and eat of his son's game, so that you may bless me (v. 31)
Isaac:	Who are you, my son? (v. 18) Who are you? (v. 32)
Jacob:	I am Esau your firstborn (v. 19)
Esau:	I am your firstborn son, Esau (v. 32)

Note the inversion of sentence structure in the last example, where the name of Esau is delayed until the end in order to heighten the dramatic effect and produce Isaac's extreme physical reaction (27.33).

Isaac does not as before engage in a detailed interrogation to discover who his visitor is. One question is sufficient. It takes longer, however, for Isaac's befuddled mind to realize who his previous visitor was (27.35).

While Esau's wild and plaintive reaction to Jacob's deception (27.34, 36, 38), is in keeping with his characterization so far, Isaac takes the reader by surprise. He is consumed by fear and shakes violently (the Hebrew of 27.33 is even more extreme than NRSV indicates). This is the most animated Isaac has been anywhere in Genesis. One might have expected him to act like this on top of Moriah, but the narrator chose not to present any of his angst as he faced death. Here, once again, he is still the victim. But he is not the only victim, as his 'blessing' on Esau shows.

In essence the blessing Isaac pronounces on Esau is the mirror image of the one given to Jacob. The fertility and prosperity received by Jacob is denied to Esau (27.39 cf. 27.28; though see comments below), and his lot will be servitude to Jacob rather than lordship over him (27.40b cf. 27.29b). In addition, the motif of conflict introduced in several ways earlier will characterize Esau's existence, 'by your sword you shall live' (27.40a). The one ray of hope is that Esau will one day break free from his subservience to his brother (27.40c).

The second blessing's reversal of the first is highlighted by the inversion of the opening images of fertility:

27.28a:	May God give you of the dew of *heaven*	A
	and of the fatness of the *earth*	B
27.39b:	Away from the fatness of the *earth* ...	B'
	and away from the dew of *heaven*	A'

Yet there is more than a suspicion of Delphic ambiguity in the second. The Hebrew preposition *min* is used in both blessings and is capable of being translated in two ways. While the context might seem to be against it, it is possible to translate 27.39b positively as 'of the fatness of the earth' (as is done for example, by KJV, NKJV, ASV). Have the two brothers been blessed equally or not? This ambiguity will engage the reader's interest as the plot unfolds (see 33.1-20; ch. 36).

Three passages set out the destinies of Jacob and Esau (i.e., 25.23; 27.27b-29, 39-40). They have taken up so much narrative space that the reader cannot miss their importance for the plot. Three main elements emerge from the three passages: the elder will serve the younger, division and conflict will characterize their relationship; the elder will be deprived of the fertility and prosperity granted to the younger (though stated ambiguously).

The oracle and blessings project beyond the story line of chs. 25–36, and envisage international relationships. Such issues lie beyond the scope of this commentary. I will, therefore, confine my interest to developments within the lives of Jacob and Esau as presented in the narrative, recognizing that more could be said.

As an actor, God seems to be absent from this episode; but how involved is he? Rebekah just happens to overhear Isaac's words to Esau (27.5). Jacob's deception works, but he comes within a whisker of being detected by both his father (27.18-24) and brother, for Esau returns 'when Jacob had scarcely gone out' (27.30). Are these simply fortuitous happenings, or does their compound effect force one to look for a divine director in the background (as in the book of Esther)? Jacob's haunting words, 'Because the Lord your God granted me success' (27.20), once again appear to be more than an evasive ploy by Jacob. (See further on, e.g., 28.10-22; 32.1-21.)

Genesis 27.41–28.22

27.41–28.9

The divisions that have characterized family relationships so far now intensify. Initially, Jacob had feared only the possibility of a curse if Isaac saw through his masquerade (27.12). Now he has reason to fear for his life. Esau has no intention of submitting to Isaac's blessing: Isaac had intoned, 'you shall serve your brother' (27.40); Esau resolves, 'I will kill my brother' (27.41). The seriousness of this development is indicated by the similarities between this story and that of Cain and Abel (4.1-16). Among numerous points of contact we might note the following. In neither story are we told explicitly why God prefers the younger to the older. Where Cain had murdered his brother, here Esau plans to do so. Cain the perpetrator was exiled eastward to the 'land of Nod' (4.16); Jacob the intended victim is exiled eastward to Haran (27.43; 28.2). Previously, Jacob and Esau have been distinguished by their pursuits (25.27; 27.3-4), just as Cain and Abel were (4.2). Esau, like Cain, hears that the earth will not yield its fertility to him (27.39; cf. 4.12). Both of them respond with anger (27.41; cf. 4.5). In some respects Esau fares worse than Cain, for at least Cain received some comforting words (4.6-7, 15); Esau receives nothing other than the ambiguous formulation of 27.39. The Cain and Abel story is not so closely related to this one that it provides the key for its interpretation, but the shadow it casts over Jacob and Esau emphasizes the divine favouritism in both and the severity of family disruption in

Isaac's camp. The nature of the family conflict is captured by juxtaposing two verses: 'Rebekah loved Jacob' (25.28); 'Esau hated Jacob' (27.41). With the senile Isaac sidelined, making plans for his own funeral (27.2; cf. 27.41), the action is confined to the explosive emotions generated by the triangle of the mother and her two sons.

Rebekah is, however, the dominant character, manipulating her husband, outthinking Esau and commanding Jacob. She it is, not Isaac, who learns of Esau's plans, just as earlier she had over-heard Isaac's plans (27.5). Since Esau's resolve to kill Jacob had been 'said to himself' (27.41), it remains a mystery how she learned of it. His words 'were told to Rebekah' (27.42)—but by whom? Was it servants spying for their mistress, or does the veiled language give room for seeing divine intervention once again? Regardless of the source of her information, Rebekah reveals her consummate skill as a plotter. Once more she says to Jacob, 'Now therefore, my son, obey my voice' (27.43), the Hebrew repeating verbatim her previous command to him (27.8). The repetition of her brusque command reminds the reader of who is in control.

Considering Rebekah's prominent role, one might pause slightly over her statement 'until your brother's anger against you turns away, and he forgets what *you* have done to him' (27.45). 'You' here is singular. But we readers know that actions so far have been a joint effort. Jacob might have got the birth-right by his own initiative (25.29-34), but the crucial blessing would never have come his way without Rebekah's nerves of steel. It is therefore a matter of 'what *we* have done to him'. Perhaps this detail suggests that neither Isaac nor Esau have discovered Rebekah's involvement. If they had, her life would have been as much at risk as Jacob's. (She is never mentioned in Isaac's analysis of the deception, nor in Esau's plan for revenge, 27.35, 41.) The fact that she can orchestrate events and yet remain undetected confirms her mastery of deception. She exits the Genesis narrative with two speeches illustrating just this. In 27.42-45 she reveals Esau's plan to Jacob and gives him direct pragmatic advice—go to Haran. In 27.46 she nonchalantly complains to Isaac about Esau's Hittite wives, and of how terrible her life would be if Jacob followed his brother's lead. Here, she nudges Isaac into giving Jacob the very advice she has just given. She gives Isaac the impression that he is in control, but she it is who has engineered the situation. Isaac is as much a victim here as he had been previously with Jacob in his tent.

The fact that Isaac moves easily into blessing Jacob, as he sends him on his way (28.1-5), shows his resignation to what happened in ch. 27. The blessing cannot be taken back; it can only be supplemented. So without coercion, he now confers on his younger son the blessings of progeny and land he himself had previously received (26.2-4). These elements of the Abrahamic promises are particularly appropriate in this context as Jacob leaves the *land* to find a *wife*. He also commissions Jacob to do what Abraham had ordered his servant to do for him. But whereas Abraham had simply told his steward to return to his country and kindred to obtain a wife (24.4), Isaac specifies the same house and the very man from whose daughters Jacob will select his wife. True to form, Isaac who trudges along in his father's footsteps for most of his life, believes that Yahweh's guidance of Abraham in the past is sufficient for him in the present. Jacob's response takes no one by surprise. Like Abraham before him (12.19-20), Jacob the bearer of the promise must flee from the consequences of his deception.

The slick manoeuvres of Rebekah are successful, but the reader's sympathies surely lie with Esau. How the news of Jacob's escape must have rankled with Esau! First, his birthright had been taken away; then his blessing; and now the opportunity for revenge. His only consolation is to attempt to gain parental approval by marrying an acceptable wife (28.6b, 8). What better way to do so than by marrying a woman from Abraham's line, one of Ishmael's daughters? For a time therefore, both sons are away from home seeking wives from relatives in foreign parts. Esau's choice of Ishmael's daughter is appropriate. The elder son passed over in favour of the younger marries the daughter of a man who suffered the same fate. What commiserations each could offer the other as they drank into the night! But for Esau, none of this can turn back the clock. Just as he turned up too late with his savoury meal, so here the horse has already bolted.

28.10-22

When Abraham had fled from the anger of Pharaoh he had returned to Bethel (13.1-3), and now the fugitive Jacob retraces his steps. But rather than its importance in the past, Bethel marks a significant new development in Yahweh's relationship with Jacob.

The divine revelation to Jacob on his first night on the run, significantly leaves Esau as the only major character in this narrative never to hear the words of God (cf. 25.23; 26.2). Jacob's dream forms a contrast to the preceding narrative. At home, intrigue and counter-intrigue by family members manipulated the situation. At Bethel, a simple divine announcement speaks simply and unambiguously. Where the human actors had previously actively taken the initiative to enforce or possibly frustrate God's will, here Jacob simply hears the divine will while sleeping. While the oracle of 25.23 always stood in the background, the previous action presented the human actors as acting autonomously, with God not explicitly mentioned. But previous suspicions about divine involvement in the plot gain strength here. The imagery of the dream, which emphasizes the close connection between the earthly and heavenly spheres, suggests that Rebekah and her family were less autonomous than they appeared to be. The perverse ambiguity of 28.13a builds on this heaven/earth dynamic by failing to make clear whether the Lord is 'beside him' (e.g., NRSV), or 'above it' [the ladder] (e.g., RSV; see, e.g., 30.14-24; 32.1-21.)

The reminders of Abraham's flight to Bethel, after being judged and found wanting by Pharaoh (12.18-20), might have raised some expectation that Jacob would likewise be judged by Yahweh for the lies, deception and callous ambition that has brought him to this spot. Rather than judgment, however, God stands by the 'ladder' with only blessing. This is all the more surprising when we recall the similar structure that reached to heaven at Babel, and that certainly presaged judgment (28.12 cf. 11.4). Isaac had similarly blessed Jacob, but only because he had been fooled. We can hardly suggest the same for God. The inscrutability of the divine will, raised first in this narrative by the oracle to Rebekah, appears again. The contrast between Jacob's narrative characterization and his divine approval raises a tension for the reader. Will the narrative soon reveal positive qualities of Jacob, thus providing some rationale for God promising, 'Know that I am with you and will keep you wherever you go' (28.15)? Or will God's favouritism remain a mystery?

Isaac had sent Jacob on his way with two elements of the three-fold Abrahamic blessing, those of nationhood and land (28.3-4). At Bethel, God himself repeats those elements but adds the third—the nations will be blessed through Jacob and his descendants (28.13-15). Though exactly how this is going to be fulfilled is still not clear. The patriarchs so far have had an uneasy relationship with the nations, to say the least, and Jacob is heading off to Haran ostensibly in order to avoid marrying into the nations like his brother has.

Despite these repetitions of the overarching patriarchal promises repeated by both his father and God, Jacob's reply reveals that his mind is elsewhere. The vow he takes does not fit well with Yahweh's dream revelation for it contains nothing concerning nationhood, land or blessing the nations (28.14), but alludes only to the spirit of God's concluding words (28.15). It is more appropriate as a response to the blessing he had stolen from Esau (27.27-29). Jacob asks for his worldly needs to be catered for (28.20), echoing Isaac's prediction of prosperity (27.28). He requests a peaceful homecoming (28.21), which would require Esau's acquiescence to the overturning of primogeniture (27.29b cf. 27.40). He is content with what he himself has wrested from Isaac's grasp, but appears somewhat distrustful of Yahweh. His vow is a challenge to Yahweh to prove himself, and if he does, then Jacob will serve him. 'If God will be with me ... then the Lord shall be my God' (28.20-21). Like Abraham he too will pay a tithe, but in contrast to Abraham's spontaneous gift to Melchizedek (14.20), Jacob's will be more of a grudging acceptance that Yahweh has been true to his word (28.22). Previously, Jacob had spoken to Isaac about 'the Lord *your God*' (27.20); Yahweh introduces himself in this scene as 'the *God of Abraham* your father and the *God of Isaac*' (28.13). Here, Jacob says that if Yahweh proves himself 'then the Lord shall be *my God*' (28.21). Until then, apparently, Jacob will remain uncommitted. How the ensuing narrative develops Jacob's relationship with Yahweh will, therefore, be of great interest (see 31.5; 33.20).

Genesis 29.1-31

29.1-14

In journeying to Haran, Jacob retraces the steps of Abraham's servant (ch. 24). Both are on a quest to find a wife, arrive at a (the same?) well, meet there a young female member of the patriarch's extended family, are invited in to meet the rest of the family, and as a result make an agreement whereby the young woman met at the well becomes the bride. There are of course some incidental differences—for example Abraham sent a servant but Jacob himself is present; Rebekah aided the servant but Jacob aids Rachel, and so on. The contrasts between Abraham's servant and Jacob are more significant. In contrast to

the request of Abraham's pious servant for divine leading
(24.12-14), Jacob has just uttered a self-centred oath at Bethel
(28.20-22). While the servant had arrived at the well laden down
with goods that impressed Laban, Jacob arrives with nothing.
Jacob's penury underlines that in contrast to the servant he is a
fugitive rather than an ambassador, and lacks everything his
stolen blessing had supposedly conferred on him.

Jacob's eager questioning of the herdsmen is contrasted by
their initial monosyllabic answers. While he is happy to have
reached his destination and kin, and with barely suppressed
excitement anticipates finding a wife, they seem quite naturally
to be a little distrustful of this stranger who has just turned up.
Once they have divulged that the young woman approaching is
Rachel, Jacob's cousin, Jacob attempts to get rid of the shep-
herds so that he can be alone with her, but his request that they
'water the sheep, and go, pasture them' (29.7), falls on deaf ears.
The extent of his eagerness can be seen in his defying accepted
formalities by kissing Rachel before he has divulged his identity,
and in addition, his removal of the heavy stone from the mouth
of the well before all of the flocks have arrived. Just as at home,
Jacob is willing to flout conventions in order to get his heart's
desire.

Rachel's character will be developed at length later in the
narrative, but here the narrator spends more time in presenting
her father Laban, whom the reader has already met in ch. 24.
The text mentions three times that Laban is 'his mother's brother'.
This repetition registers not only that Jacob has come to his relatives, but underlines precisely who Laban is. Since introducing
Laban in ch. 24, his sister Rebekah's character has been developed at some length. Will Laban display similar characteristics?
A possible hint that he will is given in 29.13b. The note that
'Jacob told Laban all these things' fails to say exactly what Jacob
told him. There is no need for him to relate the incident at the
well and his identity, for Rachel has already informed Laban of
these matters (29.12b-13a). Surely he would have to give some
explanation for why he has turned up out of the blue in Haran
(just as Abraham's servant did in 24.34-38). And if so, which
reason does he give—to escape Esau or to get a wife (see
27.41–28.9)? Did he divulge the intimate details about his deceit
of Isaac and Esau, which had been engineered by Laban's sister
Rebekah? If Jacob included '*all these things*' in his report then
Laban's emotional response 'Surely you are my bone and my

flesh!' (29.14), recognizes Jacob as more than kin (cf. 2.23), but also as someone after his own heart (see 24.28-67). And if this is so, how might the relationship between these two develop? One possibility is telegraphed when one recalls that well scenes in Genesis have produced a number of motifs, most prominent of which are: exile from the patriarchal home (chs. 16, 21, 26,), the meeting of a future wife (chs. 24,) and conflict (e.g., chs. 16, 21, 26). Here Jacob is exiled from his patriarchal home (to the 'land of the people of the east', cf. 3.24; 4.16; 13.11; 25.6). He has met his future wife. Surely conflict cannot be far behind.

29.15-30

Just how closely Laban resembles Jacob is displayed in the negotiations for Rachel. Laban's hospitality to Abraham's servant had been influenced by the gifts he brought (24.30-31), and here again his open welcome soon gets around to the issue of Jacob's contribution to the family's income. The possibility is raised that Laban is displaying a self-interest to match that of his nephew. Also his rhetorical question, 'should you therefore serve me for nothing (*hinnām*)?' (29.15), might cause some reflection when one realizes that the term also connotes 'in vain' (Ezek. 6.10; cf. 29.25). The uncle's self-interest closely matches that of his nephew displayed in the earlier part of the narrative.

Surprisingly, Jacob does not drive a hard bargain, but offers to work for seven years in order to gain Rachel's hand. This excessive offer (cf. 29.20 and Wenham 1993: 235), suggesting just how besotted Jacob is with Rachel, means that Laban does not enter into any further discussion, but takes advantage of Jacob's lack of judgment. Jacob has been transformed from a demanding negotiator (25.29-34), to a reckless lover. There is enough room in Laban's reply (29.19), to leave scope for him to dupe Jacob, for it contains no specific statement that after seven years Jacob will get *Rachel*—though obviously this is how Jacob understood it. His request to Laban is 'Give me my wife' (29.21), not 'Give me Rachel, my wife', which once again played into Laban's hands (see Kidner 1967: 160). Jacob's desire to get Rachel recalls Esau's desperation to eat (25.30-32); both brothers suffer for their lack of judgment.

Jacob's offer to work for seven years does not sit well with his mother's view that she would soon send for him (27.44), yet her words are recalled here. Rebekah had told him to stay with

Laban for 'a while (*yāmîm* *ᵃḥādîm*)'; Jacob's love for Rachel made the seven years seem like 'a few days' (*kᵉyāmîm* *ᵃḥādîm*, 29.20). Thus ironically, the seven years seemed to Jacob to be the same time his mother had suggested (though as yet, no message has arrived from Rebekah to return home). Tellingly, this is not said of the second seven-year period (29.30b).

This episode raises again the motif of the elder and younger. Just as back home there had been the elder (Esau), and the younger (Jacob), so here we have the elder (Leah), and the younger (Rachel). Leah and Esau are each the elder child, both in danger of being marginalized. But whereas Laban (29.26), and God (29.31), act for Leah, no one so far has argued Esau's case. The tussle between younger and elder had been at the centre of the deception back home; here Laban engineers a variation on that theme. Jacob's deception had been to disguise the younger as the older; Laban reverses this, substituting the older for the younger. The connection with Jacob's previous schemes is made blatantly obvious by Laban's response to Jacob's protest, 'This is not done in our country—giving the younger before the firstborn' (29.26). Laban's tone of voice is clear, conveying a veiled criticism not only of Jacob's fraud but also of the divine oracle (25.23). If as I noted above, Jacob's telling him 'all these things' (29.13), included Jacob's dealings with Esau and Isaac, Laban's words could be very well chosen. Perhaps the ruse had even been suggested by Jacob's earlier confidences. The reader can certainly see how Laban's ploy subtly replicates Jacob's earlier act. Leah's eyes are described as *rak*, which could mean that they were either weak (cf. 33.13), or lovely (cf. 18.7). However, since a contrast between the sisters is implied in 29.17, the negative connotation seems more likely. The reader will recall that Isaac's eyes were 'dim' (*khh*, 27.1). Previously the victim had poor eyesight, here it is the co-conspirator. Like his father, Jacob is also in the dark, unable to see. But at least Isaac, befuddled and senile as he was, had some misgivings. Jacob is even more intimately involved with Leah, but never suspects anything. At daybreak, after the conjugal climax, comes the anti-climax—'it was Leah!' (29.25). Measure for measure: as Jacob had deceived Isaac with kid dressed as venison, so now he is deceived by mutton dressed as lamb. The turning of the tables on Jacob the trickster is amplified by Laban's choice of words. Jacob had tricked the firstborn out of his birthright (*bᵉkōrâ*, 27.31-34); Laban has now tricked him into receiving the firstborn (*bᵉkîrâ*, 29.26). So, Jacob was more than a match for his brother and father. But in his uncle he has met someone as accomplished as his mother.

Not only has this episode shown Jacob receiving his come-uppance, it also comments on the patriarchal family in general. Jacob's protest to Laban recalls previous patriarchal deceptions in marital affairs. He expostulates, 'What is this you have done to me?' (29.25). These words reproduce exactly the protests of Pharaoh against Abraham (12.18) and Abimelech against Isaac (26.10, with a shift to the plural 'us'), and are very close to Abimelech's words to Abraham, 'What have you done to us?' (20.9). At last the patriarchal line of marital deceivers meets its match. All of these protests have been to patriarchs whose 'wife-sister' ruse has been exposed. Well, Jacob thought it was his wife, but it was only her sister—a poetic reversal!

This episode also raises a detail of the blessings pronounced by Isaac (27.27-29; 39-40). Jacob's destiny was to be lord, served (*'bd*) by peoples, nations and brothers. His arrival in Laban's household sees the first use of the root 'to serve' (*'bd*) since the blessing ceremony. Significantly the status intimated by the blessings is reversed by developments here. Jacob is presented as serving Laban (29.15, 18, 20, 25, 27, 30). This is no aberration as we shall see, for every use of this root when applied to Jacob in the subsequent narrative has Jacob doing all the serving (30.26, 29; 31.6, 41; 32.5, 10, 18, 20; 33.5, 14). The future envis-aged by the blessing is not fulfilled here or anywhere else in the Jacob story. Thus in this episode, Jacob's plans appear to be unravelling. The inversion of elder/younger priority which he had engineered to his own advantage before is now reinstated to his detriment by Laban, and in the very service he gives Laban for the wrong wife he inverts the expectations raised by the blessing he had stolen from the firstborn. Are we beginning to see some 'natural justice' assert itself in the story?

Genesis 29.31–30.43

29.31–30.13
The conflict within this family deepens. Before their birth Isaac's children had struggled in their mother's womb. Now with the birth of Jacob's children there is a struggle between the mothers. The motif continues, but with new actors. For Rachel the prize is not simply children but also victory over her sister (30.1, 8); for Leah, the goal is her husband's love (29.32). Each element of the

Abrahamic blessing has previously given rise to conflict. The herdsmen of Abraham and Lot had disputed over *land*; Jacob and Esau over *blessing*; and now, like Sarah and Hagar before them, Leah and Rachel strive over *progeny*. There might well be advantages to being the chosen people; but one of those is certainly not peace.

Yahweh hands out his own brand of justice when he enables the unloved Leah to be the only fertile wife. Even though she bears his children, however, Jacob still does not love her. The narrator's descriptions of her as being loved less (29.30) and 'unloved' (29.31) do not capture Leah's anguish. Her poignant cries for acceptance, enshrined in the names of her offspring, testify to this: 'surely now my husband will love me' (29.32b); 'Because the Lord has heard that I am hated' (29.33a); 'Now this time my husband will be joined to me' (29.34a). Her next exclamation shows that her hopes were dashed: 'This time I will praise the Lord' (29.35). Here she displays her resignation to her fate. Her only consolation is to be found in God—her husband will not love her, no matter how many children she bears. After the fourth child 'she ceased bearing' (29.35b)—for what reason we are not told. But for a previously fertile woman, it suggests that Jacob ceased having marital relations with her. Having borne four children she has served her purpose and Jacob need trouble her no further.

While the unloved wife has borne several children, the loved wife has borne none. Rachel, the younger wife, is favoured by Jacob, but not apparently by God. The reason for Leah's fertility is that God saw she was not loved. Without that divine intervention she, like her sister, would have had no children. Yahweh's intervention, on behalf of barren women has been tardy. With Sarah it took more than 25 years (12.4 cf. 21.5) and with Rebekah 20 (25.21-22 cf. 25.26). The omens are not good for a quick reversal of Rachel's barrenness.

By the time the narrative turns to Rachel's situation (30.1), her relationship with Jacob has degenerated. Their bitter words are fuelled by deep-seated animosities within that family which have transformed Jacob from a besotted lover into an angry combatant (30.1-2). Whether it is Rachel's envy of Leah (30.1), Jacob's anger with Rachel (30.2), or Rachel's shout of triumph over her sister (30.8), this is a family showing signs of serious disarray. As far as the two sisters are concerned there is no doubt that Rachel is the more vindictive of the two. Rachel expresses envy (30.1), the need for vindication (30.6), and seemingly relishes battling against her sister until she thinks she has prevailed (30.8). By contrast, Leah seems to have no such feelings. The names Leah gave to her own children (29.32-35) gave expression to the coldness of her husband. And the names she gives to her servant girls' children express a simple joy, 'Good fortune!' (30.11) and 'Happy am I!' (30.13). She does not have time to score points against her sister. One pities her forbearance, having to live with an unloving husband and a vindictive sister. One can see why she finds consolation in her children and in God.

Rachel's ploy to get children through her maid Bilhah obviously recalls Sarah's similar action with Hagar. One would think that there is already enough ill will between the characters without risking this strategy and its well known results. The connection with ch. 16 is more than superficial. Barren wives (30.1 cf. 16.1) are prevented from conceiving by Yahweh (30.2 cf. 16.2), which results in the wife offering her slave-girl to her husband (30.3 cf. 16.3). Each husband goes into' (*bô'*) his wife's slave (30.4 cf. 16.4), who obligingly conceives and bears a son (30.5 cf. 16.4, 15). The difference in the situation is that there is no contempt shown between Bilhah and Rachel as there was by Hagar for Sarah; Rachel vents her spleen on her husband (30.1) and her sister (30.8) instead. With a knowledge of the fallout from that previous episode the reader must wonder whether slave girls acting as surrogate mothers once again can in any way help the situation.

30.14-24

Reuben's return from the wheat fields with his gift of mandrakes for his mother heralds another outburst of family animosity. Once again, food takes a prominent place in the struggle between elder and younger. Jacob had gained the advantage by means of stew and savoury game. Each sister now attempts the same through mandrakes. These roots were considered to have aphrodisiacal properties (cf. Song 7.13). Rachel's behaviour here suggests they were also considered a cure for infertility. Both wives desire the mandrakes, but for different reasons. Leah no longer sleeps in Jacob's bed. This was implied by 29.35 and confirmed by her outburst against Rachel here, 'You have taken away my husband' (30.15). Leah does not need mandrakes to induce fertility (she has already had four sons), but requires them as an aphrodisiac that Jacob might desire her sexually in order that she might have more children, which she desperately hopes will cause her husband to have regard for her. The misery of her loveless marriage causes even placid Leah to develop a sharp tongue (30.15). The reason she agrees to give Rachel the mandrakes is that it gets her into Jacob's bed, if only for one night—the very thing she had hoped the mandrakes would achieve. Rachel has Jacob's love but not his children; Leah has Jacob's children but not his love. By bartering mandrakes each attempts to achieve her heart's desire.

Neither woman achieves what she had hoped. The mandrakes have no effect whatsoever on Rachel's infertility. It is Leah who conceives, not Rachel. On the other hand, God heeds Leah's desire to have more children (30.17); but Jacob remains as indifferent as ever. On delivering her third son, Leah had hoped, 'Now this time my husband will be joined to me' (29.34). After the birth of her sixth son she is still hoping 'Now my husband will honour me' (30.20). Up to now he certainty has not, and there is no evidence that he does so here. While the narrative tells us that Rachel allowed Leah to sleep with Jacob for one night, Leah gets pregnant three times (30.17, 19, 21). These pregnancies suggest that similar bargains were struck by the two women after this event, for their problems remain. They are united only by their ongoing misery.

Finally God steps into the scene and cuts through the human scheming. What mandrakes failed to provide is achieved by Yahweh's decisive act. 'God remembered Rachel' (30.22), just as previously he had Noah (8.1) and Abraham (19.29). God's acts of remembering have marked the turning point from negative to positive, judgment to salvation. Also previously, the child born to a barren woman after long delay has been the truly significant one (21.1-2). The very fact that we have been kept waiting for Joseph suggests his importance.

The struggle for conception obviously recalls the earlier patriarchal promises of progeny and nationhood. Here as before, nothing is straightforward, at least not for the favoured wife. Just as significantly, the episode broaches the topic of service, raised initially by the blessings given to Jacob and Esau. Not only does Jacob serve Laban for his wives, but he also serves Leah. Leah tells Jacob that she has 'hired' him to perform sexually that night (30.16). The result of that night's collaboration, Leah's fifth son Issachar, perpetuates in his name

Jacob's status as Leah's servant—'God has given me my hire' (30.18). This provides another ironic twist on the blessing that had announced that the elder would serve the younger. Laban's trickery has already seen the younger son serving for the elder sister; here Leah's wit means that he actually serves her. Jacob is unable even to lord it over his unloved wife. Just as God's promises to Abraham became complicated by subsequent narrative developments, so too Isaac's words of blessing, with loved wives suffering barrenness, unloved wives proving fertile, and 'lords' becoming 'servants'.

30.25-43

Significantly, Jacob sees the birth of a child to his *real* wife as a turning point in his fortunes. Jacob announces to Laban, 'Send me away, that I may go to my own home and country' (30.25). God's remembering of Noah had marked the transition between the rising and receding flood waters (8.1), now God's remembering of Rachel (30.22) marks the transition between Jacob's flight and return. Or to be more accurate, it should have done so. Even though Jacob has a personal affinity for the land previously promised to him ('my home'; 'my land', cf. 28.13, 15), he is deflected from returning quite easily by Laban. Just as his marriage to Rachel was delayed, and her bearing posterity was delayed, so too Jacob's return will be delayed. Abraham's servant had spent the minimum amount of time possible without offending family etiquette (24.54-56). Jacob seems to be in danger of never returning.

For the second time Laban and Jacob discuss wages. The first time Jacob had surprisingly agreed to the exorbitant deal of seven years service for a wife (29.18). He has now served 14 for his two wives. In renegotiating further wages once again he surprises the reader by suggesting terms even less generous than before, ('You shall not give me anything', 30.31). The reader will recall, however, that the first round of negotiations resulted in trickery by Laban. The second round does too, but this time Jacob joins Laban in a contest of wit and guile.

Deception continues unabated. Each seems to be as devious as the other. Laban removes the spotted sheep from the flock so that Jacob cannot have his wages, while Jacob manipulates the breeding so that Laban is left with the weakest animals. The truth of Laban's previous exclamation is substantiated here, 'Surely you are my bone and my flesh!' (29.14); they complement each other wonderfully. The nature of these two as accomplished cheats is reflected by wordplays found in their very acts of deception. Laban removed all the flock that were 'striped' (*'qd*, cf. root *'qb* for Jacob's name). Jacob strips 'poplar' (*libneh*) to reveal their 'white' (*lābān*) streaks in order to outwit Laban (*lābān*) (see Wenham 1993: 257).

Jacob achieves some success. The root *prṣ*, which means 'spread out, increase' is used twice in this passage (30.30, 43), and recalls God's promise in 28.14, 'you shall spread abroad (*prṣ*)'. But in staying with Laban, Jacob continues his role as a servant. The root *'bd* is used again here, 30.26 stating literally, 'Give [me] my wives and my children for whom I have served (*'bd*) you, and let me go, for you know the service (*'bd*) [with] which I have served you (*'bd*)'. These words, expressing Jacob's self-perception as a servant, are highly ironic coming from a character who risked all to achieve lordship.

Genesis 31

Jacob's return home, postponed in the previous chapter, finally takes place here. The narrative now turns back on itself. Jacob had arrived at Laban's by rolling away a stone (29.10), kissing his relative (29.11), discussing wages (29.15), and being deceived (29.23-25). He now departs from Laban with remonstrations regarding his wages (31.7, 41), deception of his uncle (31.20, 26), omission of farewell kisses (31.28), and the setting up of a stone (31.45-46; see Wenham 1993: 267). In addition, Jacob's recollection of the vow he made at Bethel (31.13), which included a clause regarding his safe return to Canaan, confirms that the narrative has turned the corner. Just how little has changed during his 20-years sojourn, however, is indicated by the verb describing his departure, 'he did not tell him that he intended to flee (*brḥ*). So he fled (*brḥ*) with all that he had ... Laban was told that Jacob had fled (*brḥ*) ... "Why did you flee (*brḥ*) secretly?' " (31.20-22, 27). Jacob does not simply leave; he is a fugitive. His position is the same as when his mother had told him. 'Flee (*brḥ*) at once to my brother Laban in Haran' (27.43). His mother had told Jacob to remain in Haran until Esau's anger had abated, when she would send word for him to return (27.45). No such word has arrived. It is Yahweh who commands Jacob to return (31.3). Is Esau still angry? Is Rebekah dead? What will Jacob find when he arrives home? And how much will he need God's promise to be with him (31.3)?

31.1-21

After a prolonged silence, Yahweh speaks. The last time Yahweh had spoken to Jacob (28.13-15), he passed no judgment on Jacob's past but simply offered promises for his future, which included a return to the land. Here again, he passes no judgment, but commands Jacob to return to the land and promises to be with him. At Bethel there had been a tension between the narrative depiction of Jacob and the divine approval. That tension continues here. While a reader might welcome Jacob's receiving a taste of his own medicine at the hands of Laban, Jacob remains the shrewd trickster in, for example, 30.37-43 and this passage. God continues to be true to his word given at Bethel, but why he should want to be remains a mystery (see, e.g., 28.10-22; 32.1-21).

While God's favouritism remains inscrutable, his support for Jacob might not be all it seems to be. The narrator gives only a terse report of Yahweh's command to return home with its accompanying promise (31.3). Jacob on the other hand, who has hardly mentioned God's name since Bethel, is positively loquacious as he catalogues Yahweh's interventions and communications during his stay at Haran. The reader is entitled to cast a quizzical eye over his speech. He exaggerates the harm done to him by Laban: 'Your father has cheated me and changed my wages ten times' (31.7). Similarly, Jacob's breeding success was not due entirely to divine intervention, which is what he claims (31.8-9), but was the result of his calculated breeding techniques (30.37-43). There is also a discrepancy between the narrative's report of the divine command (31.1-3), and Jacob's claims. He tells his wives nothing of this recent communication, but instead recounts a dream he claims to have had during the breeding season which gave him divine approval and censured Laban (31.10-12), together with a reminder of Bethel and a command to return home. This version claims far more than the narrator's account in 31.3. Jacob's reference to Bethel (31.13), reminds the reader not only of God's commitment to Jacob, but also of the self-centred vow Jacob made on that occasion. Has opportunist, cheating Jacob changed since Bethel? The only evidence to the contrary is Jacob's own speech here, where he presents himself as the innocent victim of Laban's schemes, conveniently forgetting all of his intrigues against Laban. This is no even-handed account but a propaganda exercise aimed at persuading his wives to accompany him to Canaan. Jacob's invocation of deity to justify his actions should not surprise us when we recall his words to Isaac, 'Because the Lord your God granted me success' (27.20). He can always invoke God when it suits him. Yahweh is still 'the God of my father' (31.5). God has not yet brought him home safely (28.21), so he is not yet Jacob's God (see 28.20-22; 33.18, 20).

If Jacob's protestations are not all that they seem, the same is true about his wives' complaints. Rachel and Leah had had heated exchanges as they argued over their husband (30.14-15), but here they are united in their antagonism toward their father. But do they claim too much in their depiction of the fragmentation of family relationships? That Laban has frittered away their family inheritance might well be in character, but the only evidence provided is the women's words. Their claim flatly contradicts that of Laban's sons who accuse Jacob of removing their father's wealth (31.1). And it is not immediately understandable what 'money' (31.15) they are referring to, since Jacob gave 14 years service and not a cash sum for their hands in marriage. Their protests of outrage, couched in pious terms, are compromised by Rachel's later action. While claiming that it is God who has taken away their father's wealth (31.16), Rachel is not above plain theft (31.19). This exhibits the same contrast seen between Jacob's words which claim divine action and the narrative which divulges his human scheming.

Rachel's theft of the 'household gods' (31.19), recalls Jacob's contract with Laban, where he undertook not to steal Laban's livestock (30.33). Jacob's breeding plan might have observed the letter of the contract, but certainly not its spirit. So both husband and wife have duped Laban. A play on the nuances of the verb *gnb* illustrates their partnership. The verb can mean 'steal' (e.g., 30.33; 31.19, 30, 32, 39; Exod. 20.15), 'steal away' (e.g., 2 Sam. 19.3 [4]), 'deceive' (e.g., 31.20, 26-27; Josh. 7.11), etc. Jacob had promised not to steal (*gnb*) Laban's goods (30.33), but here he 'deceived' (*gnb*) Laban (31.20) while Rachel steals (*gnb*) (31.19) from him. The two connotations of the verb underline that the mainstays of this narrative are indeed deception and conflict. Jacob sets off, taking his wives, children, livestock and property (31.17-18), following Abraham who had taken his wife, Lot, possessions and property and journeyed to Canaan (12.5). Indeed, the phrase 'to the land of Canaan' (*'arṣâ kᵉna'an*) occurs here for the first time since 12.5. The patriarchal story restarts. Just as the primaeval history began with creation and restarted with the recreation of the Deluge, so the ancestral history began with a migration from Haran to Canaan and restarts here with a replay of those events (see 8.1-5; 12.1-3).

31.22-55

There are, however, echoes of more than Abraham's initial move from Haran. One cannot help but contrast the peaceful departure of Abraham's servant from Laban's house with Rebekah (24.58-61), with Jacob's flight from Laban with Rachel and Leah. Also, this is not the first time that an uncle has pursued his nephew, but Laban's feelings for Jacob are of a different order than Abraham's for Lot (cf. 14.11-16). In addition, Laban receives a warning from God in a dream (31-24), reminiscent of the one received by Abimelech (20.3), who had been deceived by Abraham about his 'sister'. Abimelech confronted Abraham with the question 'What have you done? (*meh 'āśîtâ*)' (20.9). Laban uses the same words to interrogate Jacob concerning his wives (31.26 cf. 4.10). These echoes of deception and conflict from the Abraham story, displayed in the first half of Jacob's story, continue as Jacob returns home.

Laban's dream had told him to say nothing to Jacob, that is 'not a word ... either good or bad' (31.24; cf. 2.9, 17; 3.5, 22). It is, perhaps, an indication of the depth of their hostility that in spite of this prohibition the two of them engage in some of the lengthiest dialogue in Genesis. Their confrontation overflows with barely concealed mutual contempt, accusation and riposte laced with sarcasm. Laban begins by feigning an emotional attachment to Jacob's retinue, implying that he is taken aback by Jacob's deceit which has prevented him from providing a generous farewell. Note that it took Laban three days to discover that Jacob had fled (31.22). Previously Laban had 'set a distance of three days' journey between himself and Jacob' (30.36), as part of the convoluted duplicity between the two. The three-day delay in discovering Jacob's move might suggest that the two had kept their distance from that day on. Thus while Laban's speech might affect shocked surprise, the situation is really business as usual.

If Laban's speech cannot be taken at face value, neither can Jacob's. Jacob claims that he did not tell Laban of his plans because he thought Laban would remove his wives by force. This is news to the reader, for Jacob gave several reasons for returning in his conversation in 31.5-16 and this was not one of them. Jacob's claim that he fled because he did not want to lose his wives is ironically counterbalanced when be unwittingly endangers Rachel with his cavalier announcement that the thief who stole the gods should be executed. After Laban's unsuccessful search for his household gods, Jacob recites a litany of evils that have befallen him because of Laban's deception and manipulation (31.36-42). Here as before, Jacob conveniently forgets his intrigues with the sheep-breeding. His description of the hardships of work in the field (31.40), is selective. His complaint at the hardship does not tally with the narrator's statement that his service of 'seven years for Rachel ... seemed to him but a few days because of the love he had for her' (29.20). It is true that this is not said of his service for Leah. But Jacob's complaint is certainly not the whole truth. And his final flourish in which he interprets Laban's dream as announcing divine pity for him and rebuke for Laban (31.42), is a more than generous interpretation.

Jacob's speech is possible only because Laban does not find his household gods. Laban's failure puts him on the defensive, fuels Jacob's ire, and allows Jacob to be economical with the truth. The fact that the reader knows that the gods are there causes scepticism about Jacob's claims. One imagines that if Laban had discovered the gods it would have been he, not Jacob, who would have milked the opportunity for all it was worth, launching a tirade outlining how he had been cheated and disadvantaged by his nephew.

Rachel's motivation for stealing the household gods or teraphim is unclear, because our knowledge of their function is inadequate. For whatever reasons, they are of great value to Laban. As far as Rachel is concerned it is unlikely that they hold any religious value, since she stuffs them into a saddle and sits on them. If her claim to be menstruating is true, she would in addition be defiling the gods, (cf. Lev. 12.2; 15.9 and so on); if as seems likely she is telling a bare-faced lie, we see perhaps one more reason why the crafty Jacob 'loved Rachel more than Leah' (29.30). She has inherited from her father the same tendencies as Jacob had from his mother. Indeed, her actions replay Jacob's. Jacob had deceived his father in a tent while the old man had felt (*mšš*) him (27.22). Now Rachel deceives her father while he 'felt (*mšš*) all about in the tent' (31.34). If, as some suggest, the teraphim were associated with family blessing, the connection between the two events is almost complete. Laban's previous trick of slipping Leah into Jacob's marriage bed had been an act of poetic justice on Jacob for his charade before Isaac (see 29.15-30), but in this episode it is Jacob's family who have the last laugh. Rachel is a wife worthy of her husband.

The covenant sworn by Jacob and Laban enshrines their mutual mistrust. That each still fears the other is seen in the basic clause of the treaty in which each undertook not to work against the other (31.52). The conflict is not resolved, merely recognized and managed. The coldness between the two main antagonists is illustrated by Laban's farewell kisses for his grandchildren and daughters (31.55). There is no embrace for Jacob (cf. 29.13). The contrast at this farewell with the embrace and kisses at their first meeting speaks volumes for the path their relationship has taken.

Genesis 32

This chapter contains many reminders of Jacob's encounter with God at Bethel (28.10-22). The points of connection go beyond formal details (e.g., 'he stayed there', [*wayyālen šām*], 28.11; 32.13; the use of the naming formula *qr'* [call] + *šēm* [name], 28.19; 32.2, 30 and so on). The dramatic impact of this chapter as a whole is enriched by reading it in the light of ch. 28, to which the reader is drawn by means of such formal details.

32.1-21

The chapter begins with two brief reminders of Bethel. Jacob is met by 'angels of God' (*mal'ᵃkê' ᵉlōhîm*, a construction confined to 32.1 and 28.12), and he gives the place a name, Mahanaim ('two camps'), to commemorate his experience (32.2 cf. 28.19). Elsewhere in Genesis *mal'āk* describes a supernatural being (e.g., 16.7, 9-11; 19.1, 15; 21.17; 22.11, 15; 24.7, 40; 28.12; 48.16), and 32.1 gives one more example. Yet the word can also connote a human 'messenger', as it does in 32.3, 'Jacob sent messengers before him'. Thus the narrative moves from *mal'āk* as supernatural being to *mal'āk* as human messenger. There is a similar shift from heavenly to earthly between *maḥᵃnayim* (masculine dual) as God's two camps (32.2) to *maḥᵃnôt* (feminine plural) as Jacob's two camps (32.7-8). This easy movement from heavenly to earthly, divine to human, will be raised again in the wrestling scene, 32.22-32 (cf. e.g., Ps. 20.2; Dan. 8.9-10). Their essential connectedness has already been vividly portrayed by the staircase set up between the two in Jacob's dream at Bethel (28.12). Here, Jacob's duplication of divine activity raises once again in a graphic way the connection between his actions and divine involvement (see, e.g., 28.10-22; 30.14-24). In another way, the tension between the two is heightened later in the chapter, when Jacob's prayer, putting everything into God's hands (32.11-12), is followed immediately by his human strategies (see below).

The complexity of Jacob's character is compounded by his detailed plans for approaching Esau. At first sight this episode might seem to be a turning point in the narrative's presentation of Jacob. So far he has been a self-confident and successful trickster, turning events to his own best advantage. His return to the borders of the land, encumbered with great material prosperity, is a reminder of how well he did this. But we seem to meet a rather different Jacob here. To be sure, he is still scheming, assessing the best way to circumvent his brother's supposed anger, but his language is his most deferential so far (32.4). Also, he offers an apparently sincere prayer to God (32.9-12). So is Jacob transforming before our eyes, or should we treat his words and actions with caution?

Note that Jacob's approach to Esau goes through two stages. In 32.4-5, Jacob knows no more than when he left home: Esau has murderous designs against him because Jacob had cheated him of the blessing (27.42). Thus Jacob's aim is to 'find favour' with Esau (32.5), and he adopts an appropriately obsequious tone (see 34.1-31). But is he a genuine suppliant, as the 'lord'/ 'servant' language might suggest? Or are his words a thinly veiled attempt to warn or buy off Esau? He mentions his own prosperity (suggesting power?) in 32.5a, before asking for favour in Esau's sight. In other words, decoding the ambassadorial niceties, 'I am not the vulnerable, penniless individual I was when I fled from you last time. I have prospered greatly, in accordance with the blessing that my father gave *me*. You would be well advised to take note'. Further, he makes no explicit mention of the reason why he went to Laban's in the first place; there is no apology for previous behaviour. If Jacob does 'find favour', it will be due to Esau's magnanimity or capitulation, not Jacob's remorse (cf. use of 'find favour' in e.g., 6.8; 19.19; 39.4).

The second stage develops once Jacob knows that Esau is coming to meet him with a large company of (armed?) men. The terse report from Jacob's servants does not state what Esau's intent is. But it speaks volumes that Jacob assumes the worst: his ploy has failed; he has not 'found favour'; Esau still has murderous designs against him. And does Esau's large retinue suggest that he too has prospered, despite Isaac's 'anti-blessing' on him? Thus Jacob's aim now shifts from placation to damage limitation (32.8). The text rarely divulges the inner thoughts of characters, but here it does (32.8 cf. 32.20). We might wonder about Jacob's motives elsewhere, but here the omniscient narrator wants us to be in no doubt. Jacob is scared witless. In that state of mind he prays to God (32.9-12).

The prayer shows that two matters are clear to Jacob: his life is in danger (32.11), yet God has promised to do him good (32.9, 12). He is as humble with God as he is with Esau (32.4). He states, 'I am not worthy' (32.10). The reader must register agreement, but must also wonder whether these words, like those addressed to Esau, are engendered merely by the heat of the moment. Jacob's worthiness or otherwise has never troubled him up to now. Whether Jacob should be given the benefit of the doubt will have to be tested by how he conducts himself during and beyond his meeting with Esau. In the meantime we must reserve our judgment. His humility would carry greater conviction, however, if it were allied to penitence for the actions which have made him unworthy to receive God's favouritism. His earlier treatment of Esau is not addressed directly but is alluded to subtly. Jacob asks to be delivered 'from the hand (*yād*) of my brother, from the hand (*yād*) of Esau' (32.11). This request is somewhat ironic, since the 'hand' motif has been used to good effect previously when Jacob had been acting against Esau. Jacob's hand gripped Esau's heel (25.26), his hands were covered with goats' skins (27.16), the savoury food and bread were given into his hand (27.17), and Isaac believed Jacob to have the hands of Esau (27.22-23). His use of the idiom in a prayer pleading to be rescued from the hand of Esau recalls why he needs such deliverance.

Jacob might have prayed to God, reminding him of his promises to be with him and appealing for his deliverance, but this does not stop him from perfecting the plans he had started before he prayed (cf. 32.7-8). In fact the juxtaposition of human initiative (32.7-8, 13-21; 33.1-3) and appeal to the divine (32.9-12, 26-30) is a feature of this passage, revealing Jacob's 'belt and braces' approach. Whether one sees this as evidence of his lack of faith or his fear of risking presumption depends on one's assessment of Jacob's overall motivation, which at this moment is open to interpretation.

Jacob's gift to Esau here contrasts with the paltry bowl of soup with which he wrested the birthright from Esau in the first place.

If this repayment with interest will not 'appease' (*kpr*, 32.20) Esau what will? It is unusual to find this verb in a context such as this. It is usually confined to cultic contexts where sin is being atoned (e.g., Exod. 32.30; Lev. 1.4; 4.35, and so on). Yet even when Jacob uses the formal vocabulary for atonement he uses it only in an accommodated idiomatic sense, referring not to atoning for his previous wrongdoing, but simply to appeasing Esau.

Developments in this episode give cause for reflecting on the progress of the promises given to Jacob and Esau. The divine oracle had predicted division between the two brothers (25.23). The fact that we stand here on the verge of their reunion after 20 years' separation underlines that this has been resoundingly carried out. On the larger scale, Jacob's whole life has been one of division. Whether living at home in Canaan, or married in Haran, or sending two companies to meet Esau, Jacob's family has been divided. The same oracle and Isaac's later blessings (27.29, 40) had predicted that Esau would serve Jacob. Their separation for 20 years has delayed the development of this motif. With the two of them coming together again, it once again comes to the fore. But it is presented in a most startling way. Jacob instructs his servants, 'Thus you shall say to my lord Esau: thus says your servant Jacob ...'; 'They belong to your servant Jacob; they are a present sent to my lord Esau ... your servant Jacob is behind us' (32.4, 18, 20). These words actually invert the relationship between the two brothers which Jacob had schemed to establish; in fact, in addressing Esau as 'lord' he accords him a position greater than that in the conventions of primogeniture he had previously overturned. The service/lordship motif comes to its head in the next chapter, but the significance of Jacob's words must not be missed here. Will words be converted into action when he meets his brother?

32.22-32

There is no more graphic depiction of the recurring motif of strife than this. No sooner has Jacob sent his entourage on their way to meet Esau than he meets someone. But who exactly does he meet? The passage is a masterpiece in which mystery and ambiguity cannot be clarified by interpretation but are an essential part of its spirit. The narrator refers to the assailant as 'a man' (*'iš*, 32.24), but just once—the other uses of 'man' are supplied by NRSV (32.25, 28). Jacob on the other hand sees his opponent as divine, 'I have seen God face to face' (32.30). Both of these perspectives are combined by the assailant himself when he tells Jacob 'you have striven with *God* and with *humans*' (32.28). If we accept the narrator's designation of 'man', the question still remains: Which man? There is a scene in Ruth, where similarly neutral terms are used. Naomi tells Ruth, 'do not make yourself known to *the man*' (Ruth 3.3), even though the reader and characters know it is Boaz. When 'the man' awakes in the middle of the night 'there, lying at his feet, was *a woman!*' (Ruth 3.8). Her identity is a mystery to him but known, of course, to the reader. The use by the Genesis narrator of the neutral term 'man' is similar, but there is a major difference: the reader does not know the identity of his foe any more than the character Jacob does. By morning Jacob believes he met a divine assailant. But what caused him to think so? Was it having his hip put out of joint? Does he take the statement 'you have striven with God' as indicating the identity of the mystery opponent? Or is it his opponent's refusal to divulge his name? Does it only dawn on him when he reflects on the experience as a whole, and names the spot Peniel (cf. Judg. 6.22; 13.21-22)? Is it ever *clear* that his foe was divine? Any one of the points listed above might be taken to suggest divinity, but there are equally persuasive arguments for suggesting humanity: wrestling is a thoroughly human activity; his opponent was unable to overcome him (32.25a) and requested to be released (32.26a). A blessing does not require a deity (cf. 27.27-29, 39-40!), but if he knows that it is God, why does he ask his name? (Although see Exod. 3.13.) And what of the assailant's words in 32.28 affirming Jacob's struggle with both divinity and humanity? Are they a summary of Jacob's life to date, or an indication of Jacob's opponent *on this occasion?* The balance on each side leaves the incident shrouded in ambiguity.

One further dimension needs to be mentioned. Prior to this incident, Jacob believed that he faced a hostile Esau (32.11). Now, in the darkness, an aggressive combatant wrestles with him. Jacob had struggled with Esau in the womb; does he think he does so again at the Jabbok? Is this the reason why he craves a blessing and is so keen to know his assailant's name? The progression of and sequel to this episode (33.1-16), indicates that it is not Esau. But initially, neither the reader nor Jacob can be sure. The harder one looks the less clear the scene becomes, summed up by the paradox of the one who need only touch in order to maim (32.25), asking to be released (32.26).

Regardless of who Jacob's opponent is, it is clear that this incident which precedes his reunion with Esau replays the incident that caused their division—Jacob's deception of Isaac (27.18-29). In his father's tent Isaac was blind, and in the darkness while feeling and smelling had to ask, 'Who are you?' (27.18). Here at night, Jacob and his assailant, locked in close physical combat, ask the same question of each other. Jacob's opponent asks 'What is your name?' (32.27); Jacob enquires, 'Please tell me your name?' (32.29). The mystery wrestler refuses to reply, but unlike Isaac forces the truth out of his opponent, with Jacob revealing his true identity (32.27 cf. 27.19). Most significantly, both incidents show Jacob's desire to receive a blessing. Jacob asserts 'I will not let you go, unless *you bless me*' (32.26). He had previously told Isaac, 'Now sit up ... so that *you may bless me*' (27.19), words repeated almost verbatim by Esau in 27.31, and followed by his anguished cry 'Bless me!' (27.34, 38). Indeed this particular construction (various forms of *brk* plus first common singular suffix) is used in Genesis by only Jacob or Esau in these two episodes. Jacob remains the man obsessed by the blessing; and Esau remains deprived of it.

It should also not be missed that Jacob's re-entry to Canaan bears comparison with his exit (cf. Hos. 12.4). Whether dreaming at Bethel or wrestling at the Jabbok, Jacob sees each as an experience of God, which he commemorates by naming the spot (28.19; 32.30). One might wonder, however, whether the shift from Bethel ('house of God'), where he had a dream and received a blessing, to Peniel ('face of God'), where he struggles and suffers physical handicap, registers a significant shift in the relationship between the two.

Jacob's adversary gives him three things: a blessing, the content of which is not divulged (32.29); a new name; and a limp. The numerous problems of translation and interpretation surrounding the name 'Israel' are beyond the scope of this commentary. While many commentators see in the change of name a change of character, it is difficult to see how that fits this context. The new name Jacob receives, Israel, describes his previous actions rather than future destiny (32.28), 'You have striven with God and with humans, and have prevailed', that is, he has been 'striving' with others all his life. Note that Rachel had triumphantly announced, 'With mighty wrestlings [lit. 'wrestlings of God'] I have wrestled with my sister and have prevailed' (30.8). The remarkably similar explanation of the name Israel given here intimates that Jacob's life too has followed a similar path. The conflict between Rachel and Leah is a paradigm for Jacob's conflict with God and the world. The conflict permeating Jacob's life is reflected in the wordplay between Jacob (*ya'ᵃqōb*) and 'wrestled (*yē'ābēq*). What more appropriate place for this encounter than the Jabbok (*yabbōq*). These wordplays recall his uterine struggle with Esau, when he had grasped Esau's heel (*'āqēb*) in a wrestling hold that was enshrined in his name Jacob (*ya'ᵃqōb*). Also, Abram's name was changed to Abraham (17.5), and Sarai to Sarah (17.15), but this brought about no perceptible change in their *character*. Rather, it underlined their future destiny. Jacob's new name does not announce any change in his life, but simply registers that he continues much as before. This is underlined by the fact that after his change of name to Israel (32.28), the narrator continues to call him Jacob (32.29-30, 32; 33.1, 5, 8, and so on). So rather than predicting his future, the new name summarizes his past. The narrator has passed no explicit judgment on Jacob's previous actions. But now the wrestler does. Jacob 'has striven with God' rather than cooperated with him. So his previous actions should not be explained away as the rightful prerogative of one chosen by God. The force of this judgment, however, is affected by difficulty in identifying the wrestler. With whose authority does he speak?

If his new name sums up Jacob's past, his limp defines his future. As he hobbles towards his meeting with Esau therefore, he must trust not in the triumphalism inherent in his new name, but on God's protection, or Esau's mercy on a cripple if he is to survive.

Genesis 33

In a narrative which has had conflict at its centre, the meeting once again of its two main adversaries portends a climactic confrontation. The actual outcome is startling. Rather than combat we witness magnanimity from Esau and subservience from Jacob. By the end of the chapter, however, the two brothers are once again separated. While this is not caused by continuing conflict it reveals once again the complexity of Jacob's character.

33.1-20

Given the penchant of Genesis for providing flashbacks to previous episodes, it is not surprising that this one which reunites the adversaries should contain numerous echoes of the deceptions and stolen blessings which divided them in the first place.

Jacob ranks his family in reverse hierarchical order: slave girls in front with their children, followed by Leah and finally by Rachel with Joseph, as the advancing Esau bears down on them. Jacob goes on ahead 'until he came near (*ngš*) his brother' (33.3), the narrative using the same verb as when Isaac said, 'Come near (*ngš*), that I may feel you, my son, to know whether you are really my son Esau or not' (27.21; cf. 27.22, 25-27; 33.6-7). Eight out of its nine uses in Genesis are found in these two incidents. Just as Isaac had told Jacob, 'Come near (*ngš*) and kiss (*nšq*) me, my son' (27.26, cf. 27.27), so Esau, once Jacob approached, 'kissed' (*nšq*) him (33.4). When Jacob had robbed him of his blessing Esau 'wept' (*bkh*, 27.38); now both Jacob and Esau 'wept' (*bkh*, 33.4). Jacob makes the offer to Esau, 'Please accept (*lqḥ*) my gift (*bᵉrākâ*)' (33.11). This request quite strikingly uses the same terms used previously to describe Jacob's theft of the blessing: 'Your brother came deceitfully, and he has taken away (*lqḥ*) your blessing (*bᵉrākâ*)' (27.35; cf. 27.36).

Each of these echoes has different weight but the cumulative effect draws the reader back to those earlier incidents. The overall impact, however, is not simply to remind the reader of the earlier related episode, but to underline significant tensions between the two. Isaac's blessing on Jacob had made it clear that both nations and brothers would 'bow down' (*ḥwh*, 27.29) to Jacob. That verb is not used again until 33.3, where it describes Jacob prostrating himself before Esau! Since Jacob has been crippled in his hip, some form of bowed stooping before Esau is understandable, but he takes it to extreme lengths with a seven-fold bowing worthy of a vassal before his suzerain (33.3), in which he is followed by the rest of his retinue (33.6-7). The divergence from expectations could hardly be greater. Jacob had been destined by both oracle and blessing to lord it over his brother (25.23; 27.29), while Esau had been told that he would serve Jacob (27.40). Yet when the two are reunited the roles are inverted. So in both word ('take my gift/blessing'), and deed (bowing), Jacob is apparently throwing away his ill-gotten gains. Jacob has now served Laban, Leah and *Esau*. Esau's response is just as astonishing. Isaac's blessing had announced, 'By your sword you shall live' (27.40), yet here he adopts a pacifist role. When urged to accept the herds of animals, he refuses, saying, 'I have enough (*rab*)' (33.9). In the blessing stolen from him by Jacob, Isaac had pronounced, 'May God give you ... plenty (*rōb*) of grain and wine' (27.28). (Note that the same root is used in the

oracle of 25.23 to denote the elder, who would serve the younger.)
He has no need for anything Jacob can offer him. While Jacob
has been away grafting for material advantage by fair means or
foul, Esau has been living a life of quiet prosperity, as if Isaac
had blessed him as well as Jacob. While the context of Isaac's
blessing had seemed to preclude anything positive for Esau, the
true ambiguity of his words which allowed for prosperity is
driven home here (see 27.39b). Esau's generous attitude towards
him would come as a welcome surprise to Jacob; but how deflating
to discover the reason why.

Chapter 32 prolonged its presentation of Jacob's fears, and
delayed his meeting with Esau for so long, that at first the 'man'
at the Jabbok could plausibly be assumed to be Esau. As the
struggle continued, that possibility was eliminated. But now,
retrospectively, the connection between Esau and the mystery
wrestler is raised more explicitly. I noted above the rich play on
words between Jacob (*ya'ăqōb*), Jabbok (*yabbōq*) and 'wrestled'
(*yē'ābēq*). Esau's greeting of Jacob provides one more, for while
Jacob might expect his brother to wrestle (*'bq*) with him, Esau
actually 'embraced' (*ḥbq*) him (33.4). Once again expectations
are reversed. As Jacob had anticipated meeting Esau he had sent
his gift on ahead, saying 'Afterwards I shall see his face (*pāneh*)'
(32.20). He named the spot of his wrestling match Peniel, 'For I
have seen God face (*pāneh*) to face (*pāneh*)' (32.30). He now says
to Esau, 'To see your face (*pāneh*) is like seeing the face (*pāneh*)
of God' (33.10). Jacob's words to Esau might simply be idiomatic
etiquette (the precise form is unique to this verse). But for the
reader who has pondered on several occasions the nature of the
interrelationship between the human and the divine in the Jacob
story, his words once again enigmatically raise the issue (see,
e.g., 28.10-22; 31.1-21; 32.1-21, 22-32).

How do the two brothers emerge from this chapter? Having
seen Jacob's laming at the Jabbok and his bowing before Esau,
one might expect this chapter to show a true turning point in his
life. Some changes we might see, but the essential Jacob remains.
Esau seems to want genuine reconciliation and a life together
with Jacob (33.12, 15). Jacob too does not want the strife to
continue. But his main desire is to survive the encounter with
Esau. Once that has been accomplished, filial commitment does
not matter. He can give the impression that he will follow Esau
to Seir (33.14), because his children and flocks are tired (33.13),
and refuse contact with Esau's entourage because he does not

want to take advantage (33.15). But his words cannot be trusted, for once Esau has departed, Jacob diverts to Succoth and dwells there. Its location is unsure, some even placing it north of the Jabbok. Wherever it is, it is a long way from Seir. If his words cannot be trusted, then his actions of bowing before Esau can hardly be taken at face value. The core conflict of this story might have been put to one side, but Jacob's deception lives on. It is due entirely to Esau's generosity that the separation caused by strife has become separation within reconciliation.

Some time later Jacob moves on to Shechem (33.18). His actions here are significant in light of previous divine promises and human commitments. God has brought him back to the land as he promised (28.15). But like Abraham his only means of possessing it is through purchase (33.19 cf. 25.10). The fulfilment of the Abrahamic land promise (e.g., 15.18-21), is still a long way off. At Bethel Jacob had vowed that if God was with him so that he came to his father's house 'in peace (*šālôm*), then the Lord shall be my God' (28.21). He now 'came safely (*šālēm*) to the city of Shechem ... There he erected an altar and called it El-Elohe-Israel [God, the God of Israel]' (33.18, 20). He has returned home in peace/safely as he had asked, and he keeps his word. For the first time he builds an altar in order to signify at last, that the Lord is *his* God—'God, the God of *Israel*'. This is not an anachronistic reference to the later nation (cf. 34.7), but a personal statement by Jacob/Israel (see 28.21; 31.5).

Perhaps the most memorable feature of this chapter is not Jacob's posturing, fulfilment of vows, or flight once more from his brother's presence, but Esau's magnanimous, unspoken, forgiveness. Jacob, once he sees that he has nothing to fear from his brother, soon reverts to his old tricks. Esau shows that he has undergone a more fundamental change.

Genesis 34

Jacob might have arrived at Shechem in peace (33.18), but that state of affairs does not last long. At first this chapter might appear to be a mere aside to, or even an intrusion into, the Jacob narrative. Nothing could be further from the truth. It is an essential continuation of the story as a whole and of ch. 33 in particular. The dominant motifs of conflict and deceit, woven into the fabric of the whole Jacob story, continue here. The chapter also contains some of the finest and most acute character portrayals to be found anywhere in the book.

34.1-31

The genealogies of Genesis are patriarchal, seldom mention daughters, and when they do, rarely name them. One exception to this is Nahor's genealogy which in 22.23 mentions Rebekah. The reason for this anomaly is amply demonstrated in the ensuing narrative where Rebekah is one of the main antagonists, even eclipsing Isaac in many ways (see 27.1-17). Thus the fact that the list of sons Leah bore to Jacob should have appended to it the birth notice of Dinah (30.21), might well suggest to the reader that she will play a significant role somewhere in this narrative. That hunch is confirmed in this chapter.

The chronology implied by this episode is suggestive. Dinah, who is raped and requested in marriage, must be at least a teenager. Therefore, Jacob must have been at Shechem for a considerable time, for no more than six or seven years had elapsed between her birth and Jacob's arrival in the country (cf. 30.21; 31.41; von Rad 1972: 331). He has as yet not returned to Bethel (cf. 35.1-15). Chapter 33 ended with Jacob fulfilling part of the vow he had made at Bethel: building an altar to recognize God (33.20 cf. 28.21). But there was more to his vow than this. He had also intimated that Bethel would in future be a cultic site to which (by implication), he would return, and that he would pay a tithe to God (presumably at that location, 28.22; cf. 35.1-15). Thus his vow has been only partly honoured and as Dinah grows into adulthood he seems to be in little hurry to complete his obligation. The events of this chapter provide the occasion for Jacob to move on to Bethel.

Major motifs of the Jacob story, namely deceit and conflict, occur here once again. The sons of Jacob appear as characters in their own right for the first time. Once they have vented their rage at the rape of Dinah, their first act is one of deceit (34.13 cf. 27.35; see also 37.12-36); like father, like sons. Their coldly calculated deception centres on the conditions for marrying Dinah. Even without the narrator's warning (34.13a), the marriage contract seems suspicious to the reader. Abraham and Isaac had been adamant that their sons should not marry Canaanite women (24.3-4; 28.1-2). That circumcision of foreign men would render them worthy to marry Dinah, and Hivite women to marry Jacob's sons, is improbable from the outset. Just as Jacob had 'loved' ('*hb*, 29.18, 20, 30) Rachel, and had arranged terms with Laban for marrying her but was deceived, so now, Shechem 'loves' ('*hb*, 34.3) Dinah, arranges terms for marrying her but is deceived by her brothers. Here, however, the deception is far greater than anything seen before, for it is a life and death matter. Laban had simply substituted a different woman; Jacob's sons plan a premeditated massacre.

At first the Hivites, (Shechem the rapist apart), appear to be decent folk, naive even, fooled by Jacob's sons. There is deep dramatic irony in the speech of Hamor and Shechem before the city elders, 'These people are friendly (*šālēm*)' (34.21). This had indeed been Jacob's initial experience of the Hivites, 'Jacob came safely (*šālēm*) to the city of Shechem' (33.18). But the cover of Jacob's sons has already been blown by the narrator's note to the reader (34.13), and the speech at the city gate reveals what consummate liars they were. One would do well, however, not to have too much sympathy for Hamor and Shechem. Just as Jacob and Laban had vied with each other in out-deceiving the other, so this father and son prove to be worthy combatants for Jacob's sons, for they are economical with the truth when speaking to their elders. In advocating intermarriage as a principle they do not mention that Shechem himself is contemplating this, nor the fact that he has raped his prospective bride. If the elders had known, would they have suggested caution, being more awake to possible reprisals than the more emotionally involved father and son? When Hamor had spoken to Jacob's family he had promised that 'the land shall be open to you; live and trade in it, and get property in it' (34.10). No such agreement is mentioned to the elders. Rather, the opposite impression is given, 'Will not their livestock, their property, and all their animals be ours?' (34.23a). Is it simply the demands of persuasive rhetoric which causes Hamor and Shechem to modify the facts? To whom were they telling the truth—to Jacob's sons or to their own elders? Perhaps the conniving had been present from the outset when they approached Jacob's family. If so, they have been trumped by Jacob's sons. This provides shades of Jacob and Laban once again. The irony of the claim that all the livestock, property and animals of Jacob's family would be theirs is rammed home by Jacob's sons who 'took *their* flocks and *their* herds, *their* donkeys, and whatever was in the city and in the field' (34.28). In addition, 'all their little ones and their wives' (34.29) are taken. What happens to these juvenile and female Hivites? Do they become slaves, or are they incorporated in some way into the ancestral family? If the women become subsidiary wives, then Jacob's sons' words, 'We will take your daughters for ourselves' (34.16),

have an ironic fulfilment—certainly not what Hamor and
Shechem envisaged. More darkly, perhaps Jacob's sons have
their way with these women just as Shechem had with Dinah.
Mass rape in return for a single act.

Just as the deception theme is intensified in this chapter, so is
the motif of conflict. Previously, conflict between Jacob and
Esau or Jacob and Laban, perhaps even between Rachel and
Leah, had threatened violence, but nothing had actually
happened. Here, conflict yields its full fruit: not simply personal
animosity, but the massacre of a whole city.

The duplicity and carnage of ch. 34 forms a marked contrast
to the previous chapter. Shechem comes before Jacob's family
asking, 'Let me find favour with you' (34.11). This should have
struck a responsive chord with Jacob, for he too had used those
very words as he sent his messengers to meet Esau (32.5), and as
he prostrated himself before his brother (33.8, 10, 15). In both
cases the party making the request is in the wrong, yet neither
explicitly asks for forgiveness. Esau had responded magnani-
mously. How does Jacob's family respond when the shoe is on
the other foot? Chapters 33 and 34 juxtapose quite different
responses to wrongs committed. The depth of Esau's forgiveness
is reinforced.

What are we to make of the characters in this chapter? Dinah
is at one and the same time the most central yet most marginalized character. The only time she is the subject of a verb is in the
introductory statement, where we are told that she, 'Went out to
visit the women of the region' (34.1). It is perhaps indicative of
her fate in this story that some commentators have questioned
the propriety of even this innocent action (see, e.g., Ross 1988:
572; Wenham 1993: 310). From that point onwards she is entirely
passive, whenever mentioned always the object of a verb. She is
raped, loved and wanted by Shechem (34.2-4); discussed and
negotiated for by each family (34.6-17); taken from Shechem's
house (34.26); and the subject of a final rhetorical flourish from
her brothers (34.31). In none of this do we ever learn Dinah's
attitude. Being raped is obviously against her will. But does she
later love Shechem? What are her opinions about the negotiations and agreed conditions for her marriage? Note that Rebekah
was asked regarding her willingness to accept her marriage
arrangements (24.8, 57), so it cannot be argued that women's
opinions were never sought in these matters. Is Dinah content to
stay with Shechem? Does she consider herself to have been

treated like a whore (34.31)? Unlike several other female characters in Genesis, Dinah does not emerge from the shadow of the
males. Given social norms of sexual etiquette (e.g., Deut. 22.13-
21), the brothers' act of vengeance also removes her only hope of
marriage, presumably making her the only permanently barren
woman in Genesis. She pays the price for teaching the Hivites a
lesson. She remains Victim, Object, Silent Observer.

Shechem, Dinah's violator, is presented in more detail, but
hardly in a sympathetic manner. The impetuosity of his assault
is captured by the quick succession of three verbs, which translated literally reads, 'he saw her, seized her and raped her' (34.2).
He exhibits the same impulsiveness as Esau who forfeited his
birthright as 'he ate and drank, and rose and went his way'
(25.34). But just as Esau exhibited two sides to his nature, so
does Shechem. His lust has no sooner been inflamed and extin-
guished, than he 'loved' her and 'spoke tenderly' to her (34.3).
While he might be presented here as the split-personality tender-
rapist, the impulsive side of his nature predominates, giving the
overall picture of being a spoilt child who must get whatever he
desires. By comparison, his father Hamor is far more cautious
and calculating. He begins the negotiations for his son's marriage
arrangements with no admission of wrongdoing, couching his
proposals in generous but vague and guarded terms (34.8-10).
Shechem, however, confirms his headstrong nature, offering to
give whatever Jacob's family demands: 'Whatever you say to me
I will give. Put the marriage present and gift as high as you like'
(34.11b-12a). The actual price demanded by Dinah's brothers is
of course even higher than his youthful enthusiasm had bar-
gained for. He pays with his life.

Jacob's reaction to his daughter's rape is revealing. He
remained silent; he 'held his peace' (34.5). One might think that
he does so initially because he feels vulnerable with his sons
absent. But surely some form of protest, if only perfunctory,
should be expected, even if Dinah is only Leah's daughter. But
no reaction of Jacob to the rape itself is ever recorded; that is left
to her brothers and the narrator (34.7). It is the father of the
villain rather than of the victim who takes the initiative (34.6).
And even at the end of the chapter Jacob's indignation is confined
to Dinah's brothers who slaughtered the Hivites. Yet he objects
not to their deception (one could hardly expect that from *Jacob*),
nor to the genocide, but to the possible reprisals against him by
the aggrieved Canaanites (34.30). Jacob has become 'odious' in

their eyes. He has not endeared himself to this reader either. His major concern is for his own skin. The rape of his daughter does not threaten it, but his sons' massacre does, hence his differing reactions.

No individual son of Jacob stands out in this chapter. They act together in brotherly solidarity, whether it is herding the cattle (34.5), reacting to the news of Dinah's rape (34.7), or concocting their deception where each Hivite has his penis modified in preparation for the poetic retribution for Shechem's penetration of Dinah (34.13-15). They seem to be genuinely aggrieved at their sister's rape. NRSV translates that they 'were indignant' (34.7), but their emotions seem to be stronger than this. The root 'ṣb used here also describes God's reaction to the immense wickedness of the world in Noah's day (6.6 cf. 3.16-17). It suggests a more personal involvement in her fate, such as 'were grieved' (cf. ASV, NAS), rather than mere indignation. The nearest they get to individual action is when the massacre is carried out by Dinah's full brothers Levi and Simeon (34.25). The plundering of the city is still a group action undertaken by 'the other sons of Jacob' (34.27). As a group they take over Jacob's role, for it is they alone who respond to the marriage proposals from Hamor and Shechem (34.13 cf. 24.50, 55). They begin by referring to Dinah as 'our sister' (34.14) but conclude by calling her 'our daughter' (34.17). In the absence of any initiative from Jacob they have assumed his role as father. As the roles of father and brothers become confused, one might wonder which of them has acted correctly. Jacob's seeming indifference cannot be condoned, but the brothers' eradication of an entire city for one rape, and their possible mass rape of its women, seems an over-reaction on the other side.

While this story might seem at first sight to be an interlude in the patriarchal story, it contains the three major elements of the Abrahamic blessing. God had promised that Abraham would become a great nation. If only the marriage arrangements had not been a subterfuge to put the Hivites off their guard, then a significant step forward could have been achieved here, with the possibility of becoming 'one people' with the people of the land (34.16, 22). Such assimilation and numerical advance is scotched by the massacre. Similarly, the land promise could have received a boost if they had accepted Hamor's offer, 'the land shall be open to you ... get property in it' (34.10). But the bloodbath means that the next episode sees them on the move once again. Abraham had been ordered to 'be a blessing' (12.2). It goes without saying that this treachery does not qualify. Whatever we make of Jacob in this chapter, his assessment that he has become 'odious' to the Canaanites is correct. In fact sexual encounters, potential or otherwise, between women in the patriarchal household and foreign dignitaries, always seem to produce animosity with the nations (cf. 12.18-20; 20.9-10; 26.9-11). Previous examples had been motivated by a fear that the patriarch would be killed. Here, the patriarchal family shows that the nations have more to fear from them than vice-versa. Dinah's brothers appear to have assumed the mantle of Esau, of whom it was predicted 'By your sword you shall live' (27.40). The nations are still waiting to receive a blessing from Abraham's descendants. (For an intriguing counter-reading of this chapter, see Bechtel 1994.)

Genesis 35

35.1-15

Chapter 34 had included reminders that Jacob's vow taken at Bethel (28.20-22) had not been fulfilled completely. Those deficiencies are largely made good in this section. Since arriving in Canaan Jacob has shown no inclination to return to Bethel, and he does so here only after receiving a divine command (35.1). His return to Bethel is clouded by circumstances similar to those which accompanied him there all those years before. In ch. 28 he had arrived as a fugitive from the revenge of his brother. Now he returns, partially at least, as a fugitive from the revenge of Shechem's neighbours—a point explicitly anticipated by Jacob (34.30) and underlined here (35.5). Bethel is not only a place for human-divine encounter, but also a place of refuge for Jacob. The divine favours given at Bethel on both occasions (28.13-15; 35.10-12), contrast with the reasons for Jacob's arriving there in the first place. Thus the tension between human action and divine favour seen throughout the Jacob story continues (see, e.g., 28.10-22; 31.1-21; 32.22-32; 33.1-20).

God's command (35.1), and Jacob's speech to his household (35.2-3), both recall his previous visit. Jacob had vowed, 'If God will be (*hyh*) with me (*'immādî*), and will keep me in this way (*derek*) that I go (*hlk*) ...' (28.20). Anticipating his return Jacob says that he will build an altar, 'to the God who ... has been (*hyh*) with me (*'immādî*) wherever (*derek*) I have gone (*hlk*)' (35.3). These strong verbal links bring his vow into the foreground.

Jacob's list of conditions had continued to demand that God should provide him with bread, clothing and a peaceful return home. If God provided all of these then Yahweh would be his God, the pillar he erected at Bethel would become God's house and he would pay a tithe to Yahweh (28.20-22). God's provision (e.g., 32.5a) and a peaceful homecoming (33.18) have been achieved already. He has already acknowledged God to be his God (33.20). That commitment is reinforced here by putting away foreign gods (35.2), and his motives for hiding (*ṭmn*) the gods under the tree seem to be purer than Rachel's who hid (*śîm*) them in the camel's saddle (31.34). Once at Bethel he erects an altar and names the site 'El-Bethel', establishing it as he promised as a cultic site (28.22). The only element of his previous vow which he does not explicitly fulfil is the paying of a tithe to God. He has already given a large proportion of his wealth to his brother Esau (33.10-11). But he had promised God 'of all that you give me I will surely give one-tenth to you' (28.22b). In light of all the other evidence, perhaps we should give Jacob the benefit of the doubt and assume that the payment of tithe was included in the erection of the altar and pillar, and the giving of offerings (35.7, 14). For the first time in the narrative the reader might feel easy about assuming the best rather than worst about Jacob's actions.

This paragraph makes great use of the motif of naming by presenting several examples of naming, renaming, self-naming and duplicate naming. The naming of the grave of Rebekah's nurse is straightforward enough (35.8), if a little puzzling (see below). Luz for the second time is renamed Bethel, or rather El-Bethel (35.7). And Jacob himself is renamed Israel for the second time (35.10). God introduces himself by giving his name 'I am God Almighty (El Shaddai)' (35.11). Further on in the chapter one character is given two names: Rachel names her son Benoni but Jacob renames him Benjamin (35.18). Places also are given more than one name by the narrator, Ephrath/Bethlehem (35.19) and Mamre/Kiriath-arba/Hebron (35.27). These namings lead on to even more extensive lists of names in the genealogies that follow (35.22b-26; 36.1-43). Thus beginning in small measure in this paragraph, and gathering strength as the text continues, a catalogue of details intrudes into the narrative flow of Genesis, telegraphing to the reader that this major section of the book is about to conclude in like manner to the previous two major sections (cf. 11.10-26; 25.1-18).

It is appropriate therefore, that interspersed among the naming and genealogical details are reminders of the patriarchal promises which have bound the narrative together from the outset. Their repetition here provides a partial summary of those foundational motifs. More particularly, the covenant-dialogue between God and Abraham found in 17.1-21 is recalled here. God's self-introduction, 'I am God almighty', (17.1; 35.11), a patriarchal renaming (17.5; 35.10), and the promises of nationhood (17.6; 35.11), a line of kings (17.6; 35.11), and land (17.8; 35.12), are all present in both. Such echoes of the patriarchal promises affirm Jacob as continuing not only the family line, but also maintaining God's favour. However, they also underline that nothing promised to Abraham in ch. 17 has come to fruition, nor yet to Jacob. The stuttering progress towards fulfilment continues.

The most puzzling element in this paragraph is the death notice of Deborah, Rebekah's nurse (35.8). She is, presumably, the same anonymous nurse who accompanied Rebekah from Laban's house (24.59). Westermann considers it to be 'beyond comprehension what Rebekah's nurse is doing in Jacob's caravan' (Westermann 1985: 552). Surely she could not have accompanied Jacob to and from Haran. Whatever the answer is to this conundrum, the effect of her death notice in this context is important. The narrator has provided the death notices for Sarah (23.1-2), and for Rachel in the next paragraph (35.19), but for Rebekah, the death of *her nurse* is provided. Perhaps depriving Rebekah of a death notice, but providing one for her nurse, passes silent comment on her role in the story. Others who died were remembered; but Rebekah has died and been forgotten. (Her burial place is mentioned in passing only in 49.31). She died without ever seeing her son again (cf. 27.44-45), and appears to have said more than she realized when she told Jacob, 'Let your curse be on me, my son' (27.13; see Baldwin 1986: 149).

35.16-29

Despite God's command to, 'go up to Bethel, and *settle* there' (35.1), he now moves on. He seems as reluctant to stay as he was to go in the first place. On leaving, Rachel dies giving birth to a son. During her labour the midwife encourages her by saying, 'Do not be afraid; for now you will have another son' (35.17). This might be conventional reassurance routinely given to mothers (cf. 1 Sam. 4.20), but perhaps unwittingly the midwife reminds Rachel of her previous wish uttered at the birth of

Joseph, 'May the Lord add to me another son!' (30.24). The pathos of her previous complaint to Jacob about her childlessness, 'Give me children, or I shall die!' (30.1), now turns to deep irony as she dies in the act of giving birth. One of the curses on the first Woman had been simple pain in childbirth (3.16), but Rachel pays the ultimate price.

The ambiguity of this event, which juxtaposes the blessing of a new son's arrival with the tragedy of his mother's death, is amplified by the names given to the child. His mother calls him Ben-oni (35.18). Since she names him with her last breath, the name is usually interpreted negatively to mean 'son of my sorrow', but it could equally be translated positively as 'son of my strength' (see, e.g., Speiser 1964: 274). His father renames him Benjamin, conventionally interpreted as giving him the position of great honour as 'son of the right hand'. But it could also be seen as simply 'son of the south', a reference not only to the geographical location of his birth but also poignantly to his mother's grave. Thus both names are open to positive or negative interpretations.

Reuben is mentioned in consecutive verses (35.22-23). First he has sexual relations with his father's concubine Bilhah, and then we are reminded of his status as Jacob's firstborn son. These two points are closely connected. With the repeated reversal of primogeniture in Genesis, does Reuben's act and the narrative's reminder of who he is, 'Jacob's firstborn' (35.23), drop a hint that something might be brewing here, and that Reuben's expected inheritance of the firstborn's rights might be in jeopardy? (see 37.12-36). Reuben is the firstborn son, but by the less-favoured wife, and he has had sex with Bilhah. That Reuben's act might have dire consequences is hinted by the verbal echo of the rape of Dinah. Shechem 'lay' (*škb*) with Dinah (34.2, 7) and Jacob 'heard' (*šm'*) of it (34.5), and likewise Reuben 'lay' (*škb*) with Bilhah and Jacob 'heard' (*šm'*) of it (35.22). We never do learn what Jacob's view of Dinah's rape was; we must wait a considerable time to discover what he thought of Reuben's misdemeanour (cf. 49.3-4). Shechem's rape of Dinah is self-evidently a crime born of lust, but Reuben's motivation is less clear. Most likely he was attempting to assert his position and indicate who would inherit his father's authority, lest anyone reflecting on several reversals of primogeniture should wonder (cf. 2 Sam. 16.20-23; Brueggemann 1962: 284). Conjugal rights have already caused enough conflict in this narrative without Reuben adding to it. In fact, this is the second time that he has been involved in such affairs. In 30.14 he was the young innocent, bringing mandrakes to his mother, which produced conflict and bartering over the conjugal rights of warring wives. In this present episode Reuben is a mature and apparently scheming son who seems to have learned from his mother and Rachel some of the finer points of sexual politics.

Jacob finally meets Isaac. He has delayed longer over seeing his father than he had even in returning to Bethel, the very place where he had expressed the wish to 'come again to my father's house' (28.21). Simply returning to the land seems to have been sufficient in Jacob's mind for fulfilling the conditions of his vow. He returns to his father's house just in time for the funeral. It is customary for commentators to note that Isaac has lingered for a very long time since announcing his imminent death in 27.2. Rather than this being a problem, however, it serves an important narrative purpose. Isaac's role in the narrative has been so muted that ever since his rescue from death in ch. 22 he has hardly been alive. The action in the narrative passes from Abraham to Jacob by way of Rebekah. A lingering death for Isaac confirms his marginal role as his sons, wife and daughters-in-law carry the burden of initiative. During all of this extended narrative Isaac 'does not know the day of [his] death' (27.2). Thus the narrative gives Isaac two death-bed scenes. At the first, the decisive rupture between the two brothers is made (27.1, 7, 29, 40); at the second, they are reunited (35.27-29). The first had confirmed the divine priority of Jacob over Esau; the second lists them in reverse order, as Isaac would have preferred it, 'his sons Esau and Jacob buried him' (35.29b cf. 25.9). The narrative's description of Isaac's death and burial is done with almost unseemly haste. We are given much more leisurely and detailed accounts of his near death in ch. 22 and his anticipated demise in ch. 27 than we are of his actual death. Those incidents on Mt Moriah and in Isaac's tent were crucial events in the ongoing fate of the patriarchal promises. But Isaac has long since served his purpose, hence his summary dismissal. His death here is just one more detail in a catalogue of deaths, births, namings, itineraries and genealogies—a clearing of the decks for the next major section of the book.

Genesis 36

The extensive genealogy of Esau, which constitutes the bulk of this chapter, is just what one would expect at this point. The previous chapter had given all the appearances of bringing the

Jacob story to its conclusion, and now the line of the non-chosen is listed in preparation for the following story of Jacob's family. Ishmael had received the same treatment in 25.12-18, anticipating the story of Isaac's line. In the sequence of the genealogies the sons of Jacob (35.22b) are given precedence over the sons of Esau (36.1). But sandwiched in between these two listings is a reminder that this overturns the rights of primogeniture: 'his sons Esau and Jacob buried him' (35.29b). This makes one more silent comment on the ways of God in this narrative.

There is only one interlude in the unremitting genealogical information. The separation of Esau and Jacob, already introduced in 33.16-17, is expanded on. The two brothers had been separated for many years because of personal antagonism. They separate again here. But the reason for living separately is vastly different this time: there is simply not enough land to support them both (36.7). Just how prosperous both brothers must have become can be seen when one recalls Hamor's confident assertion to his city elders concerning Jacob's family that 'the land is large enough for them' (34.21). It is no longer large enough for Jacob and Esau. This simple fact provides food for thought in a reflection on the blessings and promises which have been woven into the texture of this narrative. That Jacob should have great material prosperity should come as no surprise, given the content of Isaac's blessing (27.28), his success in out-manoeuvring Laban (30.41-43), and general divine guidance. That Esau should find himself laden down with 'his wives, his sons, his daughters, and all the members of his household, his cattle, all his livestock, and all the property he had acquired in the land of Canaan' (36.6), is ironic in the extreme when one considers the direction this narrative has taken. Jacob's schemings, deceptions, flights and hardships, perpetrated and endured in order to secure the blessing, seem to have paid off in the long run. But Esau who had sold his birthright and lost the blessing, and who was too dull to manufacture elaborate ruses to regain them, who forgave Jacob when he had him at his mercy, and who initially refused his brother's offer 'accept my present/blessing' (33.10), *seems to be no less blessed than Jacob*. The intriguing ambiguity of Isaac's apparent anti-blessing which allowed room for true blessing rather than curse has been triumphantly exploited (see 27.39). Yet not all has been made good. The very fact that Esau's genealogy is being listed now is evidence that no matter how much wealth he displays, how many sterling qualities he might have, and no matter where the reader's sympathies lie, he is not the chosen son. The patriarchal line, and the fulfilment of the promises, should they ever come, are invested not in his children but in Jacob's. Such are the inscrutable ways of God. These are made all the more incomprehensible by the narrator's habit of foregrounding, on the one hand, Jacob's negative qualities and Esau's positive attributes on the other.

Not only is Esau presented as being in many respects no worse off than Jacob, but also as holding the advantage in certain matters. For example, Jacob had been promised that 'a company of nations ... and kings shall spring from you' (35.11 cf. 17.6). Chapter 36 provides a list of 'kings who reigned in the land of Edom, before any king reigned over the Israelites' (36.31). So both brothers produce kings, but Esau does so before Jacob and in so doing perhaps achieves a measure of nationhood before Jacob also. As the nationhood promise has progressed it will be remembered that Abraham had two sons, but only one through whom the promises could run (e.g., 17.21). Isaac had two sons, but only one was chosen. The genealogies list the numerous sons of Esau, now out of contention as the blessed offspring. Jacob's 12 sons have been enumerated (35.22b-26), but with no suggestion yet as to whether only one of them will be considered worthy to receive the mantle of blessedness.

As far as the land promise is concerned the two brothers might at first sight seem to be equals, for there is not room for both of them to live 'in the land where they were living (*māgûr*, literally 'living as a foreigner', 'sojourning', cf. RSV)' (36.7). In other words, neither Jacob nor Esau possesses any land yet. However, the last words of the chapter list the clans of the Edomites 'according to their settlements in *the land that they held*' (36.43b). While 36.43 projects into the future, there is a telling juxtaposition with the next sentence: 'Jacob settled in the land where his father *had lived as an alien (mgr)*' (37.1). So we know that Esau's descendants will possess land, but the only property Jacob owns is a plot bought for 'one hundred pieces of money' (33.19). Jacob might have been blessed but Esau has hardly been cursed.

Genesis 37–50:
The Story of Jacob's Family

Genesis 37
This major new block of Genesis begins like the previous one with a *tôlᵉdōt* formula (25.19; 37.2), fraternal animosity (25.22-23; 37.2b-11), parental favouritism (25.28; 37.3-4), and the prospect of the younger lording it over his elders (25.23d, 29-34; 37.8, 10). In both contexts divine oversight is either stated explicitly (25.23) or implied (37.5-11). Thus while the plot moves on to new scenes it does so in such a manner as to suggest that the episodes beginning here will contain variations on familiar themes.

One difference to strike the reader is its more expansive style than chs. 1-36. The narrative embroiders and dwells upon familiar motifs: the inscrutability of divine involvement; complexity of characterization; ambiguity of human motive; complication of previous expectations and so on. These concerns are seen clearly in Joseph, the dominant character in the story. It is his essentially enigmatic character that casts its shadow over the entire narrative, for much of which he is as unfathomable as God. In addition, the relationship which the ancestral family has with the wider world, a familiar motif in previous narratives as an aside to the main plot, is here brought to the centre.

37.1-11
The story begins with reminders of the land (37.1) and nationhood (37.2a) promises. Both of these elements have been threatened before and this new block begins by promising much the same. The statement that 'Jacob settled in the land ...' (37.1), does not require permanent settlement. The same term (*yšb*) was used to describe Abraham's pauses at nomadic encampments (e.g., 13.18; 20.1; 22.19), and describes Jacob's initial one month sojourn with Laban (29.14). Isaac's blessing on Jacob when he set off to Laban had expressed the wish that Jacob would 'take possession (*yrš*) of the land where you now live as an alien (*māgûr*)' (28.4). But so far

Jacob has done nothing more than Abraham and Isaac before him who 'had lived as an alien (*māgôr*)' (37.1). His hold on the land promises seems to be as tenuous as theirs had been. Indeed, by the end of the chapter, and for most of chs. 39–50, the focus shifts to Egypt. Thus Jacob's status contrasts with that of Esau and his descendants 'in the land that they held' (36.43).

Attention moves immediately from the land to Jacob's progeny (37.2b). Straightaway we see the potential for family discord. While working with some of his half-brothers Joseph brings 'a bad report of them' to Jacob. The content of the report is not given, nor whether it was justified or not. The word for report (*dibbâ*), however, suggests fabrication or slander in the majority of its uses (cf. Num. 13.32; 14.36-37; Ps. 31.13 [14]; Prov. 10.18; Jer. 20.10). On first meeting Joseph, therefore, the reader is alerted to the complexities of his characterization. Does he bring an innocent report of his brothers' bad behaviour, or does he concoct a fib in order to ingratiate himself with the father who already shows him favouritism?

The explanation that Jacob loved Joseph because he was the son of his old age might be true as far as it goes. The full reason, however, is that in his old age the wife he loved gave birth to Joseph as her firstborn (30.23-24). Such favouritism, illustrated elsewhere in Genesis, does not bode well (25.28; 29.30). We sense that open family strife, already intimated by Joseph's 'bad report', and now fuelled by Jacob's outrageous gift of a lordly garment to his favourite, cannot be far off.

Sure enough, hatred bursts on to the scene. The description of the other sons' hatred, like Joseph's 'bad report', is tantalisingly ambiguous. Syntactically, the phrase 'they hated him' (37.4), could refer to Jacob as much as to Joseph, and contextually Jacob's flagrant favouritism could support such a translation. The next verse, however, conveys their hatred of Joseph in such a way as to suggest that he is the focus of attention in 37.4, but the initial ambiguity alerts the reader to the risk that Jacob is taking. Joseph's risk is equally clear. He claims to have had dreams that picture his family bowing before him, and relates these dreams with naive gusto (37.6, 9). His announcement of the dreams drives the wedge more firmly between himself and his brothers.

The two dreams are similar but not identical. The first is transparent in meaning, with the brothers' sheaves bowing down before Joseph's. The second dream reiterates the brothers' subservience with its image of the 'eleven stars' bowing down. It adds a new element by referring to the sun and moon, which do the same (37.9). Once again, the second dream seems transparent and Jacob's interpretation seems to be the only one possible—that Joseph's brothers (eleven stars), father (sun) and mother (moon) will bow down before him (37.10). The importance of these dreams for the rest of chs. 37–50 can hardly be overestimated. They have the same function in chs. 37–50 as the divine command at creation (1.28), the promises given to Abraham (12.1-3), and the divine oracle (25.23) and Isaac's blessings (27.27b-28; 39-40), have in their respective narratives. Their significance for the rest of the narrative is not diminished by the initial uncertainty of whether these are divine dreams or simply the product of Joseph's own desire (see 38.24-30; 39.1-6; 40.1-23; 41.1-36; 42.1-17, 18-28 and so on). Note that the first dream would be fulfilled if Joseph's brothers bowed down before him, but for the second dream to be fulfilled, brothers and parents must do so (for more detail see Turner 1990a: 143-53).

In light of Jacob's preferential treatment of Joseph one might well wonder whether the first dream predicts the future or reflects the present. One can already see the possible seeds of its fulfilment in the opening scenes of this chapter. The second dream, however, raises far more questions. For brothers to bow down to Joseph might be unusual; for his father to do so almost unthinkable; but for his mother to do so is impossible. For Joseph's mother, Rachel, is dead (35.19). This blatant fact renders the second dream as a whole impossible to fulfil. If nothing else, this bizarre element indicates that there is more to the second dream than meets the eye. Jacob himself underlines this with his expostulation, 'What kind of a dream is this that you have had?' (37.10). No wonder that Jacob 'kept the matter in mind' (37.11). Readers would do well to do the same.

There are other reasons why Jacob should mull over Joseph's dreams. They present in graphic imagery the reversal of primogeniture, the institution which Jacob himself had sought to reverse. It too had been predicted of Jacob that his brother would bow down to him. But that had never occurred (see 27.29; 33.1-20). If Jacob never saw its fulfilment, might Joseph too be disappointed? Thus even those parts of the dreams which are understandable have no guarantee of fulfilment, if previous episodes in Genesis are anything to go by.

The response to Joseph's dreams is hatred (37.8) and jealousy (37.11a) from his brothers, and rebuke (37.11b) from his father. His brothers' hatred is underlined by a wordplay between Joseph's personal name and the brothers' hating him 'even more' (37.5, 8), both of which are formed from the root *ysp*.

37.12-36

The sequel to the scene of fatherly favouritism and brotherly antagonism opens by telegraphing that something nasty is about to happen to Joseph. Jacob sends Joseph off to visit his brothers at Shechem. This is the site of Dinah's rape (34.2), her brothers' bloody revenge (34.24-29), the place where Jacob's name was made odious to the Canaanites (34.30), so that the family required divine intervention (35.5). Why would the brothers choose such a provocative act as to go to Shechem? Is that why Jacob is concerned about their welfare (37.14)? And is it any less provocative of Jacob to send Joseph off in all his finery to his brothers? Was he blind to their animosity? Thus, as young Joseph sets out abroad to make an innocent visit to Shechem, like his sister before him, the negative tone of the opening verses gathers strength. To be found 'wandering in the fields' near Shechem (37.15) is a vulnerable state for a son of Jacob to be in. Jacob had arrived in peace (*šālēm*) at Shechem (33.18), yet his sojourn there resulted in anything but peace. He now tells Joseph to go to Shechem to see if all is well (*šālôm*) with his brothers (37.14), a rather foreboding task, since we know that Joseph's brothers 'could not speak peaceably (*šālôm*) to him' (37.4). Joseph does not find his brothers immediately, but has to continue his journey to Dothan. This delay increases the tension. He and they have survived the dangers of Shechem, but will he survive his brothers?

The very sight of Joseph in his distinctive garb coming into view is enough to raise his brothers' hackles. The reader's worst fears, raised by the memories of Shechem, are confirmed with the brothers' decision to murder Joseph. More than his 'bad report', his father's favouritism or the special robe which advertises his arrival, it is his dreams which trigger their fratricidal designs. The contempt and sarcasm is plain to hear: 'Here comes this dreamer (literally, 'master dreamer')' (37.19). By killing him they will negate the dreams' intolerable image of Joseph lording it over the rest of the family. Their gleeful conclusion summarizes their objective: 'We shall see what will become of his dreams' (37.20). We certainly shall.

Joseph is saved from the clutches of the other brothers by Reuben. Instead of despatching him quickly, Reuben's ploy of throwing him into a dry pit seems even more callous, condemning Joseph to a lingering death. And a poetically appropriate death at that—the depths of the pit forming an ironic contrast with the elevation predicted by the dreams. Yet Reuben has a beneficent intent, divulged only to the reader by the narrator (37.22b). In Reuben's absence, however, the other brothers are persuaded by Judah that Joseph's elimination will merely get rid of the troublesome youth. Far better to make a profit into the bargain (37.26-27). So he is sold to passing merchants (cf. 45.4).

Regardless of whether Joseph is murdered or sold into slavery, the brothers will have to explain his absence to their father. Strife between family members was a feature of chs. 25–36, and has repeatedly been associated with deception (e.g., between Jacob and Esau; Jacob and Laban). Here, the brothers' attempted deception of Jacob echoes in particular that which he himself perpetrated on Isaac (see also 34.1-31). Their sitting down for a meal while Joseph lies naked in the pit seems particularly callous. But Jacob's taking advantage of Esau and his deception of blind, senile Isaac were hardly less callous as he served up a meal for them both (25.29-34; 27.19-29). Distinctive clothing is at the centre of both episodes (27.15, 27; 37.31-33), as indeed are goats (27.9, 16; 37.31). There are contrasts too of course. The brothers had the bloodstained cloak sent to Jacob (37.32), while Jacob had gone into Isaac's tent and faced his father (27.18). Though originally planning to lie to Jacob's face (37.20), the brothers actually allowed Jacob to draw his own conclusion, 'a wild animal has devoured him' (37.33). Jacob it will be recalled, had been willing to tell a blatant lie (27.19). The verb 'to recognize' (*nkr*) is used in both scenes, in the first negatively, 'He did not recognize him' (27.23), and in the second positively, 'He recognized it' (37.33). These details present a picture of sons who have inherited their father's guile, though lacking his naked ambition perhaps. The arch-deceiver, however, is more easily deceived than his senile and decrepit father had been all those years ago. Isaac had at least asked some probing questions (see 27.18-29).

Taken as a group, Joseph's brothers act together to rid themselves of the nuisance of a younger brother. However, while Reuben's words suggest solidarity with his brothers' plans (37.22a), his intention is quite different (37.22b). Reuben is threatened as much as any other brother by Joseph's dreams, so why should he alone wish to restore him to Jacob? One would have thought that Reuben, the firstborn of Leah, and Joseph, the firstborn of Rachel, would have been natural antagonists. And since Reuben is the firstborn, he has most to lose if Joseph's dreams come to pass. Is it simply that as the eldest he feels that he should act more responsibly, or that he more than the others will be held accountable for Joseph's fate? Or are his motivations more complex than that? Perhaps Reuben's plan is to ingratiate himself with Jacob. If Joseph could not keep quiet about his dreams, he will certainly not desist from telling his father of how his other brothers had intended to kill him, but that Reuben had rescued him. If Joseph is Jacob's favourite son, there are good grounds for thinking that at this time Reuben was the least favoured. He had already staked a claim to Jacob's estate by sleeping with Bilhah (35.22; see 35.16-29). This would not only have alienated Jacob (cf. 49.4), but also Reuben's brothers, by committing incest with the mother of Dan and Naphtali (see 35.16-29). So, by rescuing Joseph, Reuben will restore his relations with Jacob and thus help him to achieve his ends. Unfortunately, the sale of Joseph to the traders scuppers these ambitions. No wonder that he cries, 'The boy is gone; and I, where can I turn?' (37.30). The alliteration, *'ênennû wa'ᵃnî 'ānâ 'ᵃnî-bâ*, graphically conveys Reuben's stuttering emotional response.

There is less doubt about the motives of Reuben's full brother Judah. His pragmatic advice is that they will gain more by selling Joseph than by killing him. His motivation is to line their pockets with 20 pieces of silver (37.28).

So three different courses of action are suggested in quick succession. Immediate death for Joseph (37.20); delayed death (37.21-22); being sold into slavery (37.27-28). This presents a picture of brothers who opportunistically seek to take advantage of the situation, rather than of a well thought out plot coming to fruition.

With such a fate for Joseph being telegraphed by all kinds of factors in the text, one wonders about Jacob's role in all of this. He knows about Joseph's tale-telling and bragging, and his own favouritism towards him. Yet he never seems to suspect the depth of his sons' antipathy towards Joseph. He sends him off to his brothers at Shechem of all places, unaccompanied. Having witnessed first hand the effects of favouritism and brotherly animosity in his earlier life one would have expected keener insight into human nature than this. Yet when he holds the blood stained cloak in his hands one cannot help but feel sympathy for him. While there might be an element of justice in seeing the arch-deceiver now being duped more consummately than he ever was by Laban, Jacob's mourning is touching (37.33-35). His torn clothes and sackcloth contrast with Joseph's fine apparel that, in part, provoked the brothers' deception. The solidarity shown by his sons in not divulging the truth, but consoling their father in his time of grief with sham concern (37.35), reveals just how much they had reviled Joseph.

There is a neat irony in Joseph being sold to Ishmaelites. Ishmael had been his father's favourite (17.18), but had ended up an outcast (21.10-21). Joseph is his father's favourite, but becomes an outcast. One is sold to the other. The branch of the family which was eliminated from the promised line by God himself, is instrumental in enslaving the one whose dreams had predicted would be the greatest of all. What Joseph makes of his deliverance from death and subsequent sale into slavery is not divulged. He remains silent and passive from the time he asks directions at Shechem until after he arrives in Egypt (though cf. 42.21). He might have escaped murder, but surely his dreams are now dead. Yet, just like his father before him, Joseph has left the promised land as the result of fraternal strife. And Jacob later had to face his brother. Will the same occur here? And as Jacob's meeting with Esau raised once again the predictions of the divine oracle and Isaac's blessing (see 33.1-20), will the dreams once again be brought to mind? (See 42.1-17.)

Genesis 38

This chapter provides an interlude by turning its attention from Joseph in Egyptian slavery to the exploits of Judah. Yet it does more than heighten the suspense regarding Joseph's fate. It builds on what has gone before, and also enriches the reading of Joseph's story once it resumes in ch. 39. For example, just as his sons, including Judah, deceived Jacob, so too in this chapter Tamar deceives Judah, which in turn anticipates how Potiphar will be deceived by his wife. In each case the deception involves presenting evidence that demands a verdict: the sons produce Joseph's bloodied cloak (37.32); Tamar produces Judah's signet, cord and staff (38.25); Potiphar's wife brandishes Joseph's garment (39.13-15, 18). The reversal of primogeniture, a key issue in Joseph's dreams, raises its head again at the birth of Perez and Zerah (38.27-30). There are more specific linguistic connections. The verb 'to recognize' (*nkr*), which had linked the deception of ch. 37 to that of ch. 27, is now picked up again here, (38.25-26). Yet again a goat is part of the intrigue (38.17 cf. 37.31). Jacob cannot be comforted (*nḥm*) at the supposed death of Joseph (37.35); Judah is comforted (*nḥm*) after the death of his wife (38.12; cf. Hamilton 1995: 431-32). Thus, just as the previous narrative foreshadows ch. 38, ch. 38 itself helps to shape the perspectives of the reader for encountering subsequent episodes.

38.1-11
Marrying a Canaanite had been ruled out by Abraham when finding a wife for Isaac (24.3), and Isaac himself commanded Jacob similarly (28.1-2). Esau's foreign wives it will be recalled, 'made life bitter for Isaac and Rebekah' (26.35 cf. 27.46). Now Judah marries a Canaanite. This not only marks a worrying departure from the tradition of the promised line, but also carries overtones of disapproval: 'Judah saw (*r'h*) the daughter ... he married (literally 'took', [*lqḥ*]) her' (38.2). This combination of verbs has been used earlier to describe the Woman's eating of the forbidden fruit (3.6); the sons of God cohabiting with the daughters of humans (6.2); the Pharaoh taking Sarai into his harem (12.15) and Shechem's rape of Dinah (34.2; though see 22.13; 30.9). So, can Judah's marriage spell anything but trouble? All of his sons are half-Canaanite and the daughter-in-law he chooses is also presumably a Canaanite. Judah's family is becoming merged with native Canaanite stock.

While Judah's marriage is irregular, his genealogical succession is recorded in reassuringly conventional language. '[Again] she conceived and bore a son' (38.3-4), announces the fertility of Judah's wife in the same words as those of 29.33-35, which described Leah's fecundity, climaxing in the birth of Judah himself. So the promise of nationhood to the ancestral family is not threatened in this generation by barren wives, as it was previously. A threat does arise unexpectedly, however, from God's judgments, first on Er for unspecified reasons (38.7), and then on Onan for practising *coitus interruptus* in order to preserve a larger portion of the family estate for himself (38.10). This leaves only Shelah to continue the line into the next generation. This small family scene might seem to have little to do with any of God's previous judgments on the grand scale. But the announcement that Er 'was wicked (*ra'*),' (38.7) recalls the same judgment

on humanity at the time of the Deluge, whose 'wickedness (*rā'â*) ...
was great in the earth' and whose thoughts were 'only evil (*ra'*)
continually' (6.5). Lot too had pleaded with the Sodomites not to
'act so wickedly (*r"*)' (19.7). Chapter 38 throws up some peculiar
points of contact also. What Er and Noah find or do in the sight
of the Lord is the inversion of their names. Er ('*r*) did evil (*r'*) in
the sight of the Lord (38.7). Noah (*nḥ*) found favour (*ḥn*) in the
sight of the Lord (4.8). Both have three sons (6.10; 38.3-5), are
parties to incestuous relationships (9.20 cf. 38.16-18), as also
was Lot (19.30-38). Furthermore, God judges the wickedness of
their associates (6.5; 8.21; 19.7, 24; 38.7, 10). God's judgment
which at first had encompassed the whole world with the Deluge,
then narrowed to the communities in the cities of the Plain, is
now meted out to individuals in a family.

With the death of his first two sons, Judah concludes that
Tamar is 'bad luck'. He banishes her to her father's house.
Despite his suggestion otherwise, he obviously has no intention
of giving Shelah to Tamar as her husband. If he fears that Shelah
will die if married to Tamar (38.11), then he will die regardless
of how old he is. Judah is just fobbing her off. Thus Tamar effectively becomes one more barren woman in the Genesis story.
Shelah, the son at the centre of this charade, was born at Chezib
(meaning 'lie'; 'deceit'). This now seems to be more than an incon-
sequential detail (38.5).

The demise of Judah's two sons provides the third opportunity
for mourning since Reuben's discovery of Joseph's sale. But while
Reuben's mourning was plaintive (37.29b-30a), and Jacob's
extravagant (37.33-35), Judah's is not recorded. To argue from
silence that Judah is being portrayed as more aloof might be
pressing the text too far. But one might well wonder when in the
next section one sees the ambiguity of 'the wife of Judah ... died;
and Judah was comforted' (38.12 literal translation). Was he
'consoled in his mourning for her, or relieved because she had
died?' (Gunn and Fewell 1993: 37).

38.12-23

Time passes and Judah's wife dies. He completes the requisite
mourning period and travels to the sheepshearing with his friend
Hirah. Judah had previously gone down (38.1); now he goes up
(38.12b), the contrasting verbs underlining a new departure in
the narrative. Tamar now reenters the fray, but her actions are
not immediately understandable. When she hears where Judah

is going she removes her widow's clothes, and donning a veil sits
by the road, thus adopting the attitude of a common prostitute
(38.15). But why is she doing this? It has something to do with
the fact that Judah has not given her Shelah as her husband,
even though the lad has now grown up (38.14b). But what is the
connection? It is only when Judah sees her and approaches her
for custom that we realize what her gambit is. She is hatching an
audacious scheme to overcome her enforced barrenness
(cf. 16.1-2). With Judah away from home and with his wife dead,
perhaps he will be open to some sexual adventure.

Judah approaches Tamar at Enaim, meaning 'two wells'.
Abraham's servant had met Rebekah and Jacob had met Rachel
at a well (24.13-15; 29.9-10). Will Judah's meeting with Tamar at
the wells be any less significant? These previous encounters had
enabled the ancestral family to continue into the next generation, and this is the very thing that Tamar craves, and Judah
prevents by his refusal to give her Shelah. After a brief, not to
say brusque, discussion concerning her fee, Judah unwittingly
has sex with his daughter-in-law. Tamar does to Judah what his
own mother Leah had done to his father (29.23-25). Chapter 37
had replayed Jacob's deception of Isaac. Chapter 38 replays
Laban's and Leah's deception of Jacob. Whatever other breaks
with convention are made in this chapter, deception continues
unabated. There is further irony in the fact that Judah's refusal
to give Shelah to Tamar is because he feared that Shelah would
die. But now, it would appear, by being duped into having sex
with his daughter-in-law they have both committed a capital
offence (cf. Lev. 20.12).

Judah emerges with little credit from this episode. Tamar
knows her father-in-law well enough to know that she does not
have to seduce him in order to get her way. Simply advertising
her availability at the roadside will be enough to trap him.
Tamar's cleverness highlights Judah's lust. He approaches his
daughter-in-law as brusquely as he had previously his wife (38.2
cf. 38.16). He has no intention of honouring the pledge he had
given to Tamar (38.11), but expects the 'prostitute' to honour
hers. He sends Hirah to retrieve his signet, cord and staff. The
fact that he sends a proxy might suggest that he prefers not to do
his own dirty work. His interest in redeeming his pledge is
consistent with his prior concern with money matters. He it was
who suggested that the brothers might as well make some profit
by selling Joseph (37.26-27). It is open to question, however,

whether his sexual lust made him pay more than the going rate
for Tamar's services. He had agreed to pay a kid, which he sends
off with Hirah. Proverbs 6.26 states that a whore's fee was a loaf
of bread. This would seem to be more usual, for if a young goat
was the usual fee charged, a few weeks' work would have given
a prostitute a sizeable flock. The pledge that Tamar forced out of
him is hardly less exorbitant than her fee, for his signet, cord
and staff amounted to his personal identity—worth far more
than the kid he is now sending. Such huge amounts reveal that
Judah's sexual drive clouded his judgment. That is why Judah
fears he will be laughed at (38.23).

Judah had thought Tamar was a 'prostitute (*zônâ*)' (38.15).
Yet Hirah enquires about 'the temple prostitute (*qᵉdēšâ*)' (38.21),
apparently a more acceptable occupation than a common whore.
Hirah is attempting to bring some respectability to this sordid
incident. But the narrator's rare act of divulging Judah's inner
thoughts (38.15, 'he thought her to be a prostitute'), means that
Hirah's etiquette might fool the townspeople, but not the
reader.

38.24-30

In 38.15 Judah approached Tamar precisely because 'he thought
her to be a prostitute (*zônâ*)'. Now he is told that 'Tamar has
played the whore (*znh*); moreover she is pregnant as a result of
whoredom (*zᵉnûnîm*)' (38.24). Judah's swift pronouncement of
capital punishment condemns his double standard more devas-
tatingly than it does her. His discovery of her indiscretion also
provides a convenient way out of Judah's obligation to give her
Shelah. Judah's death sentence on Tamar recalls God's despatch
of Er and Onan. But Er was 'wicked' (*raʿ*) and Onan selfish (at
least); but by Judah's own admission, Tamar has been 'in the
right' (38.26). The disparity between God's and Judah's judgments provides one more condemnation of Judah. Elsewhere,
the death of both parties was required if a man lay with his
daughter-in-law (Lev. 20.12). Not surprisingly, when Judah
discovers the truth, any legal requirements are conveniently
forgotten. She has duped him as triumphantly as he and his
brothers had Jacob, with the question 'see (*nkr*) now whether it
is your son's robe' (37.32), coming back to haunt him in Tamar's
words, 'Take note (*nkr*), please, whose these are' (38.25).

Judah and Tamar act in a very distant manner towards each
other. News of Tamar's pregnancy is conveyed to Judah by an

intermediary (38.24a), followed by Judah's death sentence in the third person (38.24b), while Tamar sends the incriminating evidence by proxy (38.25). Even Judah's admission of Tamar's integrity is worded, '*She* is more in the right' (38.26). There is never any face to face acknowledgment. At the end they remain as detached from each other as they had been during their impersonal act of sexual intercourse (cf. Gunn and Fewell 1993: 42; see 47.13-28).

Tamar's bearing twins to Judah, nevertheless, provides him with a form of compensation, restoring his two sons previously despatched by Yahweh. Up to this point it appeared that this branch of the ancestral family was facing extinction. Er died, quickly followed by Onan, then Judah's wife. Shelah apparently is not yet married. And Tamar faces the flames without having raised up any progeny for Er. However, whether Tamar's giving birth to twins is all good news is left open to question. The announcement 'there were twins in her womb' (38.27), replicates the announcement regarding Rebekah's pregnancy (25.24), and just as her twins were born in such a manner as to raise the question of who the firstborn was, so too with Perez and Zerah. Rebekah's twins had also struggled in the womb and beyond. Disputes between brothers, and arguments over the rights of the firstborn, seem set to continue. The fact that Esau, the spurned firstborn, had a grandson also called Zerah, adds to this impression (cf. 36.13, 17, 33). It is not only in Joseph's dreams that normal expectations are reversed.

In retrospect, Tamar's significance is clear. Like Sarah, Rebekah and Rachel before her, she has moved from barrenness to childbearing. She too has used deception to get her way, in the line of Rebekah, Jacob, Laban and Rachel (cf. Janzen 1993: 154). She does, however, elicit more sympathy than these earlier Machiavellian characters. Yet she is, quite likely, a Canaanite. If so, then she is yet one more example of a foreigner who betters a member of the ancestral family in the area of sexual/marital mores, as Abraham before Pharaoh (12.18-20) and Abimelech (20.9-10), and Isaac before Abimelech again (26.9-10), have amply demonstrated.

Genesis 39

God is mentioned often enough in chs. 37–50, with the personal name Yahweh found 11 times in chs. 38–39 and 49.18, and the title Elohim occurring 19 times throughout. But he rarely speaks (cf. 46.2-4), and to observe his actions one requires the insight of the narrator (e.g., 39.2) or Joseph's reflections (45.5; 50.20). As we shall see, however, even these latter examples are open to more than one interpretation. If elsewhere in Genesis human activity has been at the core of the narrative, then even more so here.

Despite this, the narrator is clear at the beginning of this chapter, that 'The Lord was with Joseph' (39.2a). This statement, however, reveals more about Yahweh than it does about Joseph. We should not assume that divine favour indicates a benign acceptance of Joseph's previous or subsequent activity. God's favour had rested on Jacob (e.g., 25.23; 28.10-15), yet this had not been because of any merit on Jacob's part. God's being with Joseph in Egypt, whence he has gone because of fraternal strife, should not be read more positively than God's appearance to Jacob at Bethel when he was running away from his brother's wrath.

39.1-6

When Abraham had gone down to Egypt, the Egyptians had succumbed to the physical beauty (*yāpeh*) of Sarah (12.11, 14). Now one of his great-grandsons is taken down to Egypt (39.1), and he is 'handsome (*yᵉpēh tō'ar*) and good-looking (*yᵉpēh mar'eh*)' (39.6), the very characteristics of his own mother Rachel, who was 'graceful (*yᵉpat tō'ar*) and beautiful (*yᵉpat mar'eh*)' (29.17). We can expect some sexual interest being taken in Joseph before too long.

Abraham's visit to Egypt had raised the issue of how he was going to be a blessing to the nations (12.1-3; cf. 12.10-20). He did not rise to the occasion, but Joseph increases expectations. His presence brings Yahweh's blessing on Potiphar's house (39.5; cf. 30.27).

Seeds of potential discord, however, are sown in the reader's mind. His new master, Potiphar, is described as being an 'officer' (*sārîs*) of Pharaoh (39.1). Elsewhere the term is translated 'eunuch' and on occasions conveys the narrower connotation of one who is castrated (e.g., Est. 2.3, 14-15; Isa. 56.3. On occasions eunuchs were married, see, e.g., Skinner 1930: 457). If that connotation is permitted here in 39.1, then the unit 39.1-6 has an introduction informing us of Potiphar's sexual impotence and a conclusion mentioning Joseph's sexual desirability. The potential for conflict within Potiphar's household is obvious.

Joseph's dreams had juxtaposed his lordship with others' subservience. Once he is in Potiphar's household he experiences both states himself. He is in control of everything that is Potiphar's (39.4-6); yet Potiphar is his master (39.2b-3). The juxtaposition of these two aspects recalls the motifs inherent to the dreams, reminding us to keep an eye out for their fulfilment, but also registering one more barrier to their realization.

39.7-18

Quite abruptly, Potiphar's wife is introduced, with her brusque demand for sex (cf. 38.16). In contrast to Joseph, no time is spent detailing her age or sexual allure (cf. 37.2; 39.6). She might be in the bloom of youth and ravishingly voluptuous; she might be an aging repulsive hag. So, just how much of a temptation is she to Joseph, whose good looks would suggest that he would not be deprived of female company? The narrative does nothing to criticize Joseph's refusal of course, but it would be good not to be too quick to eulogize him for this one decision.

The comparison with ch. 38 creates a context for further contemplating Joseph's situation. Both chapters present women who take the initiative in having sex with the male of their choice. Tamar, however, is presented more sympathetically than Potiphar's wife. Tamar took her initiative because of Judah's refusal to keep his word. Joseph's mistress on the other hand, with her imperious demand, simply uses her position of power to satisfy her lust. Yet perhaps even she is not presented entirely unsympathetically. If her husband is a eunuch, her desire for sexual relations can at least be understood. So the contrast between the two incidents in chs. 38 and 39 is not as simple as a switch from female justified/male condemned (38.26) to male justified/female condemned (39.7-18). There is little doubt, however, how Judah would have responded to such an approach for easy sex.

Joseph's loquacious rebuff of his mistress (39.8-9) contrasts with her blunt command, 'Lie with me' (39.7). The tenor of Joseph's response in which he rejects such 'great wickedness' (39.9), is reminiscent of Abimelech's moral outrage at Abraham's ruse which would have resulted in 'great guilt' (20.9). This present episode, however, breaks with the pattern established by such previous scenes (e.g., 12.10-20; 20.1-18; 26.6-16). Here, not only is the patriarch himself rather than his gorgeous companion desired, but also in previous sexual encounters between patriarchs and foreigners, the ancestral family has come off second best. But here that has been reversed. Joseph protests that he cannot have sex with another man's wife—a matter that did not seem to trouble Abraham or Isaac.

Joseph's rejection of her advances is recorded emphatically. First, from the narrator's perspective (39.12b), then from Potiphar's wife's perspective (39.13). She has been unambiguously spurned, and the repetition indicates that there is no point in her repeating yet again the invitation, 'Lie with me!'. The reiteration of her rebuff forms the bridge between her failed seduction and the revenge she now concocts.

Her accusation is phrased so as to give the worst possible impression. She twice says that Joseph 'came in to me (*bā' 'ēlay)*' (39.14b, 17b). The same combination of verb and preposition is used in ch. 38 to mean 'had sexual intercourse with' (38.2, 8, 9, 16, 18; cf. 29.21, 23; 30.3, 4, 16). Thus the initial impression she gives is that she has been raped. Only later is this impression modified, but her opening words to the servants, and then to her husband, are weighted to arouse maximum indignation. This is seen more clearly in a literal translation of 39.17, 'He came into me, the Hebrew slave whom you caused to come among us to mock me'. Her skill as a liar is seen clearly: she reverses the sequence of 39.12b-13 to claim that she cried out as soon as Joseph approached her (39.14); contrary to the narrative she claims that Joseph left his garment 'beside me' (39.15) rather than 'in her hand' (39.13). The former implicates Joseph as the one who removed his garment while the latter would implicate herself.

Her speech, however, accuses more than Joseph. NRSV starts with, 'See, my husband ...' but the Hebrew uses only a pronoun, 'See, *he* has brought among us ...' (39.14). She does not say, 'my husband', nor even 'your master', but impersonally and anonymously, 'he'. She then proceeds to blame Potiphar for the alleged attack, stating that his intention in employing Joseph was 'to insult us!'. Not merely to insult *me*, but *us*. Thus she not only accuses Joseph but also her husband, and attempts to unite her household against them both. Her accusation against her husband recalls Adam's accusation of God, 'The Hebrew servant, whom you have brought among us' (39.17), cf. 'The Woman whom you gave to be with me' (3.12), where Adam is equally impersonal in referring to his wife. Both speeches reveal strained relations if not outright animosity.

She is equally dismissive of Joseph, whom she refers to not as 'Joseph', nor as 'this Hebrew slave' but merely as 'a Hebrew man'.

The reasons for her animosity to Joseph are plain. But we must speculate as to why Potiphar is also the object of her vitriol. Perhaps, if Potiphar is a eunuch, her disdain for him is because he cannot have sex with her, while her anger towards Joseph is because he will not have sex with her. She is left thoroughly frustrated. The narrative presents her as someone who craves intimacy, conveying this through repeated uses of the prepositions *'el* or *'eṣel*, translated here as 'beside' or 'by': 'he would not consent to lie beside her' (39.10); 'he left his garment beside me' (39.15); 'she kept his garment by her' (39.16); 'he left his garment beside me' (39.18). In her request and accusation, and the narrator's description, her pathetic desire to have Joseph or his garment 'beside her' is revealed.

This is not the first time that Joseph has lost his clothing. He was stripped by his brothers who used his cloak to cover their tracks (37.23, 31-33). Similarly here, Potiphar's wife uses his cloak to deceive her husband (39.16-17). The first occasion marked a major transition in the narrative, where the hopes expressed in Joseph's dreams seemed to be annihilated. Its use again here marks another major development in the plot. The repetition of the garment (*beged*) motif is particularly appropriate here for the root *bgd* is occasionally used to connote adultery (Jer. 3.8; Mal. 2.10-16. Cf. Hamilton 1995: 465). The noun was also used in the previous episode in connection with Tamar's entrapment of Judah (38.14, 19).

39.19-23

Potiphar's reaction to his wife's report is swift and decisive. Some commentators are unconvinced that he fully believed his wife, because he does not order Joseph's execution for his alleged attempted rape (cf. Deut. 22.23-27). In addition, it could be argued that Potiphar's reaction is mild when compared with the bloody revenge of Dinah's brothers (34.25-29), or Judah's summary announcement of capital punishment on Tamar (38.24). It should not necessarily be assumed, however, that imprisonment was all that Potiphar had in mind for Joseph. For example, is Joseph's sojourn in prison merely an interlude before his trial and subsequent execution? Two of Joseph's fellow inmates illustrate the uneasy existence of being a prisoner in this gaol. The chief cupbearer is released to enjoy his freedom, but the chief baker is executed (40.20-22). Either fate conceivably awaits Joseph. Being placed in prison recalls the earlier act of placing Joseph in the pit, which was part of the brothers' murderous designs (37.22-24). While it is true that the text does not say with whom Potiphar became enraged (39.19), leaving open whether it was with his wife or Joseph, the more natural reading, I believe, is that Potiphar has been hoodwinked by his wife.

The chapter draws to a close by drawing on motifs with which it started. Chief among these is the assertion of Yahweh's presence with Joseph. The Lord's presence had made Joseph 'a successful man' (39.2), something noted by Potiphar also, with the result that Yahweh blessed Potiphar's house too (39.3, 5). We learn now that within prison 'the Lord was with Joseph and showed him steadfast love' (39.21) and that the chief gaoler trusted Joseph implicitly because 'the Lord was with him' (39.23). The result of this divine favour is that Joseph returns to the status he had at the beginning of the chapter. The chief gaoler puts (*nātan*) matters into his hand (*yād*, 39.22), just as Potiphar had 'put him in charge (*nātan b^eyādô*)' (39.4; cf. 39.8). Previously Joseph had been in charge of the house (*bayit*), now he is in charge of the prison, literally 'the round house' (*bêt hassōhar*).

Much space is devoted to underlining that Yahweh was with Joseph. Yet he was stripped and sold by his brothers, is a slave in a foreign land, was unjustly accused by his master's wife and now finds himself in prison, possibly awaiting a worse fate. What would his lot have been if the Lord had not been with him, we might well wonder. The juxtaposition of Joseph's true position, that is, the divine presence, in addition to the predictions of his dreams, and his now lowly estate might hint that some hidden purpose is being served in all of this.

Genesis 40

Joseph, in prison because of his refusal to 'sin (*ht'*) against God', (39.9), is joined by two others who have 'offended (*ht'*) their lord' (40.1). Whether the imprisonment of Pharaoh's officials is any more justified than Joseph's is difficult to determine. The term used for Pharaoh's anger (*qṣp*) can convey human response to a formal offence (Lev. 10.16), as well as a fit of pique (2 Kgs. 5.11; Est. 1.12). The way in which Pharaoh deals with the two later in the chapter provides no rationale for the different treatment he metes out. So miscarriages of justice might afflict more than just Joseph.

All three are confined 'in the house of the captain of the guard (*śar haṭṭabbāḥîm*)' (40.3 cf. 40.4). This same title was used earlier to designate Potiphar (37.36; 39.1). How many captains of the guard are there? If 'the captain of the guard' here is a circumlocution for Potiphar, then Joseph has remained under some form of 'house arrest' at Potiphar's. This is strongly implied by the information that they were all incarcerated 'in his master's house' (*bêt ˒ᵃdōnāyw*, 40.7), a term previously used to describe Potiphar's residence (39.2). The captain of the guard's attitude to Joseph certainly recalls that of Potiphar. Joseph had 'attended' (*šrt*) Potiphar who 'made him overseer' (*pqd*, 39.4-5). Now in prison, the captain of the guard 'charged' (*pqd*) Joseph with the other prisoners while he 'waited' (*šrt*) on them (40.4), who like Potiphar are officers/eunuchs (*sārîs*, 40.2, 7). If this captain of the guard is indeed Potiphar, and is to be distinguished from the chief jailer (39.21-23), then Joseph has once again 'found favour in [Potiphar's] sight' (39.4). Is this due to Joseph's sterling values again becoming evident because 'the Lord was with him', or does it suggest that his anger against Joseph is abating because of growing questions about his wife's accusation?

Joseph is serving once again, as he was at the beginning of the previous chapter. People are also dreaming again, which recalls the beginning of the whole story (37.5-11). Those initial dreams had foretold a future far different from Joseph's current state. So the fulfilment of dreams in this chapter raises once again the question of whether Joseph's dreams will be fulfilled. His brothers had sarcastically named Joseph 'the master of the dream' (37.19). And he now fills that role as a dream interpreter. Joseph offers his services with the words, 'Do not interpretations belong to God?'. This is, apparently, a rhetorical question with which all characters agree. His next words are, 'Please tell them to me' (40.8). Thus Joseph is claiming to have access to the mind of God (cf. 40.12, 18). The subsequent fate of the cupbearer and baker confirm Joseph's prowess as an interpreter of dreams (40.21-22). But does it also confirm that Joseph speaks for God? Joseph claims that interpretations come from God, yet in ch. 37 his brothers and father knew intuitively the meaning of Joseph's dreams.

The fulfilment of the dreams not only confirms the accuracy of Joseph's interpretation. It also highlights the uncertainty of Joseph's future. For if imprisoned dreamers can suffer such contrasting fates, one tasting freedom and the other execution, what does the future hold for 'the master of dreams' himself? Joseph's choice of words in his appeal to the cupbearer is revealing. The term he uses for the dungeon (*bôr*) in which he is imprisoned is the same as that used for the pit into which his brothers put him (37.20, 22, 24, 28-29). It was telling his own dreams that resulted in Joseph being put into that pit. It is his interpretation of dreams that raises the possibility of being released from this dungeon. But such expectations are quickly dashed when the cupbearer simply forgets Joseph. This act of ingratitude marks the nadir of Joseph's experience so far. He has always retained something of a favoured status. The story began with him as favoured son, then he descended to being favoured slave; then to favoured prisoner. But now, he is a forgotten prisoner (40.23).

Genesis 41

Dreams and their interpretation were instrumental in Joseph's descent to Egypt. At the time, the dreams of Pharaoh's servants in prison had seemed to offer no release for Joseph. But now Pharaoh dreams. This initiates a chain of events that links with Joseph's interpretations in prison, and ultimately with those boyhood dreams of lordship.

41.1-36

Joseph is forgotten, in prison and wishes to be released; but he can interpret dreams. Pharaoh has enormous personal freedom and power, but is perplexed by his dreams. Their respective strengths and needs indicate that each has the ability to assist the other. The Pharaoh's second dream, which presents contrasting images of ears of grain recalls Joseph's first dream of prostrated sheaves (37.6-8), and makes his appearance in this chapter all the more likely. It can only be a matter of time before they come together.

These dreams are, presumably, not the only ones that the Pharaoh has had in the last two year. That he employs dream interpreters is evidence of that. So why do these dreams stump them? Their general tenor seems fairly obvious. Whether their inability is due to their incompetence or to their desire not to offend the monarch with bad news (cf. Dan. 2.4-11; 4.7), is of less importance than its function of telegraphing Joseph's imminent involvement. With the Egyptian interpreters sidelined we await the arrival of the master of 'the dream' (37.19).

Events at court finally jog the memory of the chief cupbearer. He remembers his 'faults', from the same root *ḥṭ'* which was used to describe his offence against Pharaoh (40.1). But which faults does he remember—this previous offence or his desertion of Joseph? It would be folly to raise again how he had previously offended Pharaoh, now that the troubled monarch is confronted by professional incompetence to interpret dreams. The reasons for his imprisonment are skipped over lightly, with a quick reference to Pharaoh's anger, and no intimation as to the reason, nor whether it was justified (41.10). His review of the dreams he and the baker had had hints at the transparent import of Pharaoh's dreams. Just as they had dreams with positive (vine and wine cup, 40.9b-11) and negative (cakes and birds, 40.16b-17) images, so Pharaoh's dreams have auspicious (fat cows, 41.2; plump grain, 41.5) and inauspicious (thin cows, 41.3-4; wizened grain, 41.6-7a) images. Pharaoh's dreams are clearly a mixture of good and bad news.

Joseph's arrival at court is delayed only long enough for him to shave and change his clothes. The clothing motif suggests that once again Joseph's status is about to change. When his brothers stripped him it marked his descent from favoured son to slave (37.23). When Potiphar's wife disrobed him it sealed his transition from trusted slave to prisoner (39.12). He can surely descend no lower than he has now. Jacob's initial gift of the robe to Joseph had elevated him among his brothers. His change of clothing in order to come before Pharaoh suggests that the clothing motif has now come full circle.

Pharaoh's speech reveals that he already anticipates the worst. His description of Joseph's ability as an interpreter is generous, going somewhat beyond the cupbearer's report (41.12 cf. 41.15). When he describes his dreams, in comparison to the narrator, he emphasizes their negative aspects. For example, in describing the thin cows he adds, 'Never had I seen such ugly ones in all the land of Egypt' (41.19). Almost all of 41.21, which describes the thin cows remaining thin after gorging themselves, is added. He adds more negative epithets in 41.19, 23 (cf. 41.3, 6). In 41.24 he reduces the two positive epithets of the narrator to one (cf. 41.5). So although Pharaoh has called in the master interpreter, he himself is indulging in some interpretation himself—and it is negative.

In his dialogue with Pharaoh, Joseph once again raises his relationship with God. He has no innate ability to interpret dreams, 'It is not I; God will give Pharaoh a favourable answer' (41.16). Yet he provides the interpretation immediately after hearing Pharaoh's description of the dreams, without consulting God (cf. Dan. 2.17-23; but see also Dan. 4.19-22). Indeed, he has already decided on his general interpretation before he has heard the dreams. How can he promise Pharaoh a 'favourable (*šālôm*) answer' (41.16), before Pharaoh has related his dreams? In fact, given their respective positions, one wonders whether Joseph's answer is more favourable for him than it is for Pharaoh. His interpretation is straightforward, and simply confirms what a reader could have deduced in broad outline. But Joseph goes far beyond dream interpretation. He also gives advice on the future agricultural policy of Egypt—none of which is suggested in the dreams. If interpretations come from God, have these political suggestions also? (Pharaoh seems to think so, cf. 41.39.) The policy he suggests will obviously require a skilled overseer. While Joseph does not explicitly offer his services, he nudges the Pharaoh in his direction. It will be necessary to appoint a 'discerning and wise (*ḥākām*)' man (41.33). And the only reason Joseph now stands before the throne is because of the inability of Pharaoh's wise men (*ḥᵃkāmîm*, 41.8). Joseph suggests that overseers should be appointed (*pqd*), which the reader will recall is what Joseph has been on more than one occasion. Potiphar 'made him overseer (*pqd*)' (39.4-5), while in prison Joseph was 'charged' (*pqd*) to look after the cupbearer and baker (40.4). If Joseph's release from prison was telegraphed in the earlier part of the chapter, his appointment to high position is here also.

Joseph states that the doubling of Pharaoh's dreams means that 'the thing is fixed by God, and God will shortly bring it about' (41.32). If that is so, then what about Joseph's own doubled dreams? And are the numerous intimations that Joseph's status is about to change, harbingers of the fact that we shall soon 'see what will become of his dreams' (37.20)?

41.37-57

Joseph's promotion occurs without delay. The Egyptian court is remarkably compliant when Pharaoh elevates Joseph to second in the kingdom. The incompetence of the court has just been demonstrated. An unknown Hebrew slave who has been paroled from prison shows his skill and is then promoted over their heads. This would normally be a situation tailor-made to produce professional jealousy (cf. Dan. 6.1-5). In addition, the Pharaoh does not investigate the reasons for Joseph's imprisonment, nor the seriousness of his crime. Thus Pharaoh is presented as an absolute monarch who can release prisoners on a whim (cf. the cupbearer and baker). He is, however, also capable of being manipulated by Joseph's interpretations and subtle suggestions (see above). One might well ask why the Pharaoh and his court assume that Joseph's interpretation is correct when 14 years must pass before it can be verified. Is this further evidence that the Lord is with Joseph?

Previous hints that Joseph's declining status is about to change are confirmed here. Prior to imprisonment Potiphar had placed him over his house (*'al bêtô*, 39.4); now Pharaoh puts him in charge over his house (*'al bêtô*, 41.40). Just as Potiphar appointed Joseph over everything except his food and wife (39.6, 9), so Pharaoh places Joseph over everything except his throne (41.40). It seems to be Joseph's destiny to be placed over (*'al*) most things: over his brothers (37.8), Potiphar's house (39.4), Pharaoh's house (41.40), the whole land of Egypt (41.33, 41, 45). All except the first of these have been accomplished. And it is the manner of his promotion which brings his relationship to his brothers back into focus. Pharaoh treats him like a prince, giving him a signet ring, a gold chain and 'garments of fine linen' (41.42). The story has returned to its starting point when Joseph was dressed by his father in lordly garb with long sleeves (37.3). Should we now expect Joseph to act as he had before when so attired—as an insensitive braggart, milking the favouritism he held in the eyes of the one with power, giving 'bad reports'? Or have the passing years and experience of injustice knocked those traits out of him? (See 42.1-17.)

Joseph is drawn increasingly into Egyptian society. He is given an Egyptian name (cf. Dan. 1.7), and an Egyptian wife, the daughter of an Egyptian priest. Like Judah before him, Joseph marries a foreigner. The ethnic purity of the ancestral family, of such importance to Abraham (24.3-4) and Isaac (28.1-2), is beginning to unravel. The corollary of being drawn increasingly into Egyptian society is a growing alienation from his family. At the birth of Manasseh he announces that God has made him 'forget all my hardship and all my father's house' (41.51). By mentioning his father's house he has obviously not forgotten it in the same way that the cupbearer forgot him. But he now sees his destiny as lying elsewhere. Since being in Egypt he has been in the house of Potiphar (e.g., 39.2, 4, 5, and so on), incarcerated in the 'round house' (e.g., 39.20-23), and now elevated to Pharaoh's house (41.40). But his father's house, in which this story began and to which his dreams referred, is far from him. Throughout seven years of plenty and into the famine, Joseph, second in power only to Pharaoh himself, makes no attempt to contact his family in Canaan. But then, 'all the world' came to Egypt (41.57). Can Joseph and his family be kept apart much longer? And what then? (See 50.1-14.)

Genesis 42

In chs. 12–36 the barrenness of matriarchs was in the foreground (e.g., 11.30; 25.21; 29.31). We are now reminded of the barrenness of the land. While mentioned briefly before (e.g., 12.10; 26.1-2), the occasional inadequacy of the promised land to support the ancestral family now comes sharply into focus. More and more of Joseph's family leave the land to which Abraham had migrated.

42.1-17

Jacob realizes that 'there was grain in Egypt' (42.1). If only he knew what else, or rather who else, was in Egypt! His reason for not sending Benjamin with his brothers is not because he is too young to travel, nor solely because he loves him more than any of his other sons (42.38). Rather, he fears that harm might befall him (42.4). While harm could come to Benjamin from the Egyptians, Jacob might well fear more than foreigners. Catastrophe had struck Benjamin's brother when he had left home. But Joseph had been killed by a wild animal when he was separated from his brothers, rather than when he was with them. Or so it seemed. Does his reluctance to send Benjamin suggest that he has harboured suspicions about the cause of Joseph's death? He had kept Joseph's dream in mind (37.11); has he also kept Joseph's death in mind?

The last chapter presented Joseph as the master of dreams, and saw him enlisted as master of grain distribution. In this chapter his brothers arrive in Egypt. The necessary elements have been assembled to recall Joseph's first dream in which his brothers' sheaves of grain bowed down to his. Now as Joseph stands amid the grain his brothers prostrate themselves before him (42.6 cf. 37.7). Yet Joseph's behaviour is most peculiar. Though he recognizes his brothers he does not greet them or introduce himself. Rather, he acts as if they were total strangers, and in so doing evokes earlier episodes. When his brothers had deceived Jacob with Joseph's blood-soaked cloak, they requested their father, 'see (*nkr*) now whether it is your son's robe or not. He recognized (*nkr*) it' (37.32). Similarly Tamar returned Judah's pledge and asked him to 'Take note (*nkr*), please, whose these are ... Then Judah acknowledged (*nkr*) them' (38.25b-26a). Here, when Joseph saw his brothers 'he recognized (*nkr*) them, but he treated them like strangers (*nkr*)' (42.7). The obverse of this situation is then stated, 'Although Joseph had recognized (*nkr*) his brothers, they did not recognize (*nkr*) him' (42.8). In the previous incidents Jacob and Judah publicly acknowledged the evidence presented. Here, by contrast, Joseph's recognition is only internal; his actions deceive his brothers. Previously, it was the deceived who acknowledged the evidence. Here, Joseph deceives by his refusal to acknowledge publicly his brothers. Joseph's action is peculiar enough, but when contrasted with Jacob's and Judah's is doubly so (see 41.37-57).

Why does Joseph behave in this way? The narrative provides only hints. Previously, Joseph had 'forgotten' his father's house (41.51), but when he meets his brothers he 'remembers'—not their throwing him in the pit, nor their selling him into slavery—but specifically his dreams (42.9). The narrative links Joseph's remembrance of his dreams with his peculiar behaviour: 'And Joseph remembered the dreams which he had dreamed about them and he said to them, 'You are spies' (42.9, literal translation). Thus it is in his dreams that we must seek a rationale for his bizarre actions. Note, however, that the prostration of Joseph's brothers has not fulfilled his dreams. The imagery of his first dream pictured his brothers' sheaves bowing down to his (37.7). But only 10 of his brothers are present in Egypt. And the second dream includes not only all 11 brothers but also Joseph's parents doing the same (37.9-10). Thus if Joseph has remembered his dreams, he must realize, as he sees his brothers prostrate before him, that his dreams have not yet been fully realized. His behaviour might well be motivated by this realization.

His accusation that his brothers are spies is unexpected and serious. His allegation carries the reader back to Joseph's dreaming youth at home. As a lad, Joseph had acted like a spy in bringing back a bad report of his brothers to Jacob. The term (*dibbâ*) used to describe Joseph's action in 37.2 is also used to describe the spies' report in Num. 13.32; 14.36-37. So Joseph accuses his brothers of doing what he had once done, even though he knows that they are innocent. His brothers' reply, 'your servants have never been spies' (42.11), is an assertion that Joseph could never truthfully make about himself. They also protest that they are 'honest men'. Yet the reader, unlike Joseph, is aware of how they deceived Jacob concerning Joseph's supposed death. But their protestation of honesty raises the question of how honest Joseph himself is being, by falsely accusing them of a serious offence. On this point there seems little to choose between the brothers. The 10 protest, 'We are all sons of one man' (42.11). They certainly are—all 11 of them.

Despite their denials, Joseph continues to turn the screw. The men claim to be 10 brothers, with a father and younger brother at home and another 'who is no more' (42.13). Joseph disputes this and announce a test that will prove 'whether there is truth in you' (42.16). They must produce their younger brother. But there is no logical connection between this test and the dispute it is supposed to settle. The men might well have a younger brother, but they could still be spies. Even if they parade another younger male before their accuser, how is Joseph to know whether this is indeed their brother? Readers know that the accusation is unfounded and the nature of the test confirms that this is just a ruse. And with a little reflection the brothers too could have seen this. But Joseph's motives for acting like this are nowhere explicitly stated. Since, however, Joseph's manipulation of his brothers was triggered by his remembering his dreams, a motivation for seeing Benjamin is hinted at. Benjamin's arrival will create the possibility for his prostration, and with it Joseph's dreams will be one step nearer fulfilment (see 37.1-11). The extent to which he will go to achieve this is seen in his swearing by Pharaoh (42.16)—no other Israelite character in the Bible swears by anyone other than Elohim/Yahweh (cf. Deut. 6.13; Josh. 23.7).

In addition, the seriousness of Joseph's intent is shown when he imprisons them for three days. Imprisoning his brothers could be seen as revenge, replicating their previous imprisonment of him in the pit (37.24). But a more telling connection exists between Joseph's imprisonment of his brothers on trumped up charges with his own imprisonment on the slanderous word of Potiphar's wife (39.14-20). In each case the accusers know that their accusations are lies. Indeed, their allegations are partly analogous. Potiphar's wife accused Joseph of attempted rape. Joseph claims that the brothers wish 'to see the nakedness (*r'h 'erwâ*)' of Egypt (42.9, 12). The same phrase is used elsewhere in the context of sexual offences (e.g., 9.22-23; Lev. 20.17). Thus Joseph's accusation contains sexual innuendo. In his position of power, Joseph appears to be as manipulative and vindictive as his former mistress was.

42.18-28

Joseph's behaviour becomes increasingly enigmatic. He now softens his demand and requires that only one brother remain in Egypt while the rest go to get Benjamin. Is he lowering his guard and showing evidence of genuine concern for his brothers beneath his austere exterior? Or does his move from a harsh to a more lenient approach simply replicate his brothers' decision not to murder him but to sell him into slavery (37.26-27)? On the other hand it is worth considering that oscillating from harshness to gentleness is an age-old ploy of hostage takers. A brutal confrontation followed by kinder words dispose the victim to please the interrogator at all costs.

One possible motivation for Joseph's behaviour, however, can be safely eliminated. A common suggestion is that Joseph is merely testing his brothers to see whether they have reformed, will confess their sins against him and demonstrate their love for Jacob and Benjamin. If this is Joseph's motivation, it is a mystery why he has suddenly become obsessed with the welfare of his father and brother when he has lived for years in Egypt without making any attempt to discover anything whatsoever about his family. If the whole world, including his brothers, can come to Egypt (41.57), then the Egyptian potentate could certainly go to Canaan (cf. 50.4-7). In Egypt he has cared nothing about his family, as he himself confesses (41.51). An equally fundamental objection is that Joseph has no grounds for believing that Jacob and Benjamin would be badly treated by his brothers. Joseph was not sold into slavery because, like Benjamin, he was the son of Rachel, but because he was a tale-telling brat who boasted of his dreams, in which all family members, not just his 10 older brothers, were destined to bow down. And as 42.22 states, not all brothers were in favour of mistreating Joseph (cf. 37.22). As far as Jacob is concerned, the reader knows that he was cruelly deceived by his sons, but Joseph does not. By the time his stained cloak was spread out before Jacob, Joseph was in Egypt (37.28). So Joseph has no grounds for suspecting that his brothers would mistreat Jacob. Additionally, if he requires a confession of guilt from his brothers, then they provide one: 'We are paying the penalty for what we did to our brother' (42.21). Joseph's behaviour induces their confession, but the fact that he continues as if nothing had happened, merely stepping aside for a while to weep (42.24), indicates that such a confession is not his aim. His private weeping is as enigmatic as his public speech and action. As 42.9 indicated, Joseph's behaviour is motivated by his dreams, not by concern for family welfare.

Before Joseph sends his brothers on their way, he selects Simeon as hostage. Joseph's choice might well be arbitrary, but could be caused by Reuben's speech in which he reminds his brothers of how he had pleaded for clemency toward Joseph (42.22). Perhaps Joseph learns here for the first time of Reuben's pleas, and thus passes over Reuben as the firstborn and chooses the next in line, Simeon. Whatever the reason, Leah's second son is held as the bait to catch Benjamin, Rachel's second son (Sternberg 1985: 291).

There is yet one more enigma when Joseph replaces the money in the brothers' sacks. If he had handed the money over openly and declared that the grain was a gift, it would have been unusual but unambiguous. But what does this surreptitious refund signify? Is it an act of generosity, suggesting Joseph's over-arching motives in this puzzling episode? Or is it one more sadistic trick which will enable him to imprison all of them for theft when they return? The reader is in the same quandary as the brothers who were 'bewildered' (42.28, NEB) at this turn of events.

Joseph's reunion with his brothers has a precedent which brings it into sharper focus. Esau had also come face to face with a brother who had wronged him (ch. 33). Like Joseph he too had been separated from his brother(s) for 20 years (31.38, 41; 37.2; 41.46, 53). When he met Jacob he was in a position of power, surrounded by 400 men, just as Joseph is surrounded by the might of the Egyptian empire. But Esau acted in sharp contrast to Joseph. Esau had wept as he and Jacob embraced each other (33.4). Joseph weeps, but in private, not on his brothers' necks, while they are terrorized by his charade of self-concealment and false accusation. Esau's response to meeting Jacob is to welcome and forgive a brother who had seriously wronged him and to offer the hand of reconciliation. Joseph's response does not have to duplicate Esau's. But the contrast with Esau's treatment of Jacob makes Joseph's actions appear all the stranger.

Joseph's allusion to God (42.18), and his brothers' panic-stricken cry, 'What is this that God has done to us?' (42.28), brings into focus once again God's role in this story. With no explicit words or acts from God, like the brothers, we as readers are left to ponder God's involvement, which at this stage at least, is as enigmatic as Joseph's actions.

42.29-38

The bemused brothers arrive back home without Simeon. When Joseph had disappeared, they had left Jacob to draw his own conclusions from the bloodied cloak. But here they must face him and give an explanation for Simeon's absence. In recounting their experience in Egypt they deviate slightly from the account in 42.1-28. Some details are realigned, but the most striking differences are the omissions and additions. For example, they do not tell Jacob that they were all imprisoned for three days, nor that their lives are at risk if they do not return with Benjamin (cf. 42.20). Naturally, they report nothing of their own conversation in which they deduced that their dilemma is retribution for their previous maltreatment of Joseph. Also, they make no mention of their discovery of money in one of their sacks. On the other hand they seem to invent a promise that they will be allowed to trade in Egypt if they do return with Benjamin (42.34). Thus they minimize the negative and accentuate whatever positive there is. Their report, therefore, underestimates the gravity of the situation. It is hardly surprising that Jacob does not agree to allow Benjamin to return with them (see Wenham 1993: 410).

If their doctoring of the evidence was an attempt to shield Jacob from the full implications of the situation, then they are only partially successful. For when they open their sacks they discover that the problem of the returned money is greater than they thought. Previously they were only aware that one brother had the money (42.28). But now, with Jacob looking on, they discover that each of them has money in his sack. None of them understands what is happening. But none suggests that this is a good omen—they are all 'dismayed' (42.35). Jacob judges the money in the sacks to be an omen that Simeon has joined Joseph in oblivion, soon to be joined by Benjamin should he go to Egypt (42.36). Thus it is not surprising that Jacob spurns Reuben's irrational suggestion that if anything goes wrong, Jacob can kill his two grandsons (42.37)!

Jacob's final words indicate the pecking order that still prevails in this family. He bewails the fact that Joseph is dead and that Benjamin 'alone is left' (42.38). He is the only son of Rachel left, of course. Yet Jacob has nine other sons standing before him. But they are of a different order. If Benjamin were in an Egyptian prison and Simeon was required for his release, there can be little doubt that he would already have been on his way.

The story has turned full circle: a brother failing to return (cf. 37.29-31); the father remembering only Joseph's demise (42.36 cf. 37.33-34); showing favouritism (42.38 cf. 37.3); once again anticipating a journey to Sheol (42.38 cf. 37.35). The difference this time is that Jacob is not alone in being deceived. And overarching all this, the bewilderment of the brothers and mental anguish of Jacob, is the fact that Joseph has remembered his dreams (42.9).

Genesis 43

43.1-15

While the family eke out their existence, Simeon remains in prison. Finally the Egyptian grain runs out and Jacob must face the inevitable. Despite telling his sons to return and buy more food (43.2), Jacob knows that the task is more complex than that. If Benjamin does not go, there will be no more food. The heated discussion with Judah and his brothers simply rehearses what they all know. There is little point now in telling his sons that they should have given the Egyptian evasive answers (43.6). They had unfortunately presented themselves as 'honest men' (42.11), a virtue lost on Jacob. Jacob is portrayed as a dithering aged patriarch who will not accept his sons' counsel. Judah says as much in 43.10, 'If we had not delayed we would now have returned twice'. Chapter 42 had seen a shift in Jacob's mood from decisive (42.1-2) to diffident (42.38), a posture picked up at the beginning of ch. 43. It is not only Joseph who can present two faces.

Just as in the report they gave to their father in 42.30-34, Judah here presents a diluted account of their conversation with Joseph. Nowhere does he tell Jacob that if Benjamin does not accompany them then they will be executed (cf. 42.20), nor the implication that if they do not return, Simeon will be executed (42.19-20). These omissions are probably designed to prevent Jacob becoming even more agitated. But it is a reminder that for all kinds of reasons, some laudable, some not, neither Jacob, nor Joseph, nor his brothers find telling the truth easy. There is, however, more than a hint that Judah's character is in the process of change. He offers himself as surety (*'rb*) for Benjamin. Previously he had given a pledge (*'ērābôn*, 38.17-18) to Tamar. With Tamar, he himself had admitted his wrong (38.26), but in ch. 43 his concern for his father shines through.

Reuben had previously made a rash suggestion in an attempt to persuade Jacob to send Benjamin (42.37), but to no effect. Simeon, of course, is not present. So Judah now takes the initiative. Rather than Reuben's strategy of offering his sons, Judah puts himself forward as being personally responsible should anything happen to Benjamin. He chooses his words carefully, 'so that we may live and not die' (43.8), the very words used by Jacob when he sent them to Egypt in the first place (42.2 cf. 47.19). The echo of his earlier words must surely convince Jacob that Judah's advice makes sense.

Finally persuaded, Jacob decides to send a gift to the Egyptian. Jacob had previously sent a gift (*minḥâ*) to assuage the anger of Esau (32.13, 18, etc.), and everything had worked out well on that occasion. He appears to be using the same tactic here, though the huge contrast between Joseph's and Esau's response to meeting long lost brothers makes such an approach questionable (see 42.18-28). Sending such choice produce (43.11) is a favour indeed in the middle of a famine. Giving this present also unwittingly replays Jacob's former preferential treatment of Joseph. Such favouritism had been one of the contributing factors to Joseph going to Egypt in the first place. Also, ironically the gifts he sends include gum, balm and resin—items that the Ishmaelite traders had carried down to Egypt along with Joseph (43.11 cf. 37.25). An increasing number of motifs from the opening episodes of the narrative are now recurring, suggesting that the problems which began there could possibly be nearing some sort of resolution (see 42.29-38).

In the end Jacob acknowledges that he has no choice in the matter. The omnipotent Egyptian can manipulate them in whatever manner he sees fit. He sends his sons on their way resigned to the fact that 'if I am bereaved of my children, I am bereaved' (43.14).

43.16-34

Once Joseph sees that Benjamin has arrived, his attitude to his brothers moves into a new phase. Previously he had adopted a harsh and belligerent stance towards them, before becoming more lenient (42.7-17 cf. 42.18-20). He now appears to be positively generous, inviting them to eat with him. Not surprisingly, the brothers are suspicious. They must have expected some form of inquisition and interrogation of Benjamin, rather than generous hospitality. The money in their sacks defied explanation and now this! They fear the worst: the Egyptian will accuse them of stealing his silver and enslave them (43.18). Yet it was Joseph himself whom they sold for silver into slavery (37.28). Thus one more echo of the opening movements of the narrative foreshadows an impending resolution. But what form that resolution will take is far from clear at this point. And the issue of the money they found in their sacks is an example of this. Fearing the worst, the brothers tell the truth about the matter, (though see the slight discrepancy between 43.21 and 42.27-28). Yet the matter is dismissed by Joseph's steward as being of no consequence. No money has been reported as stolen, and the occurrence is put down to the inscrutability of divine intervention. Does the steward utter more than he realizes, or is he stabbing in the dark? The reader, who knows that Joseph ordered the placing of the silver in the sacks, is as nonplussed as the characters. Why does he never raise the matter with his brothers? If it is simply an act of generosity, then why does he return it in a manner designed to cause unease to his family?

As if to underline that his accusation of spying was just a ruse, Joseph releases Simeon before meeting his brothers (43.23). One would have expected interrogation of Benjamin before Simeon's release, if Joseph had been serious in his claims.

When the brothers present their gift to Joseph they bow before him. Benjamin is with them, and so here we have the true fulfilment of Joseph's first dream. All of his brothers are now present (see 42.1-17). The gift they bring, however, was brought on Jacob's initiative (43.11), and his sons refer to him as Joseph's servant. So there is a hint that this is some form of tribute from Jacob, and that he is in some way present by proxy among his prostrate sons. Thus, there are hints that the fulfilment of the second dream, which predicted subservience of all family members, cannot be far away.

When he meets his brothers he goes through the formal pleasantries of inquiring after their welfare and that of their father. Their reply, 'Your servant our father is well; he is still alive' (43.28), is true up to a point. He is certainly alive, but suffering mental anguish because of the trauma he is going through (42.38; 43.14). The brothers themselves were responsible for causing their father grief in the past, when they pretended that Joseph had been killed. But Joseph himself is causing just as much now by refusing to reveal that he is still alive. But surely his reticence must now end. Benjamin has arrived. Yet with just a hurried word of greeting he rushes out to weep. His previous weeping was difficult to fathom, but here it is caused by 'affection for his brother' (43.29). With such positive emotions, surely an open reconciliation must be imminent.

The feast that Joseph serves to his brothers would be an ideal opportunity for him to reveal the truth to them. But the only thing revealed is his favouritism for Benjamin who receives five times more than the rest. If by this Joseph is trying to drive a wedge between the brothers, he fails. For despite such flagrant favouritism, they all 'drank and were merry with him' (43.34). If he wants one final demonstration of his brothers' honesty and integrity, then he has it. Surely, the reader thinks, he will tell them *now*. But he does not; the charade continues.

Genesis 44

44.1-13

Joseph once again sends his brothers on their way without divulging his identity. As before he replaces their money in their sacks. This time, however, he puts his silver cup in Benjamin's sack. When he had placed money in their sacks before it had been, apparently, an act of generosity. The matter had exercised the brothers but it was never raised by Joseph. Presumably he is being generous again. Putting his silver cup in Benjamin's sack is consistent with his favouritism already displayed (43.34). In this light, his command to his steward to apprehend his brothers and charge them with theft (44.4) is quite startling. Joseph orders his steward to ask the men, 'Why have you returned evil for good?'. That question could well be asked of Joseph. His brothers have shown themselves to be decent men. They acknowledged their previous discovery of money in their sacks (43.21) and brought him a gift (43.26). If Joseph did not accuse them of theft before, why does he do so now?

Not surprisingly, the brothers are taken aback by such accusations. Their stunned reply, 'Why does my lord speak such words as these?', is certainly understandable. But is it a little hasty? They know that money has inexplicably turned up in their sacks before (42.28, 35). If that has occurred, then the discovery of a silver cup would not be implausible. Their indignation leads them to make the rash suggestion that if any of them is guilty, that person should be executed and the others enslaved (44.9). Their protests and offer recall Jacob's when accused of stealing Laban's teraphim (31.32). But Rachel's subterfuge saved him on that occasion (31.34.35). The brothers are more naive and vulnerable. Strangely, the steward dilutes their offer. He is content with slavery for the culprit. The rest may go free. Does the steward have a more balanced view of justice, or is it because he feels uneasy, knowing that they have the cup because he put it there (cf. 44.1)? The speed with which they unload their sacks and open them up, eager to demonstrate their innocence, shows just how defenceless they are, totally at the mercy of Joseph's whims.

The incident only makes Joseph's character all the more baffling—he hides the cup to ensnare Benjamin; yet his silence over the money suggests that once again he is being generous to his brothers. Surely one would have expected the opposite, since he has already shown favouritism to Benjamin above the other brothers (42.34). Grief stricken at the discovery of the cup, they return to meet their tormenter. Will Joseph ring any more changes in his bizarre toying with his brothers?

44.14-34
Once again his brothers bow down before him. He has already witnessed partial and complete fulfilments of his first dream (37.10 cf. 42.6, 43.26). While these have been the result of Joseph's peculiar behaviour, his motivation must surely be more than to keep replaying this scene repeatedly. He accuses them using extreme terms, 'What deed is this that you have done?' (44.15). This is similar to previous accusations of gross wrong: the Lord God to the Woman (3.13); Pharaoh to Abram (12.18); Abimelech to Isaac (26.10) and Jacob to Laban (29.25). In these examples the accuser knows that a wrong has been committed. Joseph, however, knows that the accused are innocent, and this contrast merely underlines the sadistic nature of Joseph's charges.

Are we to take Joseph's claims concerning his practice of divination at face value? (It is prohibited in, e.g., Lev. 19.26; Deut. 18.10; cf. 2 Kgs. 21.6). Previously he has claimed that the interpretation of dreams comes from God (40.8; 41.16, 25), rather than through 'secret arts'. Is he simply telling one more lie in order to terrorize his brothers? He has already thoroughly disoriented them by making money and a silver cup mysteriously appear in sacks of grain, and even exhibited knowledge of their respective ages (43.33), and being hostile, hospitable and generous towards them in quick succession. He now claims to have access to secret powers. If true, this would only add to their confusion and sense of helplessness, for 'if the foreigner can divine, then he should know that they are not guilty' (Westermann 1986: 133).

Judah's stuttering reply (44.16), graphically conveys the brothers' sense of powerlessness before this unfathomable potentate. What indeed can they say? One thing he does say is, 'God has found out the guilt of your servants'. Obviously Judah and his brothers know that they are not guilty of Joseph's accusation. Is Judah simply expressing resignation to events, since this incident lies beyond the realm of human understanding? Does he feel that a plea of guilty, though unwarranted, is more likely to result in clemency than if they engage in heated debate with the damning evidence before them? Or, in the background can a confession of their previous offence against Joseph be detected? Regardless of how his words are understood, the utter bewilderment of the brothers is clear.

Judah's offer of imprisoning all the brothers (44.16b) is refused by Joseph, who asks for only Benjamin, with the rest going free. His intended parting line, 'go up *in peace (šālôm)* to your father' (44.17), can hardly be anything but mocking, in light of the situation he has created, and a striking contrast to the apparent concern he had shown earlier when asking, 'Is your father well (*šālôm*)?' (43.27; see Janzen 1993: 174). In response to this, Judah steps forward and delivers one of the longest monologues in Genesis. The amount of narrative space devoted to this speech (44.18-34), and its content, which provides a summary of the action in Egypt and Canaan from 42.6 up to this point, demonstrate its significance and hint that a turning point in the narrative has been reached. Joseph's response will tip the whole story one way or the other.

In essence, Judah's speech is a plea to Joseph not to imprison Benjamin because it would bring about the death of his father (44.22, 29, 31 cf. 44.34). To prevent this, Judah offers himself to be imprisoned (44.33). His speech is usually taken to show how much the brothers have reformed, their present concern contrasting with their previous enslavement of Joseph and deception of Jacob. But Judah's speech raises additional contrasts. His compassion for Benjamin and Jacob contrasts with Joseph's indifference. He never contacted his family during all his years in Egypt. As a slave he could not; as a potentate he did not. Also, the contrast between the brothers' previous and current behaviour could be explained by the differences between Joseph and Benjamin, rather than by a presumed reformation of the brothers. That is to say, Benjamin is not a braggart like Joseph was. The contrast in the brothers' attitude to Joseph and Benjamin could demonstrate just how insufferable Joseph had been.

On the other hand, Judah's speech reveals the brothers acting as they had at the beginning of the story. Judah reports Jacob's words concerning Joseph, 'one left me, and I said, "Surely he has been torn to pieces"' (44.28). But only Jacob believes that. Judah and *Joseph* know that he was not torn to pieces. So by recording his father's delusion, Judah continues the masquerade.

As in the brothers' reports given to Jacob (42.29-34; 43.3-7), Judah's recollection of their initial meeting with Joseph is rather benign. For example, he omits the accusation of spying (42.9-14), his temporary imprisonment of all of them (42.16-17), his imprisonment of Simeon for a considerable time (42.19, 24). The implied threat of execution (42.20) is diluted to not seeing Joseph again (44.23 cf. 43.5). And Judah appears to think it wiser not to mention anything about the mysterious appearance of the money in their sacks. Thus Judah's speech plays down the aggressively hostile tone of Joseph's previous behaviour. But he accentuates the picture of Jacob's grief. For example, he reports words by Jacob which emphasize how precious Benjamin is—the only remaining son of Jacob's (favourite?) wife (44.27). Twice he mentions the potential death of Jacob. First by claiming that Joseph was told this at their first meeting (44.22), although the narrative is silent on that, and then at the end of his monologue repeating the certainty of Jacob's death. Judah's speech is thus a model of diplomacy: the negative aspects of Joseph are downplayed and the case for clemency is subtly strengthened. Judah presents himself as a man of integrity, which puts pressure on Joseph to equal him. And in all of this Judah makes no appeal for his own welfare, or for his brothers generally, or for Benjamin in particular, but specifically for his father. Just how will Joseph respond to this?

Judah's monologue was prompted by a disagreement with Joseph over the appropriate punishment for Benjamin's 'crime'.

It is instructive to see how the brothers and Joseph differ over this matter. Several possibilities are canvassed (44.9-10, 16, 17, 33), but consistent differences emerge. The brothers have advocated either permanent separation of all brothers from Jacob (through either execution or enslavement), or freedom for all brothers except Judah. On the other hand, Joseph has consistently advocated slavery for Benjamin and freedom for the rest. The brothers' suggestions would mean that Jacob would never come to Egypt. If they never returned home, Jacob would assume the worst and die thinking that all of his sons had suffered Joseph's fate. And if Judah alone was enslaved, Jacob would not return to rescue him. When Simeon had been imprisoned, the only reason the brothers returned was because the food ran out—not concern for Simeon. Only Joseph's consistent stance of Benjamin remaining and the rest returning would bring Jacob to Egypt, together with his sons, prostrating himself before Joseph and pleading for Benjamin. He had kept Simeon on false charges of spying, saying that if they wanted to see Simeon again they would have to return with Benjamin (42.19-20). One can see Joseph working towards the next contrived concession: 'If you want to see Benjamin again then you must return with your father'. For the prostration and subservience of all the family is necessary for the fulfilment of Joseph's second dream (37.9-10). When Joseph had first met his brothers at the granary he 'remembered the dreams that he had dreamed about them' (42.9). Apparently, he has not subsequently forgotten them.

His brothers, however, consistently resist leaving Benjamin in Egypt. How will Joseph deal with this refusal?

Genesis 45

The narrative has been building up to this scene. Joseph's pretence is put to one side and some tensions are resolved. But the essentially enigmatic nature of Joseph's character continues.

45.1-15

Joseph has wept before, but has hidden or controlled it (42.24; 43.30). Judah's speech achieves something that neither hearing his brothers' confession (42.24) nor seeing Benjamin again (43.30) could achieve. Thus, the reasons for his open weeping here must be found in the content of Judah's speech. Judah's transparent concern for Jacob stands in stark contrast to the games Joseph has been playing with his father's life. Judah's speech prompts

Joseph not merely to reveal his identity, 'I am Joseph', which in itself would bring the charade to an end, but to continue, 'Is my father still alive?' (45.3). In fact the latter question is more important than the former statement, but the question makes no sense without the former revelation of who was asking it.

Not only has Joseph wept before, he has also asked whether Jacob is still alive (cf. 43.7), and enquired generally about his welfare (43.27). He does so once again here in response to Judah's speech. The repeated enquiries indicate that Jacob's death or survival is a key issue for Joseph. So why has Joseph acted in a way which has threatened to kill Jacob (e.g., 44.31)? I would suggest that previously he had wanted to know whether his father was still alive in order to ascertain whether one more detail in the second dream could be fulfilled. In other words, his questions about Jacob were not motivated simply by genuine concern but largely by a desire to fulfil his destiny. Now, having heard Judah's graphic description of Jacob's anguish, he asks the question because he is motivated by true compassion for his father: 'your father' (43.27; 44.17) becomes 'my father' (45.3). It is often asserted that Judah's speech reveals that the brothers have changed. What is more likely, is that the speech produces a change in Joseph.

The stunned silence of his brothers (45.3b) contrasts with Judah's prolonged speech. It is now Joseph's turn to launch into a lengthy monologue. He begins by absolving his brothers of blame for his enslavement, seeing in the course of events God's plan to preserve life and the ancestral family (45.5b, 7). But since this is the first time such an explanation has been offered, for how long has Joseph believed this? Presumably not from the beginning, during his service in Potiphar's house and subsequent imprisonment, nor even when he met his brothers again. He remembered his dreams (42.9), but received no further insight. The dreams, the fulfilment of which can plausibly be seen as motivating Joseph's subsequent behaviour, contained no revelation concerning divine plans for saving the family from famine. In addition, it is after he has interpreted Pharaoh's dreams that he announces that he has 'forgotten' his family (41.51). Thus his assertion here has all of the hallmarks of an idea that has only now dawned on him. Joseph is searching for a reason that will bring coherence to the jumble of events and finds it in the inscrutable will of God. His realization here contrasts with what he has been doing previously. He states that 'God sent me before you to preserve life' (45.5b). It is thus ironic in the extreme that Joseph should have acted in a manner which threatened the life of Jacob, as Judah has now forcefully shown him (45.22, 31). The contrast confirms that Joseph's conclusion about the preservation of life is not what has been motivating him in his scenes with his brothers.

Only now does Joseph embrace and weep over his brothers. Esau had done this the moment he had been reunited with Jacob (33.4). Joseph does it only after a long delay of deception and self-concealment. Again, the contrast indicates that Joseph's actions were not necessary. It is difficult to see what the entire charade of false accusations, imprisonment and threatened enslavement has got to do with preserving life (45.5b). Joseph's pious words are uttered only after Judah has boxed him in. They give an explanation for why his brothers sent him to Egypt. But they provide no explanation for his maltreatment of them. Previously, the brothers knew neither the identity nor the motivation of the bizarre Egyptian. The only thing he reveals here is his identity (see 46.28-34).

Nevertheless, some form of closure is provided by the statement, 'his brothers talked with him' (45.15). The complications of this narrative began when they 'could not speak peaceably to him' (37.4).

45.16-28

As soon as Pharaoh and his court hear that Joseph's brothers have arrived they are pleased. Pharaoh immediately orders what one would have expected Joseph to have done the first time he met his brothers, if the welfare of his family had been close to his heart. Pharaoh commands them to return to Canaan and bring their father and belongings and live in luxury in Egypt (45.18-20).

When Joseph sends them on their way he decks them out in fine garb, but cannot resist showing flagrant favouritism once more to Benjamin. He provides him with five times as many garments and a present of silver. This recalls the unfortunate precedent set by Jacob in giving Joseph his distinctive clothing at the beginning of the story. The clothing motif has occurred at crucial points in the twists and turns of this unpredictable story, indicating a decisive shift in each episode (e.g., 37.23; 38.14; 39.12; 41.14). Thus as the story seems to be heading to a natural resolution, elements which were part of the earlier complications raise their heads once again. One more might be implied in Joseph's remarks to his brothers, 'Do not quarrel (*rgz*) along the way' (45.24). The term he uses, however, has a range of meanings, including fear, tremble, rage, etc. (cf. 1 Sam. 14.15; 2 Sam. 7.10; Isa. 28.21). These connotations could also be appropriate here. They might well fear what Joseph would do to them when they all returned. They have already seen his emotions fluctuate wildly, and just as importantly, Joseph has not provided any explanation for his odd actions. As a result, Joseph might well wonder whether they might harbour animosity for the way in which he has treated them and be consumed with rage on the journey.

When they reach home and tell Jacob the news, it is not surprising that 'he was stunned; he could not believe them' (45.26). What the text does not spell out is what Jacob *has* believed all these years: that Joseph was dead, torn to pieces by beasts, on the evidence presented by his sons. He still does not know that they deceived him, for they had simply presented the evidence. Perhaps he is deceived into thinking that they too were misled. Or, perhaps this news strengthens doubts that he might have about their involvement (see 42.4). Whether Jacob realizes the truth about these matters or not, the reader can see that the arch-deceiver has been out-deceived. Jacob had previously bettered Isaac, Esau and Laban. But in his old age he has been deceived by his own sons. There might well be elements of retribution in Joseph's treatment of his brothers. But with Jacob hardly less so. Joseph has presented a false persona before his brothers and father in order to claim the promise of his dreams, just as Jacob had masqueraded as Esau before his father in order to receive the blessing (27.18-29).

Genesis 46

46.1-27

Jacob set off 'with all that he had' (46.1), just as Abraham had done when travelling in the opposite direction (13.1 cf. 31.21). Stopping at Beer-sheba he offers sacrifices and God speaks to him in a night vision. Previous movements into and out of the promised land have been accompanied by visions (e.g., 12.1-3; 28.12-15), though not in every case (12.10). So such a vision is not surprising in itself, but this is the first unambiguous and direct involvement of God since the narrative began in ch. 37.

Previously, there have been dreams which required interpretation (e.g., 37.5-10), or assertions by characters or narrator that God was involved (e.g., 39.2; 45.5). But here, God himself speaks directly and unequivocally. The rarity of such an utterance in this narrative, coupled with its content which sanctions the abandonment of the promised land until after the death of Jacob (46.4), highlights its significance. This is especially so when one recalls God's appearance to Isaac with its directive, 'Do not go down to Egypt' (26.2). In addition, the present divine revelation is made to a character who has not occupied centre stage in the narrative. As its major character one might have expected Joseph to have received any explicit divine insight. Yet so far, while he has certainly spoken about God, it is arguable whether God has spoken to him. Not even his dreams are unambiguously divine. On the other hand, Jacob has had several communications from God (28.13-15; 31.10-13[?]; 35.9-12). What Jacob's dream here shows, however, is that Joseph's assessment of God's involvement in the story (45.5, 7) is correct. Joseph had told his brothers that God had engineered events so that life generally and his family in particular would be preserved. Here God tells Jacob that in Egypt he will make him into a great nation, as promised to his ancestors. God's opening and closing discourses with Jacob, as with Abraham, concern various aspects of the ancestral promises (12.1-3; 22.15-18; 28.13-15). But true to form, God's revelation to Jacob also shows that the fulfilment of the promises will be anything but straightforward: the promised nation will arise but not in the promised land (46.3 cf. 15.13).

The ancestral story had started with Abraham setting out with no seed, and now Jacob moves on with comparatively numerous seed. Thus while the nationhood promise has not arrived, it is on its way to fulfilment. The catalogue of descendants emphasizes the number seven, tying it in with other genealogical information in Genesis. The total number of Jacob's descendants who either went down to Egypt or were born there is 70 (46.27). The list includes the number of sons each son fathered. The seventh son is Gad, who fathers seven sons. In addition, the numerical value of the consonants in his name is seven (see Sasson: 1978: 171-85). Other multiples might be noted: Rachel and her maid Bilhah have 21 (7 x 3) children. Leah and Zilpah between them have 49 (7 x 7) descendants. Such numerical preoccupations were frequent in the genealogies of chs. 1–11 (see 2.1-4a; 4.17-25; chs. 5, 10). The enumeration of Jacob's family here echoes the listing of the world's 70 nations in ch. 10 and thus telegraphs that Israel is on the way to nationhood. In recalling the genealogies of the primaeval history, it suggests that just as there the predictability of genealogical succession indicates divine oversight. The Lord was not only with Joseph (39.2, 23), but is also with Israel.

46.28-34

Jacob commissions Judah to lead the family to their rendezvous with Joseph in Goshen. This is fitting, since Judah's speech (44.18-34) had induced Joseph's self-revelation. In addition, Judah's role here produces a balance where the son who suggested Joseph's enslavement (37.27), and thereby separated father from son, should be the one who leads the way to their reunion. On the other hand, the choice of Judah is surprising, because the entire ancestral family has just been listed, in which Judah was only fourth in order of priority. So the way in which Judah has gained ascendancy among the brothers, despite the Tamar incident, shows that it is not only Joseph's lordship over his brothers that challenges the usual conventions of primogeniture (see 49.1-28).

The situation is set up for the fulfilment of that element of Joseph's dream which predicted Jacob bowing before Joseph (37.9-11). Joseph is the eleventh of 12 sons, yet has become 'lord of the land' (42.30), and 'like Pharaoh himself' (44.18), to whom Egyptians and brothers alike bow the knee (41.43; 42.6; 43.26). Yet Jacob does not bow the knee. Joseph 'presented himself' (46.29) to Jacob, who retains all the prestige of family patriarch. Jacob has been involved in two reunion scenes, the first with his brother, the second with his son, both of which refuse to fulfil narrative predictions. Rebekah's divine oracle had predicted that Esau would serve Jacob (25.23), and Isaac's blessing that Esau would serve him and bow (*hwh*) before him (27.29, 40). Yet when the two meet again, it is Jacob who comes bowing and scraping before Esau, seven times no less (33.3). Jacob had interpreted the dream of 37.9-10 to predict that he would bow (*hwh*) before Joseph. But he never does. Thus, in reunion scenes, Jacob's actions invert the expectations set up at the beginning of the narratives (see 45.1-15). One can make a good case for saying that the failure of the expectations is caused by characters' insistence on forcing their fulfilment (for more detail on this recurring aspect of the Genesis narrative, see Turner 1990a: 177-80).

Jacob has anticipated death without Joseph more than once before (37.35; 43.14). Now that they are reunited, he can anticipate it with peace. There will, however, be a delay. Joseph lived with Jacob in Canaan for 17 years (37.2). As if to balance the books, Jacob will live in Egypt with Joseph for 17 years (47.28).

Once the weeping and embracing are over, Joseph instructs his family on how to approach the Pharaoh, so that they will be able to settle in Goshen. His advice is rather surprising given the fact that he has already promised them Goshen (45.10). Pharaoh himself had said as much with his offer of 'the best of the land' (45.18), which is Goshen (47.6). But now, it appears, this concession will have to be wheedled out of the Pharaoh. Joseph's advice, however, comes from a master strategist who had been promoted to his present position by giving Pharaoh broad hints, rather than outright demands (41.25-36). His brothers would do well to listen to him.

Genesis 47.1-28

47.1-12

When meeting Pharaoh, Joseph's brothers go one step further than he suggested. Joseph had hoped that the mere mention of his brothers' occupation would result in their being settled in Goshen (46.33-34; cf. 45.10), as the Pharaoh's own words seemed to indicate (45.18, 20; 47.6). They leave nothing to chance, however, and request settlement in that area, which is granted with alacrity by Pharaoh. Thus true attitudes are concealed beneath the diplomatic niceties. What appears to be royal generosity, is actually a manifestation of Egyptian social prejudice. The brothers' request saves Pharaoh the embarrassment of explaining why he has chosen Goshen for them. Goshen is the 'best part of the land' for shepherding, and as a result is peopled by social undesirables (cf. 46.34).

The migration from Canaan to Goshen raises once again the land promise that has been a major motif throughout the ancestral history. An alternative name for Goshen, the land of Rameses, is used in 47.11, underlining that this land is not their land. It is not the land promised to Abraham (cf. 13.14-17; 15.18-21; 17.8). Yet it is, ironically, the first land that they have been *given* (*ntn* 47.11). Their only possession in the true land of promise is a grave and a small plot of land, and even they had been purchased (23.13-16; 33.19).

Jacob enters Egypt as the head of his household and Joseph presents him as such to Pharaoh (47.7). As if to thank the Egyptian potentate for his benevolence, Jacob blesses him. This is the first example of Jacob giving a blessing. Previously, he has received blessings (e.g., 28.3-4, 13-15; 32.26-29), or failing that, stolen them (27.18-29). It has been a long time coming, but even Jacob in the end obeys the original Abrahamic command 'be a blessing' (12.2). Yet despite such an obsession with blessings, Jacob's words to Pharaoh reveal a disillusioned old man. His assessment of his life is 'few and hard have been the years of my life' (47.9). By comparison with his forefathers his years have hardly been 'few'. His 130 years compare favourably with Abraham (175), Ishmael (137) and Isaac (180), and Jacob has not yet died, by which time he is 147 (47.28). But his words reveal a sadness of tone. The accumulation of blessings has not impacted on his life in a positive way. He sounds disenchanted, and on that note exits from Pharaoh's presence. The reader surmises that his death notice cannot be long in coming.

As the family settles down in Goshen Joseph busies himself over their welfare (47.12). At last, the favouritism that has bedevilled this family seems to be at an end, with Joseph distributing provisions to his brothers 'according to the number of their dependants'. But then, one might recall, Benjamin has 10 sons (46.21), more than any of his brothers. Thus once again Joseph gives his full brother Benjamin more than he does to any of the rest (cf. 45.22).

47.13-28

The famine hits Egypt and Canaan and we now see how Joseph's wisdom works in practice. Joseph collects revenue from both countries (47.14) in exchange for grain. So he not only saves his family who leave Canaan, but also Canaanites who remain there and come to Egypt to buy grain. But it is difficult to maintain an entirely benevolent reading of Joseph's actions. In 47.15a, we read that all of the money in Egypt and Canaan had been spent on Joseph's stockpiled grain, and that the Egyptians came to Joseph, offering first their livestock (47.16-17) and then themselves in slavery (47.18-19). Both of the variant readings of 47.21, 'he made slaves of them' (Samaritan and LXX) and 'he removed them to the cities' (MT), make abundantly clear that whatever Joseph did, he separated them from their land. It is now state property (47.20).

It is not clear whether Canaanites, like Egyptians, are reduced to slavery once their assets are exhausted. If they are, then the only groups to escape this fate are Joseph's family and the priests into whose line he has married (47.22, 26; 41.45, 50; 46.20). If only the Egyptians are enslaved, then what of the Canaanites? Presumably once their money was gone, they would starve to death. Either scenario questions the predictions in the ancestral narrative that Abraham's descendants would be a blessing to the nations (12.3; 18.18; 22.18; 26.4; 28.14). Forfeiture of one's land and forced enslavement might be preferable to starvation, but they are hardly blessings. A moment's reflection on Joseph's own experience of enforced emigration and enslavement is enough to establish this.

Life might be bleak for most, but not apparently for Joseph's family. Their vocation as keepers of livestock ensured their settlement in Goshen (46.6, 32, 34; 47.6). We now see Joseph removing livestock from the Egyptians and Canaanites. But who receives these livestock? Pharaoh had previously told Joseph to put the most capable of his brothers in charge of the royal livestock (47.6). The dispossessed themselves acknowledge to Joseph that 'the herds of cattle are my lord's' (47.18). Is this the way that Joseph's family 'gained possessions' (47.27) in Goshen? And if the ancestral family are profiting at the expense of the dispossessed and enslaved, this is a most surprising turn of events. In 15.13 God told Abraham that his descendants would find themselves in a foreign land, where they would be enslaved and oppressed. We now see Abraham's descendants in a foreign land, but it is Abraham's descendant Joseph who enslaves its inhabitants and oppresses them. That is to say, Joseph does to foreigners what the reader had anticipated foreigners would do to Israel. Once again, expectations raised by the narrative have been turned on their heads. In ch. 15 no motivation for the enslavement and oppression of Abraham's descendants was given. Should the divine prediction ever be fulfilled, perhaps Joseph's treatment of the Egyptians provides one.

Joseph's motivation for his actions is presumably 'to preserve life' (45.5; cf. 47.15, 19, 24). He is not the first to find himself confronted with that task. Judah's actions in denying Tamar a husband were similarly motivated. Yet his actions are condemned from his own lips (38.26). One function of ch. 38 therefore, might well be not only to contrast Judah and Joseph, but also to highlight their similarities (see 38.24-30; Wildavsky 1994).

This section draws to a close by anticipating Jacob's death. The length of his Egyptian sojourn and his age at death are given before his actual death is recorded. Just as Joseph had lived 17 years in Canaan before going to Egypt (37.2), so Jacob lives for 17 years in Egypt after leaving Canaan. This chronological inclusion telegraphs that the action of this story, and with it that of the book of Genesis as a whole, is coming to a conclusion.

Genesis 47.29–48.22

47.29–48.7

Jacob requests Joseph to make a solemn oath by placing his hand under his thigh. Only two such oaths are made in the Bible, both in Genesis, and in each case it is connected with being inside or outside the land of Canaan. In 24.2-9 Abraham made his servant swear that Isaac's wife would come from outside of Canaan. Here Jacob makes Joseph swear that he will be buried inside Canaan. In making that oath, Joseph grasps the very thigh/hip (*yārēk*) that was put out of joint when Jacob last entered Canaan (32.26, 32-33). These two oaths highlight the importance of the land in the ancestral promises, a point that needs to be reemphasized now that the entire family are living beyond its borders.

Jacob takes a long time to die. In his speech to Pharaoh he had intimated his imminent demise (47.9). The narrator has already given him a brief obituary notice (47.28). His approaching death is once again anticipated (47.29), which provides the occasion for his request to Joseph to make the oath about his final resting place. News then comes to Joseph that his father is ill. Anticipations of his death have divested it of any tension, and the reader must surely be impatient to see the end of him. Isaac too had lingered on the edge of the grave (27.2; 35.27-29), but Jacob is much more active, and as the chapter proceeds indulges consciously in some actions that he had previously perpetrated on an uncomprehending senile Isaac. Isaac had been unaware that primogeniture was being overturned before his fading eyes. Here, as we shall soon see, it is Jacob's intention from the outset.

After summoning Joseph and his two sons to his bedside, Jacob recalls the blessing he received from God at Luz (Bethel). It is not a comprehensive summary of either incident in chs. 28 or 35, but limits itself to the two elements of nationhood and land. These are the two issues of greatest interest to Jacob at this time. He has just extracted an oath from Joseph that he will bury him in Canaan (47.29-30). His aim here in summoning Joseph and his sons, it appears, is to ensure genealogical succession within the embryonic nation living in Egyptian exile.

However, the logical connection between his remembrance of former blessings and his subsequent action is not clear at first sight. What connections are there between the blessing delivered at Luz/ Bethel (48.4), the adoption of Joseph's sons (48.6-7), and the death of Rachel (48.7)? Perhaps the elements of nationhood and land found in these former blessings provide a clue. Joseph's sons relate to both of these elements. They had been born to an Egyptian wife (41.50-52) beyond the borders of Canaan. Their legitimacy as descendants of Abraham is thus open to question. By formally adopting them as Jacob's own sons, not simply grandsons, their status is affirmed. They are counted as Reuben and Simeon, the first two sons of Leah (48.5). But since they are Joseph's children, they will be counted as sons of Rachel. It seems, therefore, that by this means Jacob has posthumously increased Rachel's offspring. If this is the reasoning behind his actions, then one can understand why he then moves on to recall the death of Rachel (48.7), who died in childbirth, and was thus prevented from having more sons.

48.8-22

The parallels between this blessing scene and that in ch. 27 cannot be missed. Isaac and Jacob are drawn together by their questions, 'Who are these?' (48.8) and 'Who are you?' (27.18); their desires, 'that I may bless them' (48.9) and 'that I may bless you' (27.4); their visual impediments, 'Now the eyes of Israel were dim with age, and he could not see well' (48.10a) and 'his eyes were dim so that he could not see' (27.1); and their intimacies, 'he kissed them and embraced them' (48.10b) and 'he came near and kissed him' (27.27). But more striking than any of these similarities of detail is the main action of the scene in which Jacob reverses primogeniture. Isaac had done this unwittingly, but Jacob does so deliberately.

As Jacob's intentions become clear, we see that his earlier reversal of the son's names when he announced their adoption was not an oversight (48.5 cf. 48.1). Yet just how effective his actions will be is open to question. The scene in ch. 27 showed how Isaac was duped into blessing the wrong son. But the rest of the narrative challenges the view that Jacob was blessed as the reader was led to believe he would be, or that Esau was not blessed (see, e.g., 33.1-20; ch. 36). Will Jacob's attempt to reverse primogeniture be any more successful?

This question is raised forcefully with the reversal of expectations contained in Joseph's second dream (37.9-10). The dream had predicted that father and mother would bow before their son, but here the son prostrates himself before his father (48.12). Coming hard on the heels of the reminder of Rachel's death (48.7), which occurred before that dream was dreamed, thus rendering its image of his mother bowing down impossible, the reader can feel justified in casting a quizzical eye on any statements that purport to predict family relationships.

Not only does Jacob show partiality to Ephraim over Manasseh, but also to Joseph over the rest of his brothers. His gift to Joseph of a portion of the land of Canaan is more than a reminder to his exiled son that Canaan is his true home. It singles Joseph out from his brothers (48.22), and reveals the same favouritism working at the end of the story as was present at the start (cf. 37.3). The fact that Jacob announces this in the absence of Joseph's brothers suggests his awareness that old animosities might not have died. It also shows that despite the hardships that have made the years of his life 'few and hard' (47.9), he cannot help himself from showing the same favouritism that contributed to his hardships. It signals that true peace and reconciliation might not yet have arrived for this family (see 50.15).

The blessing of his grandsons show Jacob's face set against the conventions of primogeniture. Here, however, unlike the situation between himself and Esau, the reversal of expectations is not presented as being God's will. However, neither God's silence nor Jacob's speech lessens the enigma of the act. Why, just for once, cannot the firstborn be promised precedence?

Genesis 49

Jacob's obsession with obtaining blessings at the beginning of his story (27.18-29; 28.20-22; 32.26 and so on), is balanced by his dispensing blessings to Pharaoh (47.7), Joseph and his sons (48.8-20), and now to his 12 sons at its end. Yet as one considers Jacob's words in this chapter, one wonders whether 'blessing' is altogether the correct word. His words run the full gamut from fulsome blessing to virtual curse. Jacob's assessment of his sons' past and future puts him in the position of power, isolating past actions for praise or censure and predicting future destiny. But one might well speculate what kind of blessing Jacob himself would receive from an independent observer.

Just how efficacious will these blessings be? The respective blessings on Jacob and Esau were shown to be anything but predestinarian (see, e.g., 27.18-29; 33.1-20.) He summons his sons telling them to 'hear' (49.2), using the same term as Joseph's 'listen' (*šim'û*, 37.6), when he divulged his dreams to his brothers. And those dreams have similarly only been fulfilled in part. No matter how precisely humans attempt to mould future events, and no matter how precise divine prognostications sound, there is always room for surprise.

The difficulty of categorizing Jacob's pronouncements as blessings is illustrated by his words to his firstborn Reuben (49.3-4). Jacob pronounces him to be 'excelling in power' (49.3b), yet as 'unstable as water' (49.4a). Thus positive and negative statements are juxtaposed. Jacob's negative words are occasioned by Reuben's having gone 'up on to your father's bed', presumably a reference to the incident where Reuben lay with Bilhah. Jacob's reaction to this outrage has been long delayed. At the time, the only reaction recorded was that 'Israel heard of it' (35.22). While Reuben might well be receiving his just deserts, it also reveals a somewhat vindictive side of Jacob, who waits until his deathbed (cf. 49.29) to vent his spleen on his son. In addition, Jacob's assessment is hardly evenhanded. Since this is supposedly a chapter of blessings (49.28), one might have expected some positive aspects of Reuben to be recalled. He was the one, after all, who saved Joseph's life (37.21-22, 29; cf. 42.22). While this matter might be unknown to Jacob, he had witnessed Reuben's magnanimous if somewhat impulsive gesture, when trying to persuade Jacob to send Benjamin to Egypt (42.37). One gets the impression that Reuben is being treated somewhat unfairly. One reckless act of sexual impropriety, ignored by Jacob up to this point, appears to outweigh any virtue he might possess.

Jacob displays a similar attitude to Simeon and Levi. He condemns their violence outright here. Presumably, this is a reference to their actions at Shechem (ch. 34). Jacob's attitude to their violence seems to have changed, however. At the time his only concern was fear for his life (34.30). He did not bring forward any moral objections to the act itself. Yet here, he condemns their violence and anger apparently as a matter of principle. Additionally, he has no good word to say about either of them, yet when Simeon was imprisoned by Joseph he affected deep emotional trauma (42.36). The effect of Jacob's blessing on Reuben was to remove him from his status as firstborn. If we expected the next sons in line to take over that role, then we are disappointed. Both Simeon and Levi are cursed, with the hope that they will be divided and scattered (49.7).

Jacob's treatment of Reuben and Simeon in the first two blessings, throws his comments in the preceding chapter regarding Ephraim and Manasseh into sharp relief. There he pronounced that Ephraim and Manasseh will be his, just as Reuben and Simeon are (48.5). Yet when he comes to these two sons in this chapter, the negative far outweighs the positive. Does this indicate that Reuben and Simeon are being removed to make way for Ephraim and Manasseh? If so, then it will not be clear to the assembled brothers, who were not privy to the events of ch. 48. Or does it suggest that being 'just as Reuben and Simeon are' (48.5), is not in fact such a blessing as Ephraim and Manasseh were led to believe? Jacob might be as devious at the end of his life when he is dispensing blessings as he was at the beginning when he was acquiring blessings by deception.

Reuben, Simeon and Levi, the three eldest sons, have in turn been removed from the preeminent position by Jacob's miserly 'blessings'. The preeminent position to the family is now taken by Judah, the fourth in line (see 46.28-34). Indeed, Jacob blesses him with almost identical words to those that he himself had stolen from Isaac, 'your father's sons shall bow down before you' (49.8 cf. 27.29). Such a detail merely highlights the nagging question that a reader might legitimately ask about the efficacy of these blessings (49.26a notwithstanding). Isaac's prediction concerning the subservience of Esau to Jacob was reversed in 33.3-15. And Jacob himself has never bowed down to Joseph, as his dreams had predicted (see 42.8; 43.26-28), but again the prediction was reversed (see 48.12). Joseph's dreams had predicted, in part, subservience of his brothers, and this has been fulfilled more than once. But now Jacob predicts that Judah's brothers, a grouping which necessarily includes Joseph, will bow before Judah. In addition, images of royal authority more appropriate to Joseph's status in Egypt (49.10), are applied to Judah. It reads like an attempt to reverse Joseph's dreams. What will have precedence, boyhood dream or deathbed blessing?

Compounding such reservations is Jacob's remarkably one-sided appraisal of Judah. He receives unqualified praise, yet the narrative has more than once dwelt on his failings. When the brothers had plotted Joseph's fate it is true that Judah had counselled against killing him, but not in order to release him, rather to enslave him (37.26-28). His assignation with Tamar had forced from him the confession that, 'She is more in the right than I' (38.26). While it could be argued that Jacob did not know about the former incident, the latter public display and subsequent birth of children (38.27-30) could hardly have been kept from him. While Judah is not presented as an unqualified villain (cf. 44.18-34), Jacob's blessing brackets out all censure. Yahweh's inscrutable attachment to Jacob is replicated in Jacob's treatment of Judah. (For a counter-reading see, e.g., Good 1981: 111.)

There now follows a series of brief blessings on Zebulun, Issachar, Dan, Gad, Asher and Naphtali. This series begins promisingly with a positive blessing on Zebulun, containing images of protection (49.13). Issachar had been conceived when his mother Leah had 'hired' Jacob for the night (30.18). Issachar's name (containing *śkr*, hire) had originally referred to the mode of his conception, telling us more about the father than the son. Here, however, the concept of 'hire' is transferred to the son who will become 'a slave at forced labour' (49.15). God had told Abraham that his descendants would be slaves for a limited period (15.13), but Jacob's pronouncement seems to suggest his perpetual destiny. The image of Issachar as a 'strong donkey' (49.14a), a beast of burden, emphasizes his role as servant.

The blessings on Dan, Gad, Asher and Naphtali (49.16-21), children of the concubines Bilhah and Zilpah, are appropriately brief. Their exact connotations are elusive. For example, is Dan's biting at horses' heels (49.17), a continuation of his positive function as judge in Israel (49.16), or does the image of 'snake/serpent' carry more negative overtones (cf. 3.14-15)? Are Asher's rich food and delicacies (49.20), an indication of material blessing or a rebuke for inordinate luxury? The blessing on Naphtali contains major problems of translation that are beyond the scope of this commentary. The most transparent is the blessing on Gad, but even here the most that this son has to look forward to is that he will give as good as he gets (49.19).

The most enigmatic verse in this section is, however, 49.18, an abrupt outburst by Jacob as he completes Dan's blessing. Is it a statement of quiet confidence in Yahweh? Or might it suggest, rather, a sense of frustration? Prior to this point only Judah has received true commendation, with the emphasis decidedly toward the negative, or enigmatic. Thus Jacob's statement, 'I wait for your salvation, O Lord', registers his awareness that his sons and the blessing he had fought for so hard himself, have brought more problems than actual blessing.

Not surprisingly the blessing on Joseph is the longest (49.22-26). Its imagery is no less elusive than any of the others. The general positive stance it takes is, however, quite clear. Note that this is the only blessing to invoke God (49.24-25). The reference to those who attacked Joseph is striking (49.23). Within the context of the Joseph story the attackers must surely be the brothers. Thus 49.24 which depicts how Joseph repulsed such an attack with the help of God, would refer to how he trumped his brothers by rising to high office in Egypt. This context shows that Jacob believes that Joseph 'was set apart from his brothers' (49.26) by divine decree.

The final blessing, that on Benjamin (49.27), continues the flow of short blessings which began with Zebulun's and which was interrupted by Joseph's. As with elements in the blessings on Dan (49.17) and Gad (49.19), it is not clear whether Benjamin's 'devouring' and 'dividing' as a wolf is intended to be positive or negative.

The concluding remark by the narrator indicates that these blessings are related to the lives of the tribes (i.e., descendants), of Israel/Jacob and not just to individuals (49.28). What the tribes might make of them lies beyond the narrative framework of Genesis. However, how might we expect Jacob's sons to leave his presence after hearing such an outline of their respective destinies? Presumably not with the same sense of elation with which Jacob had emerged from his father's tent all those years before when he had fooled Isaac into giving him the blessing. The blessings might well be 'suitable' (49.28), but the majority of them are hardly desirable. The 'blessings' on Jacob's sons, as embryonic tribes, do not bode well for the promise of nationhood originally given to Abraham. Numerically they are edging slowly towards becoming a nation. But if Jacob's 'blessings' bear any relation to reality, what kind of nation will they be? Even allowing for obscurities in the language used, a loose coalition of divided (49.7b), oppressive or subservient (49.8b, 15b) and warring tribes (49.17, 27), it would seem. This is hardly the fulfilment of God's promise that Abraham would become 'a great nation' (12.2). But then, how many other predictions made in

Genesis have had simple confirmations? Whether Jacob's words will be ratified or not is one item to occupy the reader who moves on beyond the confines of Genesis.

Despite the fact that Jacob had claimed Manasseh and Ephraim to be his sons (48.5), when he calls his sons together and blesses them in this chapter, not only are they not present, but he makes no mention of them. The private confidences transacted between Jacob, Joseph and his two sons in ch. 48 remain a secret. This is just as well, if Jacob's assessment of the characters of his sons in this chapter is accurate.

The blessings are followed quickly and briefly by Jacob's demise. Jacob's request to be buried with his ancestors in the family grave at Machpelah is understandable. In burial he will be reunited with his parents and grandparents. Yet ironically his corpse will lie there with Leah, the less-favoured wife. Rachel, the wife he loved, died and was buried 'on the way to Ephrath' (48.7). Thus the ongoing division within the ancestral family is registered once again. The brothers Jacob and Esau lived and died separately, and the sisters Rachel and Leah cannot even share a common grave with their husband.

Genesis 50

50.1-14

Joseph mourns at Jacob's deathbed just as God had promised (46.4). At that same time God had also promised that Jacob would return from Egypt, and now the narrative turns its attention to this.

Joseph waits until the end of the embalming and mourning period. This period is probably to be construed as lasting 110 days (40 plus 70, 50.3), thus anticipating Joseph's own death notice where we are informed that he died aged 110 years (50.26). Joseph's request to Pharaoh to take his father's body to the family burial plot in Canaan is couched in court diplomacy. Jacob had indeed requested Joseph on more than one occasion to bury him in Canaan (47.29-30; 49.29-32). In recounting Jacob's desire to Pharaoh, Joseph mentions only Jacob's desire to be buried with his kin, rather than the stark statement, 'Do not bury me in Egypt' (47.29), which could easily be taken as an anti-Egyptian sentiment.

Jacob's funeral arrangements reiterate where 'home' is for this family. But his burial demonstrates just how Egyptianized the family has become. The Canaanites who observe the funeral cortege comment, 'This is a grievous mourning on the part of the *Egyptians*' (50.11). They are unable to distinguish between the Egyptians and Jacob's family in the entourage (cf. 50.7-8). Jacob's burial passes ironic comment on the progress of the patriarchal promises. First, the promise of land is recalled. Jacob's insistence on burial in Canaan underlines where the land of promise is. But while Jacob's return is permanent—he is in a coffin—the rest of the family return to Egypt once Jacob is entombed. Also, the comment on the naming of the place of mourning, 'it is beyond the Jordan' (50.11), emphasizes that the patriarchal family and the promises have now moved on, beyond the land of promise. As far as the nationhood promise is concerned, the fact that the entire group are taken to be Egyptians calls attention to the precariousness of national identity. In the last few chapters the term 'Israel' has been used increasingly to designate the nation rather than the individual (e.g., 47.27; 48.20; 49.16, 24, 28). But now that this 'nation' returns to its promised land, it is indistinguishable from the Egyptians. The threat of assimilation is noted.

The burial of Abraham and Isaac had brought together their respective sons to show their final respects (25.9; 35.29). Such reunions had, however, only been temporary. All of Jacob's sons are present at his burial too. Like Isaac and Ishmael, and Jacob and Esau before them, the brothers had been living separately, with Joseph at the court while they resided in the land of Goshen. With Jacob now deceased, will the fractures in the family get wider? And with Joseph in a position of power, what might the brothers expect from him?

50.15-26

The facade of brotherly unity is revealed for what it really is as soon as the brothers return from the funeral. The brothers fear that with Jacob out of the way, Joseph's true animosity for them will be revealed (50.15). Their anxiety shows that the reconciliation achieved in ch. 45 did nothing more than paper over the cracks. Perhaps their journey to Canaan and back refreshed their memories of how they had travelled that road before, on their trips to Egypt to buy grain, and of how Joseph had toyed with them and their father mercilessly. Their suspicions of Joseph's attitudes toward them recalls their demeanour toward him at the beginning of the story. Just as they had once 'hated'

Joseph (37.4-5, 8) they now wonder whether he 'still bears a grudge' (50.15) against them. Strained relationships are just as evident at the end of the story as they were at the beginning, in Jacob's presence or in his absence.

Not only does the account come to a close with reminders of the familial tension that has run throughout, but also a reminder of how well accomplished this family is in the art of deception. The brothers claim that their recently departed father had instructed them to ask forgiveness from Joseph for their previous actions (50.16). There is no record of this in the previous narrative and it is intrinsically implausible. They cannot claim that Jacob had said that Joseph must forgive them, for this command would have been directed to Joseph himself and not the brothers. In addition, the narrative never records whether Jacob had been told what the brothers had done. One thing that their devious report does, however, is to underline that Joseph has never formally forgiven his brothers. The closest he came was to announce that his sufferings were part of God's will (45.5-8). On the other hand, his brothers have not yet formally confessed or asked for forgiveness. Their present approach falls short of this also. They are motivated by self-preservation, not contrition. The full extent of the brothers' desperation can be seen in their bowing before Joseph with the confession 'we are here as your slaves' (50.18). Previous prostrations were done when they did not know Joseph's identity (42.6, 36; 43.28; 44.14). They now know who he is, and they know that this action fulfils to the letter the dream that predicted their subservience. They might be 'your brothers' (50.17), but are now 'your slaves' (50.18), a contrast in designation which plots the move that has occurred in the story as a whole. Such self-conscious grovelling speaks volumes concerning their genuine feeling of terror.

Joseph's weeping in reaction to his brothers' speech is just as enigmatic as his weeping when he 'tested' them (42.24; 43.30; 45.2, 14-15). The difficulty in assigning a single convincing motive for Joseph's weeping here at the end of the story, confirms his status as the most complex and mysterious character in Genesis. Does he take their report at face value and is he upset that his father has misunderstood him? Or, that his father has rightly surmised what his plans are and scotched them? Or does he see through his brothers' ruse and recognize it for the deception that it is, and weeps that his brothers can still misunderstand him? (cf. Hamilton 1995: 704). Is he simply relieved that his brothers have finally confessed the wrong that they did, and is overcome with relief? Or does he weep when forced to confront the fact that he has not yet formally forgiven his brothers? In fact it is striking that not even in this scene does Joseph respond by saying 'I forgive you'. He tells them not to be afraid and reassures them (50.19, 21), but on the basis of God's overriding plan 'to preserve a numerous people' (50.20), not on the basis of his forgiveness. Invoking the divine will supplies a reason for the brothers' treatment of him, but not for his treatment of them. Indeed, nowhere does Joseph ever request forgiveness for his treatment of his brothers and father. His statement, 'Am I in the place of God?' (50.19), is somewhat equivocal in this context. It could be reassuring—namely, they need not fear Joseph because matters of vengeance can be left to God. On the other hand it is also a way of avoiding an act of forgiveness, for forgiveness ultimately can come from God alone (cf. 39.9). Jacob spoke similarly to Rachel (30.2) to convey the idea that he was being asked to do something he could not do. It is perhaps worthwhile recalling the reconciliation between Jacob and Esau (33.4). Esau also did not intone the words 'I forgive', but his spontaneous reaction to seeing Jacob again spoke louder than words. Joseph's playing cat and mouse with his family continues to sour their relationships and leaves them unsure of his true motives. He assures them that they are safe but provides no unambiguous proof that they are forgiven. The fraught relationships between Joseph and his brothers are thus left unresolved at the end of the story.

His words are notable when read against the larger context of the whole book. Some have suggested that Joseph at the end of Genesis corresponds to Adam at the beginning. For example, just as Adam was created in God's image and ruled over God's domain with his wife given to him by God, so Joseph is dressed in royal attire by Pharaoh and placed over all the land of Egypt and given a wife from the priestly family. (1.27-28; 2.22 cf. 41.40, 42, 45). (See Dahlberg 1976: 363-64, for a rather different interpretation; cf. Sailhamer 1992: 215.) If such points of contact are suggestive, then perhaps one more could be put forward. Just as Adam overreached himself in wanting to become 'like God' (3.5, 22), Joseph too has succumbed to the same temptation in his role as Egyptian potentate, summed up in his pregnant rhetorical question, 'Am I in the place of God?' (50.19).

Other aspects of the patriarchal story are also left unresolved. On the one hand Joseph marks continuity with his ancestors.

This is underlined by being told twice that he died aged 110 years (50.22, 26). It has often been noted that Joseph's age at death has a neat mathematical relationship to the lives of the previous three generations:

Abraham:	$175 = 7 \times 5^2$
Isaac:	$180 = 5 \times 6^2$
Jacob:	$147 = 3 \times 7^2$
Joseph:	$110 = 5^2 + 6^2 + 7^2$

Thus Joseph's age is the sum of the squares of the ages of the preceding generations. He brings this section of the family history to a neat conclusion that can be expressed numerically.

Yet the story as a whole cannot be set out with such precision. For example, the progress of the ancestral blessings and promises has taken a tortuous route, rather than an inexorable linear unfolding. There is a hint of this even in Joseph's death notice. For while Joseph is the youngest but one of the brothers, he is the first to die (50.24 cf. Exod. 1.6). This is a rather jarring note to read just a little while after Jacob's fulsome blessing of Joseph 'who was set apart from his brothers' (49.26). And the final note of the book of Genesis, 'he was embalmed and placed in a coffin in Egypt' (50.26), hardly brings to a satisfying resolution the promises of nationhood, land and blessing that have sustained much of the story line since 12.1-3. The story of Genesis obviously has unfinished items on its agenda which the reader will take forward into Exodus.

Indications of what some agenda items will be for the next book, and the way in which they will be developed, are hinted at, however, in the final words of Genesis. As far as the promise of land is concerned, there is a recognition that they are all in the wrong land and that God will take them back to where they all know they belong—Canaan (50.24-25). This is significantly the only place in the story where Joseph has given any hint of knowing the land promise (though see 40.15). Even Joseph who has lived 93 out of his 110 years out of the land, knows that he does not belong in a coffin *in Egypt*. The nationhood promise is also to the fore in this concluding section. Indeed, Joseph sees this as bound up with the divine will that lies behind his coming to Egypt (50.20). The 'numerous people' that God is preserving obviously includes the emergent nation comprising Jacob's family, but is not confined to that. For the story makes it clear that Egyptians, and probably Canaanites, have also been preserved (47.13-28). Thus some aspect of Abraham's descendants being a blessing to the nations surfaces (cf. 12.2). It must also be conceded, however, that Joseph's 'blessing' of the Egyptians included their enslavement (47.18-21). And the return to Canaan will see Canaanites dispossessed of their land (15.13-16). Thus the three main strands of the ancestral promise which started the story—land, nationhood and blessing, are present at the end, but they remain as complex as ever and their fulfilment as far away as ever. The delay is illustrated in the contrast between Jacob's and Joseph's funeral. Why is Joseph not buried with Jacob and his ancestors at Machpelah? Because the family must wait for God to act. Or rather, God is waiting for the family to become a great nation in Egypt before he can bring them out of Egypt, with Joseph's corpse, and enter the land of Canaan (15.13-16; 46.3-4).

The first and last words of Genesis begin with the Hebrew preposition b^e ('in'). The first word concerns time: 'in the beginning' ($b^e r\bar{e}$'$\hat{s}\hat{\imath}t$, 1.1). The last word concerns space: 'in Egypt' ($b^e mi\d{s}rayim$, 50.26). The time and space created by the story of this text between those two points has a complexity that belies the seemingly simple surface texture. But those two points map the extent of Genesis' interests, from the breadth of creation to the minutiae of family squabbles and bereavements. The contrast between Joseph's corpse, embalmed and lying in state in Egypt, with the thrust of the ancestral story—that this family will become a great nation in a land far away, and will be a blessing—clearly emphasizes one thing. This story will continue. The strangely downbeat conclusion to the book highlights that fulfilments of promises await the future. If the future of the ancestral family in Exodus and beyond replicates in any way the journey taken in Genesis, it will be a complex and captivating one.

Bibliography

Alexander, T. Desmond
   1983   'Genesis 22 and the Covenant of Circumcision', *JSOT* 25: 17-22.
   1989   'From Adam to Judah: The Significance of the Family Tree in Genesis', *EvQ* 61: 5-19.
Alter, Robert
   1981   *The Art of Biblical Narrative* (London: George Allen & Unwin).
Anderson, Bernhard W.
   1978   'From Analysis to Synthesis: The Interpretation of Genesis 1-11', *JBL* 97: 23-39.
Baldwin, Joyce G.
   1986   *The Message of Genesis 12–50: From Abraham to Joseph* (Leicester: Inter-Varsity Press).
Bar-Efrat, Shimeon
   1989   *Narrative Art in the Bible* (JSOTSup, 70; Sheffield: Almond Press).
Bechtel, Lyn M.
   1994   'What if Dinah is not Raped? (Genesis 34)', *JSOT* 62: 19-36.
Berlin, Adele
   1983   *Poetics and Interpretation of Biblical Narrative* (Sheffield: Almond Press).
Brueggemann, Walter
   1982   *Genesis: A Biblical Commentary for Teaching and Preaching* (Atlanta: John Knox).
Cassuto, U.
   1964   *A Commentary on the Book of Genesis* (trans. I. Abrahams; 2 vols.; Jerusalem: Magnes Press).
Clines, David J.A.
   1990   'What Does Eve Do to Help? and Other Irredeemably Androcentric Orientations in Genesis 1–3', in *idem. What Does Eve Do to Help? and Other Readerly Questions to the Old Testament* (JSOTSup, 94; Sheffield: JSOT Press): 25-48.
Coats, George W.
   1983   *Genesis: With an Introduction to Narrative Literature* (FOTL, 1; Grand Rapids: Eerdmans).
Dahlberg, Bruce T.
   1976   'On Recognizing the Unity of Genesis', *TD* 24: 360-67.
Emerton, John A.
   1987   'An Examination of Some Attempts to Defend the Unity of the Flood Narrative in Genesis: Part I', *VT* 37: 401-420.
Eslinger, Lyle
   1979   'A Contextual Identification of the *bene ha'elohim* and *benoth ha'adam* in Genesis 6:1-4', *JSOT* 13: 65-73.

Exum, J. Cheryl
    1993   'Who's Afraid of the "Endangered Ancestress" ', in Cheryl Exum and
            David J.A. Clines (eds.), *The New Literary Criticism and the Hebrew
            Bible* (JSOTSup, 143; Sheffield: Sheffield Academic Press).
Gibson, John C.L.
    1981   *Genesis*, I (The Daily Study Bible; Edinburgh: Saint Andrew Press).
Gunn, David M., and Danna Nolan Fewell
    1993   *Narrative in the Hebrew Bible* (Oxford Bible Series: Oxford:
            Clarendon Press).
Good, E.M.
    1981   *Irony in the Old Testament* (Bible and Literature Series: Sheffield:
            Almond Press, 2nd edn).
Hamilton, Victor P.
    1990   *The Book of Genesis 1–17* (NICOT; Grand Rapids: Eerdmans).
    1995   *The Book of Genesis 18–50* (NICOT; Grand Rapids: Eerdmans).
Hauser, Alan J.
    1982   'Genesis 2–3: The Theme of Intimacy and Alienation', in D.J.A. Clines,
            David M. Gunn and Alan J. Hauser (eds.), *Art and Meaning: Rhetoric
            in Biblical Literature*, (JSOTSup, 19; Sheffield: JSOT Press).
Helyer, Larry R.
    1983   'The Separation of Abram and Lot: Its Significance in the Patriarchal
            Narratives', *JSOT* 26: 77-88.
Hendel, Ronald S.
    1987   'Of Demigods and the Deluge: Toward an Interpretation of Genesis
            6:1-4', *JBL* 106: 13-26.
Janzen, J. Gerald
    1993   *Abraham and All the Families of the Earth: A Commentary on the
            Book of Genesis 12–50* (International Theological Commentary;
            Grand Rapids: Eerdmans).
Kidner, Derek
    1967   *Genesis: An Introduction and Commentary* (TOTC; London: Tyndale
            Press).
McEvenue, Sean E.
    1971   *The Narrative Style of the Priestly Writer* (AnBib, 50; Rome:
            Pontificio Ist Biblico).
Miller, Patrick D.
    1978   *Genesis 1–11: Studies in Structure and Theme* (JSOTSup, 8; Sheffield:
            JSOT Press).
Molina, Jean-Pierre
    1980   'Noé et le déluge', *ETR* 55: 256-64.
Rad, Gerhard von
    1972   *Genesis: A Commentary* (OTL; Trans. J.H. Marks; Philadelphia:
            Westminster Press, rev. edn).
Rashkow, Ilona N.
    1992   'Intertextuality, Transference, and the Reader in/of Genesis 12 and
            20', in Danna Nolan Fewell (ed.), *Reading Between Texts* (Louisville,
            KY: Westminster/John Knox Press): 57-73.
Rendsburg, Gary A.
    1992   'Notes on Genesis xv', *VT* 42: 266-72.
Robinson, Robert D.
    1986   'Literary Functions of the Genealogies of Genesis', *CBQ* 48: 595-608.

Ross, Allen P.
    1980   'Studies in the Book of Genesis, Pt. 2: The Table of Nations in Genesis
            10: Its Structure', *BSac* 137: 340-53.
    1988   *Creation and Blessing: A Guide to the Study and Exposition of the
            Book of Genesis* (Grand Rapids: Baker Book House).
Sailhamer, John
    1992   *The Pentateuch as Narrative* (Grand Rapids, MI: Zondervan).
Sasson, Jack M.
    1978   'Genealogical "Convention" in Biblical Chronography?', *ZAW* 90:
            171-85.
Ska, Jean L.
    1992   'Sommaires proleptiques en Gn 27 et dans l'histoire de Joseph',
            Bib 73: 518-27.
Skinner, John
    1930   *A Critical and Exegetical Commentary on Genesis* (ICC; Edinburgh:
            T & T Clark, 2nd edn).
Speiser, E.A.
    1964   *Genesis* (AB; Garden City, NY: Doubleday).
Sternberg, Meir
    1985   *The Poetics of Biblical Narrative: Ideological Literature and the
            Drama of Reading* (Bloomington: Indiana University Press).
Trible, Phyllis
    1984   *Texts of Terror: Literary-feminist Readings of Biblical Narrative*
            (Philadelphia: Fortress Press).
Turner, Laurence A.
    1990a   *Announcements of Plot in Genesis* (JSOTSup, 96; Sheffield: JSOT
            Press).
    1990b   'Lot as Jekyll and Hyde: A Reading of Genesis 18–19', in David J. A.
            Clines, Stephen E. Fowl and Stanley E. Porter (eds.), *The Bible in
            Three Dimensions: Essays in Celebration of Forty Years of Biblical
            Studies in the University of Sheffield* (Sheffield: JSOT Press): 85-101.
    1993   'The Rainbow as the Sign of the Covenant in Genesis ix 11–13', *VT*
            43: 119-24.
Wenham, Gordon J.
    1986   'Sanctuary Symbolism in the Garden of Eden Story', in R. Giveon
            et al. (eds.), *Proceedings, Ninth World Congress of Jewish Studies,
            Division A: The Period of the Bible* (Jerusalem: World Union of
            Jewish Studies): 19-25.
    1987   *Genesis 1–15* (WBC; Waco, TX: Word Books).
    1993   *Genesis 16–50* (WBC; Waco, TX: Word Books).
Westermann, Claus
    1984   *Genesis 1–11: A Commentary* (trans. J.J. Scullion; Minneapolis:
            Augsburg).
    1985   *Genesis 12–36: A Commentary* (trans. J. J. Scullion; Minneapolis:
            Augsburg).
    1986   *Genesis 37–50: A Commentary* (trans. J.J. Scullion; Minneapolis:
            Augsburg).
Wildavsky, Aaron
    1994   'Survival Must not be Gained through Sin: The Moral of the Joseph
            Stories Prefigured through Judah and Tamar', *JSOT* 62: 37-48.

Index of References

Index of Authors

Lightning Source UK Ltd.
Milton Keynes UK
UKOW01f0014260118
316864UK00003B/208/P